MANUAL OF LIBRARY AND INFORMATION SCIENCE

MANUAL OF LIBRARY AND INFORMATION SCIENCE

DR. P. BALASUBRAMANIAN
M.A., M.L.I.Sc., M.Phil., PGDCA., PGDPR, Ph.D.
Deputy Librarian,
Manonmaniam Sundaranar University,
Tirunelveli, Tamilnadu

and

DR. A. BALADHANDAYUTHAM
B.Sc., M.A., M.L.I.Sc., M.Phil., Ph.D
Assistant Professor,
Department of Library and Information Science,
Madurai Kamaraj University, Madurai, Tamilnadu

REGAL PUBLICATIONS
New Delhi-110027

MANUAL OF LIBRARY AND INFORMATION SCIENCE

ISBN 978-81-8484-165-7

Typeset by
S.S. COMPOSERS
3190, Mohindra Park, Shakur Basti, Delhi-110034.

Printed in India at
MAYUR ENTERPRISES
WZ Plot No. 3, Gujjar Market, Tihar Village, New Delhi-110018.

Published by
REGAL PUBLICATIONS
F-159, Rajouri Garden, New Delhi-110027.
Phone: +91-11-45546396
E-mail: regalbookspub@yahoo.com

Contents

Preface

We are extremely happy to place before the readers our new Book on *"A Manual of Library and Information Science."* This Book is written in accordance with the syllabus prescribed by the Indian Universities for the Bachelor degree and Master degree in Library and Information Science.

In this book, there are five units of which Unit I describes the foundations of Library and Information Science. Unit II describes the Library Management and its importance. Unit III discusses the Information sources and its types and functions. Unit IV describes the Reference Services. Unit V discusses the Digital Library and its characteristics. An attempt has been made to cover the interest of the students and professionals of Library and Information Science.

Views and suggestions for the betterment of this book are always welcomed. We are grateful to the authors of many books whose books we studied and consulted. We thank Regal Publications, New Delhi, for their help in bringing out this book in the shortest possible time.

Dr. P. BALASUBRAMANIAN
Dr. A. BALADHANDAYUTHAM

LIBRARY AND SOCIETY

ROLE OF A LIBRARY—MODERN CONCEPT

Library plays a vital role in improving the educational standards and research efforts. History shows that the library development is standing on its most promising springboard. Unlike the past, there is much more recognition and appreciation for librarianship. Librarians in most of the countries, including developing countries like India, command respect in the societies. Their value is acknowledged without much reservation and has considerably advanced, though still there is a long way to go to reach a satisfactory scenario. Today, library is a product of advancement and is an acknowledged social agency. So strong is the communication between the library and society that the libraries tend to prosper.

India has been the cradle of one of the earliest civilization. Intellectual enquiry and philosophical thinking were the factors that shaped the Indian civilization. The ancient Indian Literature like Rigveda, Upanishads, etc. are all based on philosophical thinking and still today they are considered as philosophical treaties. The vedic age would, therefore, be a good starting point for the study of libraries in India. The story of the library can be studied under three heads, namely, ancient, medieval and modern.

The first Library in modern India was established in 1784 attached to the Asiatic Society of Bengal. Immediately after the death of Tippu Sultan in 1799, the manuscripts preserved in his library were sent to the Asiatic Society of Bengal and some to the universities of Oxford and Cambridge. This can be witnessed from the palm leaf manuscripts which are still preserved in the Saraswathi Mahal Library at Tanjore, Tamil Nadu. After the establishment of the Asiatic Society of Bengal, the Asiatic Society of Bombay was established in 1804. Two more societies with public libraries grew up in Calcutta the Delphin Society in 1811 and the Calcutta Library Society was established in 1818 with a library open to the public. In 1830 another public library, called the Bombay Library was founded in Bombay. The Calcutta public Library was established in 1835 by the English Community in Calcutta. The Connemara Public Library which was established in Chennai in 1890 also deserves special mention and this library today functions as the State Central Library of Tamil Nadu.

Library is the product of our Cultural maturation. It is essentially a response to the total communication patterns of modern Society. The word library has been derived from the Latin word *Liber* which means "a book." The use of the word library to denote a building, a room, set of rooms in which collection of books is housed and organized is also common. The most appropriate meaning of the term library is that "a library houses an organized collection of documents to preserve them and make them available for use." The most important word in this definition is "use." This is being reflected in Ranganathan's definition as "a library is a public institution or establishment charged with the care of a collection of books and the duty of making them accessible to those who require use of them."

This definition prescribes two basic functions of a library. The first function is "The care of collection of books." That is, protecting books from the four major enemies of books like fire, water, vermin and human beings. Naturally the dominating spirit in this function was caretaker ship. The second function assigned by Dr. S.R. Ranganathan to Libraries "the duty of making the books accessible to those who require the use of them" is in direct opposition to the age long tradition of caretaker librarianship.

Libraries play a vital role in the development of the

Society. Knowledge of the aims and progress of the society may be obtained by reading and keeping abreast of events through literature. The recurring theme is that all literature should be available to all people freely without fear or favour, through the medium of libraries. To effect this ideal, librarians should be prepared to co-operate with other influences such as formal education, the mass media, and other social, political, agencies for positive and intelligent use of leisure.

Library in Modern Society

Libraries in the modern society feature vitally in socio-economic welfare and socio-political changes. They are crucially related to the country's artistic, aesthetic and intellectual activities. This remarkable functioning of training the mind and the spirit of man enabling him to work of the social, cultural, ethical, spiritual, political and material advancement of the society is the basis of all library academic pursuits.

The present libraries function is more a service agency against the conservation function of former days. As Service agency the modern library perform vital function for the elevation of the society. Library plays a vital role in improving the educational standards and research efforts. People will not make the fullest, most fruitful use of libraries unless they are well-educated. It is a necessary complement to all education services, providing the material essential for the utilization of the capacities developed by education and opportunity for their further development is the individual. The library enables every man to enlarge his mind with the refined pleasure of great literature.

Library and education are sister services. Education implies discipline and cultivation of the intellect. It enables the individual to know himself and the life around him. The importance of formal education imparted through a school, a college or a university can hardly be over-exaggerated. It is now being increasingly realized that self-education permeates the entire life of the individual from the cradle to the grave.

The most appropriate agency of continuing education for people of all ages is a public library. It serves as a center for arousing and stimulating materials and programmes to satisfy their desire for knowledge. The society has an obligation as other to feed the people with food for thought though libraries. Education and Library are therefore, two most important factors of social metamorphosis. Therefore, the library if it is to achieve its fullest role in society is not passively to make books available when needed by a potential reader, but actively to stimulate the use of books. In stimulating the reading habits, the academic (especially school level), and public libraries play a vital role. Libraries can do best work for children and old people by guiding them in choosing his/her book. The aim of the library must be to sell itself, go out and promote its services.

Library must inculcate in the minds of individuals that reading is of far greater significance for the creation of intellectual, moral, aesthetic, social and political values. Libraries offer special types of services to help in the advancement of research in society.

Functions of Libraries

Dr .S.R. Ranganathan records some important functions of the library which are stated below.

1. To raise the economic resources of humanity to the extent necessary to maintain the ever increasing population, in comfort and free from want of any kind; and also.
2. To help in the elevating, self-dependant use of leisure with the aid of freely served books, pictures, sound records, and other graphic materials; and
3. To help in increasing the opportunity for the spiritual awakening of one and all of the members of humanity.

Since the library is inter-twined in purpose and function with society's needs, it may be asserted that library is the agency promoting educational research, informational, recreational, civic sense, aesthetic, appreciation. McColvin has rightly recorded that today we have reached the stage where we advocate universal library provision not merely because the masses need knowledge, but also because we firmly believe that medina will not be able to exercise wisely their rights and powers unless they do intend enjoying access to the mine of knowledge. Also Shera characterizes the present age as being largely concerned with the utilization of applied science in the design of society, and writes that we are therefore, very much dependent upon the successful communication of information, one of the most basic social activities.

Social Origin and Development

In order to determine whether or not the library is a social organization we shall have to find if the library has its roots in the society. A society is a collective forum of individuals, their activities and their beliefs. Libraries of the old days were not functioning as social institutions because in early times the library was considered to be the property of an individual or of a particular group. Then books in the library were kept under locked cupboards. It reflects that the early libraries were not functioning as social organization but as private property. But, there were sufficient and justifiable reasons for this.

In ancient times books were written by hand, and one or limited copies were available. It was an immensely difficult and costly affair to make multiple copies of manuscripts. Therefore, very rich people like kings and big jamindars, could afford to bear the heavy cost on reproduction, as well as on safety of books. Had the manuscripts were then kept open for the use of one and all, valuable records of cultural heritage of the society would have perished. A few learned public were allowed to handle these carefully. But for the safe custody by the individual owners, this valuable cultural heritage would have died in infancy. Here we may compare the ancient manuscripts with small seedlings and plants which when kept safely in conditioned environment, grow big and the society later reaps the benefits of their shadow and fruits. Likewise, the society could not have benefited by the knowledge these valuable manuscripts contained, had these were not protected by the individual owners.

Social Objectives

Documents are kept in the library for democratic use by all members of the society. The library aims at providing reading and other materials for ensuring healthy intellectual growth of all the members of the society. Its objectives are social and democratic, i.e. society-oriented. The Five Laws also lay marked emphasis on this objective. This also proves that the library is a social organization.

Library: A Social Organization

Any organization may be considered to be a Social Organization if it fulfils the following major conditions:

- its origin and development is associated with the society and its objectives are social
- it endeavors to inculcate (in the members of the society) religious, ethical, moral, intellectual and cultural values and side by side it teaches, directly or indirectly, right behaviour and conduct
- it keeps in touch with other social organizations and maintains a cordial relation with these, and
- it strives to continue to remain as a live institution.

Therefore, the library can be considered to be a social organization if it possesses the following qualities:

- Social origin and development
- Social objectives
- Quality of Adaptation of social order
- Relation with other organizations
- Liveliness

Adaptation to Social Order

The library has always been open and adapted to changing social order. It has never stuck to rigid and orthodox procedure and services. Rather, it has been changing with change in the society. Under changed circumstances, it adopted open access system, started public relation and extension activities, introduced computerization and engaged itself in fulfilling the intellectual, educational, informational, and cultural needs of the society. It is always willing to make earnest efforts to change with the society.

Relation with other Social Organization

The concept of cooperation is inherent in libraries. The library is a firm believer of cooperation. On one hand libraries cooperate amongst themselves (through Inter-Library Loan, Cooperative acquisition, cooperative cataloguing network, etc.). On the other hand, the library maintains relation and cooperation also with other social organizations such as educational, literary, cultural and service institutions.

Methods for Becoming Social Organization

The library of today is not only a study centre but also a social centre. Libraries of all countries are functioning as social centers by extending their activities and services such as organizing exhibitions, lectures, dramatic presentation, competition, reaching people through book mobile. Nowadays the library is concerned with the provision of books for relaxation and pleasure with assistance to students and provision of up to date technical scientific and sociological information. All these factors, i.e., its origin, development, objectives services management and finance reveal that the library is a social organization.

Library: For Better Citizen

As stipulated by UNESCO in its manifesto for public libraries, right of access to information is the basic right of an individual in a democratic society. Active and informed participation of each and every individual and group in the country's affair is essential for a real democratic set-up. A democratic society needs such citizen as are exposed to the environment around them and are well acquainted with the cultural social political and economic heritage and development of the country. At the same time they should also be able to take right decision at right time.

Library is an agency which can serve this purpose most efficiently, effectively, and economically. The role and responsibility of a library to make better citizen is more important and vital than providing facts and figures. Every society has realized this as will be evident from the Kenyan committee report which put on record the public interest in libraries has greatly increased and public library is no longer regarded as a means of providing casual recreation of an innocent. It is recognized as an engine of great potentialities for national welfare, and as an essential foundation for the progress in education and culture without which no people can hold its own in the struggle for existence.

Libraries and Culture

Culture is closely related to social life. It is passed from generation to generation either through personal contact or through recorded knowledge. Thus the culture of the ages treasured and conserved in recorded documents neither dies nor diminishes unless the recorded documents or their store houses —libraries are destroyed. In a cultural revolution communication is indispensable. Books in libraries are the most powerful means of communication. Libraries contain manuscripts, books, periodicals, etc. The society as a whole or a region of it is an era is found embodied in the pages of documents. These valuable cultural kits are transmitted from one generation to another. Books are a means of maintaining wisdom through the ages.

Library: An Information Centre

Human society has traveled a long journey from Stone Age to the age of the information technology. The age of information technology, in which we are living today and the technological revolutions that we are witnessing today are founded on the pillars of information. Our present society is thus information-based society. It would be pertinent to mention here that information is being generated today with such an alarming speed.

There is vast ocean of information in every discipline. The world is deluged with information. The more we learn, the more is left to be learnt. Every individual in the society whether he is a student, a researcher, a specialist, a layman, a professional, an industrialist, a worker, a child or an aged person needs information of one kind or the other. The flood of information has therefore to be controlled analyzed and channelised so as to derive maximum benefit. This implies taking steps to ensure that the available information reaches the right user.

Library: An Education Centre

The library is the most effective and economic medium for spread of education and dissemination of information. Education is a process and from childhood to old age every one continuously passes through this process. In the whole life the human passes through or receives education in two forms: formal education and informal education. The library plays vital role by helping the citizen pursue both forms of education. It is for this reason that the library is dubbed as "People's University."

Library and Formal Education

In formal education, men and women receive education of a specified level based on specified syllabi. This form of education is imparted in academic institutions, such as schools, colleges, universities, research institutions, etc. The library does occupy a significant place in academic institutions. Educationists and scholars hold that it is a "better proof of education to know how to use a library than to possess university degree."

According to the UGC (UK) "The character and efficiency of a university may be gauged by its treatment of its central organ, the library..."An adequate library is not only the basis of all teaching and study, it is the essential condition of research without which additions can not be made to the sum of human knowledge." The library has become still more important in academic set-up due to change in the nature of education.

During the past, formal education was based on dictation: the teachers used to dictate and speak and the students used to listen to. This system has been done away with in western countries and in India also we are following new methods with appreciable speed and success. The present day education is no more an one way system in which the student had passive participation. In the changed system the student is expected to have active participation. The teacher mainly kindles the curiosity of students, makes them aware of basic facts, teaches them methodology and refers them to book to find detailed information for them, which is discussed later in tutorials, etc.

Parry committee wrote in this connection, "Lecture and text book method is no longer regarded as the sole method for teaching." It recommended that if one of the main purposes of university education is to teach students to work on their own, reading by students must be preferable to attendance at a lecture unless the lecture is superior in presentation or contents to the available literature. Students are thus referred to books both by teachers and librarians. This leads to active participation of students in educational system. Education of today is becoming more and more library-oriented, which is evident from the fact that academic libraries of today are always full of students, researchers and teachers alike. It has rightly been said, a university is as good as its library. The library is therefore indispensable for the society for meetings its educational needs.

Library and Non-formal Education

Men and women do not cease to receive education after completing their formal education because the process of learning does not stop after school, college or university education. Education is a continuous process, and therefore the human beings continue to receive education before and after receiving formal education. There are people who, for many factors, do not find opportunity to receive formal education. Formal education is like a pond of education with limited boundaries, whereas non-formal education is like an ocean of education which knows no bounds. The library helps immensely in non-formal education and adult education.

Libraries in Higher Education and Research

Libraries occupy a place of prominence in higher education. These are not only essential for teaching and study. But are equally important for research programs without which no further addition to human knowledge is possible. The education commission headed by Dr. S. Radhakrishnan has laid stress on the importance of libraries in higher education. No system of higher education can produce effective results without a strong library at its centre. Educational requirements and methods have greatly changed and broadened. Both faculty and students are becoming more and more. dependent on libraries. Therefore, knowledge of the use of libraries effectively is not only important but also essential for getting maximum benefit out of the books and recorded materials.

Libraries in Self-education

Self-education has its own meaning and importance. Education should not cease with the completion of formal education at a school, college or a University. The self-education starts at the point where the formal education ends. Actually education is a continuous process and one should make efforts to gain knowledge throughout life. Libraries play an important role in making such efforts fulfilled.

Library-centered Teaching

The methods of teaching are rapidly changing. It is no more considered proper to keep the teaching activities confined to the four walls of the class room. The students need to be brought into contact with the experiences of the past and present by using books in libraries. Some advanced countries have launched library-centered teaching programmes in their institutions. Library centered teaching will get the young minds out of the dull and monotonous class-room-centered teaching. It will save them from being thrust will undigested notes. Library-centered teaching will promote mutual respect between the teachers and the taught.

KINDS OF LIBRARIES

The enormous quantitative growth of literature and equally the user necessitated in the setting up of different types of libraries at different levels with different purposes. Formally a single library for the entire mass existing to the most information needs. With the expansion in the field of education at all levels specially in higher education there is a demand amongst the students and teaching staff to have libraries in their own respective institutions. Similarly, the post-industrial era witnessed the growth in the number of industries, firms and commercial organistions. Competition compels one to keep running in the race, with the bandwagon effect (success-breeds-success). This necessitated the setting up of special libraries.

Now if we examine the library sphere in any part of the world it is a three-tier system consisting of:

- Public Library System
  - o Public Libraries
  - o National Library
- Academic Library System
  - o University Library
  - o College Library
  - o School Library
- Special Library System.

Each one of them has its own specific objectives, structure, organization and function. Hence the features and activities are totally different from the other. Each one of them is discussed separately in the forthcoming paragraphs.

PUBLIC LIBRARY

A library which is opened to everyone, irrespective of age, sex, educational attainment and social and economical status is called a Public library. A public library is also known as "People's University." Public libraries are established under the clear mandate of law to ensure nation-wide library service. Public library is an institution for diffusion of knowledge, creating equal and ample opportunities for everyone to take his course in the most suitable way.

UNESCO Manifesto (1927) defines a public Library as a Library:

(1) Which is established under "the clear mandate of Law";
(2) Which is Maintained wholly from public fund";
(3) Which levies no 'direct charge' (fees) from its users for and of its services; and
(4) Which is open 'for free and equal use by all members of the community' regardless of race, colour, region, sex, nationality language, or levels of educational attainments."

Functions

The UNESCO manifesto has defined the functions of a public library as:

- *Education*: To foster and provide means for several development of individual or group accurate at whatever stage of education, closing the gap between the individual and recorded knowledge.
- *Information*: To bring to the individual or group accurate information quickly and in depth particularly on topics of current concern.
- *Culture*: To be one of the principal centers of cultural life and promote a keener participation, enjoyment and appreciation of all the arts.

Leisure: To play a part in encouraging the positive use of leisure and provide materials for change and relaxation.

Objectives

Dr. S.R. Ranganathan hails the library as a 'Social Institution' and he lays down the following as its objectives;

(1) To help the life long self-education of one and all;
(2) To furnish up-to-date facts and information on all subjects to one and all;
(3) To distribute in an unbiased way, all shades of recorded views and thoughts to one and all as a help in discharge of their political functions in respect of local, national and international affairs.
(4) To contribute to productivity drive by informing top managements of the latest trends in respective areas of interest;
(5) To provide one and all a harmless and elevated use of leisure;
(6) To preserve the library remains of the humanity for posterity, as vehicles of culture and as source materials for research; and in general; and
(7) To work for continued social well-being, as the agency in charge of all socialized recorded thought.

Thus a library has educational, informational, political, economic, industrial, cultural and antiquarian objectives. Provision of reading materials in a public library means—

(1) To facilitate informal self-education of all people in community;
(2) To enrich and further develop the subjects on which individuals are undertaking formal education;
(3) To meet informational needs of all;
(4) To support the educational, civil and cultural activities of groups and organizations; and
(5) To encourage wholesome recreation and constructive use of leisure time.

Provision of materials is the first step. The follow-up service is more important. The services of the modern public library include—

(1) Organization of materials to make it easily available and accessible.
(2) Lending of materials for the individual's available of usage.
(3) Reference and information work guidance to assist the different types of users according to their needs.
(4) Extension services to stimulate maximum usage through publicity programmes/public relations.

Convinced of the fact that books and reading have a powerful influence on society, the public library under dynamic leadership can become an active and effective education. Public libraries co-ordinate with academic institution like schools, college and universities to assist in their formal and informal educational activities. It can also act as an agency of adult education. Welharm S. Learned (1924) strongly holds the view that "the public library is indispensable basis for a community intelligence services."

The other field to be mentioned is the work which has been and is being done by public libraries to alleviate the problem of adult literacy. As the library of the 'People's University' one of the functions of the public library is to follow-up mass education programmes by providing books of all types, viz. Service or the illiterates, neo semi-literates and literates.

In pursuance of its recreational function, the chief role of the public library is to provide material for recreation, entertainment, adventure and escape Recreational uses of library services shadowed imperceptibly in to those of an educational opportunity comes a readership that requires access to information and to recorded knowledge on a greater scale than before.

Most public libraries extend their work to special classes of readers in many different ways. These include—

- book delivery service to the aged and housebound;
- book service to the hospitals including physically and mentally handicapped and prisons and other institutions in their areas.

Dr. S.R. Ranganathan says that "public Libraries generate material happiness, mental joy and spiritual delight; they are social institutions charged with the duty of providing the means for perpetual self-education of one and all; and they contribute to the circulation of ideas, the harnessing of leisure, the demands of democracy, the spread of literacy and the success of commercial and industrial organization."

Clientele

The public library serves a wide spectrum of users. The clientele of the public library include—

- School children
- Housewives
- Students
- Scholars
- Businessmen, etc.

Collection

Since the public library users are varied in nature the collection is also of diverse type. The collection of a public library comprise of—

- Text books
- Reference books
- Newspapers
- Magazines
- Journals, etc.

Services

The services offered by the public library are—

- Lending service
- Reference service
- Inter-library loan
- Referral service
- Reprographic service, etc.

It is the secret of success of several self-made personalities. Public library is a social institution for continued communication of knowledge. Public library sphere today is not limited to a depository, reservoir or a circulation centre, but it serves as a guide to valuable records of human knowledge and it is today one of the most important agencies of educating the masses.

NATIONAL LIBRARY

The feeling that there must be a place where the country's intellectual heritage may be collected, preserved and kept for use by the present and coming generations, resulted in the setting up of National libraries. In France the library established by the king was declared national property in 1795 and was granted the right to obtain the deposit copies of all printed publications of the country. Later national libraries started collecting and preserving literature on their country, her people, language, culture, etc. published anywhere in the world.

The role and functions of national libraries tend to vary from country to country. The epithet 'national' was first introduced by the French radical writers in the 18th century and the term meant to them the people of a country. And in 1704 the 'Libri Du Roi' or the Royal Library at Paris become Bibliotheque National, the French National conversion having declared it a national property and granted it their to obtain deposit copies of all printed publications of the county. The other older National libraries include those of Denmark, the Netherlands, Sweden, Britain, Ireland and the USSR.

Definition

The definition of a national library, as adopted at the general conference of UNESCO in 1970, is as under:

> "Libraries, which irrespective of their titles are responsible for acquiring and conserving copies of all significant publications published in the country and functioning as a "deposit" library, either by law or under other arrangements. They will also normally perform some of the following functions: produce a national bibliography, hold and keep up to date a large and representative collection of foreign literature including books about the country, act as the national bibliographical information centre, compile union catalogues, publish the retrospective national

> bibliography. Libraries which may be called "national" but whose functions do not correspond to the above definition should not be placed in national library category."
>
> "Library is called national when it is the official depository of printed works, a general access library, information and bibliographical centre, and a centre of coordination, planning, and stimulating of the entire library system of the nation."

Sir Frank Charles Francis, Director of Libraries of the British Museum described National library as a library which has the duty of collection and preserving for posterity of the written production of that country. The Librarian's Glossary and Reference Book refers to the national library as "a library maintained out of government funds and serving the national as a whole. Usually books in such libraries are for reference only. They are usually copyright libraries. The function of such a library is to collect and preserve for posterity the books, periodicals and newspapers published in the country. This is best done by a law acquiring publisher to deposit copies of all publications in other countries' best do this." The Encyclopaedia of library and information science defines National library as "a library is called a national one when it is official depository of printed works; a general access library; a bibliographical information center; and a center of co-ordination, planning and stimulation of the entire library system of the nation."

The functions and duties of the national library indicated and implied from the above definitions, lead to a two-tier organization of a national library. The first tier will function as the deposit unit or complex, where every national document will be perfectly preserved. The other tier will functions the services unit of the national library. Owing to the diversity of national information needs, the single national library has to develop into a network of a number of national libraries, particularly in the thrust areas like agriculture, medicine and science and technology.

According to Dr. S.R. Ranganathan a national library system should consist of—

- National Copyright library,
- National Depository Library, and
- a system of National Service Libraries pertaining to different subject feels.

Functions

The following are the basic functions of a National Library:

(1) The primary function is preserve the literature produced in a particularly country under the terms of Copyright Act;
(2) To acquire comprehensive, representative current foreign literature;
(3) To compile catalogue of materials in possession and also Union catalogue of the Country's holding;
(4) To publish a current national bibliography and also re-respective national bibliographic when needed; and
(5) To set-up a national references of any bibliographical service throughout the country and act as a clearing house for enquiries to and from various centers in the country and overseas.

It is worthy to mention here that some of the public libraries function either for their countries as a whole or for the cities in which they happen to be located. The National library of Singapore is also the public library for that country which is small in area, while the National library of Tunisia acts as the public library for the city of Tunis in which it is situated.

To conclude, it can be said that "the national library of a country is a library or a network of libraries that collects and conserves all national documents and also significant useful non-national documents produced in other and executes the use of the collection to meet the national information needs."

Organizational Set-up

The organizational set-up of national libraries of different countries varies according to the needs and functions to be performed by them. In his Library Development Plan, Ranganathan writes that the organizational set-up of a national library should be similar to that of a big public library. He ascribes the following departments:

(1) The Home Section;
(2) The National bureau of copyright;
(3) The National bureau of International exchange;
(4) The National library for the blind;
(5) Contact libraries abroad for propagation national culture;
(6) The National library for the seafarers;
(7) The National bureau of Inter-library loan;
(8) The National bureau of bibliography;
(9) The National bureau of technical services; and
(10) The National library secretariat.

Collection

Since the National library procures all the documents published in the country, the collection consists of—

- o Text books
- o Monographs
- o Microfilms
- o Reference books
- o Newspapers
- o Magazines
- o Journals

Clientele

The clientele of the National library is of multi-focal nature. The clientele of the National library include—

- School children
- Housewives
- Students
- Scholars
- Businessmen, etc.

The national library also takes care of special types of users like blind, the seafarers, the Physically Challenged, etc.

Services

The national library is competent enough to serve a wide range of users in more than one way. Through home section or local service it serves the local population. The services rendered by the National Library include—

- Lending service
- Reference service
- Inter-library loan
- Referral service
- Reprographic service
- Translation service
- Microfilm

The national library occupies the highest position in the national library system of a country. But yet, the national library still functions like a big public library.

National Library of India

The National Library of India is the largest library in the country. It is an institution of National importance under the 'Department of Culture, Ministry of Tourism and Culture, and Government of India'. The library is designated to collect, disseminate and preserve the printed material produced in the country. The library is situated on a scenic 30 acres Belvedere Estate, in Kolkata, formerly Calcutta City.

Aims of the National Library of India

- Acquisition and conservation of all significant national production of printed material, excluding ephemera.
- Collection of printed material concerning the country, no matter where it is published, and as a corollary, the acquisition of photographic records of such material that is not available within the country.
- Acquisition and conservation of foreign material required by the country.
- Rendering of bibliographical and documents services of current and retrospective material, both general and specialised.

- Acting as a referral centre purveying full and accurate knowledge.

History—Calcutta Public Library (CPL)

Calcutta Public Library was established in 1836. It was not a Government institution. It was running on a proprietary basis. Every person subscribing Rs. 300 in one payment or three instalments was to be considered a proprietor. Poor students and others were allowed to use the library free of charge for a specified period of time. The then Governor General, Lord Metcalf transferred 4,675 volumes from the library of the College of Fort William to the Calcutta Public Library. This and donations of books from individuals formed the nucleus of the library. Prince Dwarkanath Tagore was the first proprietor of the Calcutta Public Library.

Both the Indian and foreign books, especially from Britain, were purchased for the library. In the report of 1850 we find that the library started collecting books in Gujarati, Marathi, Pali, Ceylonese and Punjabi. Donations were regularly made by individuals as well as by the Government of Bengal and North Western Provinces.

The Calcutta Public Library had a unique position as the first public library in this part of the country. Such a well organised and efficiently run library was rare even in Europe during the first half of the 19th century. Because of the efforts of the Calcutta Public Library, the National Library has many extremely rare books and journals in its collection.

The Imperial Library

The Imperial Library was formed in 1891 by combining a number of Secretariat libraries. Of these, the most important and interesting was the library of the Home Department, which contained many books formerly belonging to the library of East India College, Fort William and the library of the East India Board in London. But the use of the library was restricted to the superior officers of the Government.

Amalgamation of CPL and Imperial Library

Lord Curzon, the then Governor General of India, was the person who conceived the idea of opening a library for the use of the public. He noticed both the libraries — Imperial Library and Calcutta Public Library—were under-utilised for the want of facilities or restrictions. So, he decided to amalgamate the rich collection of both of these libraries. He was successful in effecting the amalgamation of Calcutta Public Library with the then Imperial Library under certain terms.

The library, called Imperial Library, was formally opened to the public on 30th January 1903 at Metcalf Hall, Kolkata. The aims and objectives of the Imperial Library, well defined in a Notification in the 'Gazette of India' as—'It is intended that it should be a library of reference, a working place for students and a repository of material for the future historians of India, in which, so far as possible, every work written about India, at any time, can be seen and read.'

John Macfarlane, the Asst. Librarian of the British Museum, London, was appointed as the first Librarian of the Imperial Library. After his death, the famous scholar and linguist Harinath De took over the charge of the library. After his death J.A. Chapman became the librarian. Mr. Chapman showed keen interest in the affairs of the library and tried hard to improve its status. After his retirement, Khan Bahadur M.A. Asadulla was appointed as the librarian and he continued as the librarian till July 1947.

The policy of acquisition broadly adhered to by the Imperial Library was enunciated by Lord Curzon in his speech at the opening ceremony of the library,—"The general idea of the whole Library is that it should contain all the books that have been written about India in popular tongues, with such additions as are required to make it a good all-round library of standard works of reference."

Declaring the Imperial Library as the National Library

After the independence the Government of India changed the name of the Imperial Library as the National Library, with an enactment of the Imperial Library (change of name) Act, 1948 and the collection was shifted from the Esplanade to the present Belvedere Estate. On 1st February 1953 the National Library was opened to the public, inaugurated by Maulana Abul Kalam Azad. Sri B.S. Kesavan was appointed as the first librarian of the National Library.

Collections

Indian Languages Collection

National Library receives books and periodicals in almost all the Indian languages. These are received under the Delivery of Books and Newspapers (Public Libraries) Act, 1954. (D.B. Act). Language divisions acquire process and provide the reading materials to the readers in their respective languages. Hindi, Kashmiri, Punjabi, Sindhi, Telugu and Urdu language divisions maintain their own stacks. Other language books are stacked by the stack division. Language divisions are also responsible to answer the short and long range reference queries.

The library has separate Indian language division for—

- Assamese,
- Bengali, Gujarati,
- Hindi,
- Kannada,
- Kashmiri,
- Malayalam,
- Marathi,
- Oriya,
- Punjabi,
- Sanskrit,
- Sindhi,
- Tamil,
- Telugu, and
- Urdu Languages.

English and Foreign Language Collection

The National Library has an invaluable collection in English language, because of the systematic collection development by Calcutta Public Library as well as by the Imperial Library. Imperial library had a good number of Arabic and Persian works and few other foreign language books. In 1985 European Languages Division was reorganized and five separate divisions were formed. They are:

- East Asian Languages Division,
- Germanic Languages Division,

- Romance Languages Division,
- Slavonic Languages Division,
- West Asian, and
- African Languages Division.

Rare Books Collection

The National Library has innumerable number of rare books and other reading materials. Earlier, these items were stacked with other books. But, in 1973, a separate Rare Books Division was established to take care of the rare books. At present the books published prior to 1860 are considered as rare books. Along with such materials, manuscripts and microfilms of the library are also stacked in this division.

Science and Technology Collection

As per the recommendations of the 'Reviewing Committee' (1968), Science and Technology Division was set-up in 1972 in the National Library, India. The basic function of this division is to collect and disseminate the core material in science and technology. At present the division holds about 17,000 books and monographs and 800 titles of current periodicals. The division provides reading facilities to the users. This is the only division which has an open access stack system.

Indian Official Documents

All the publications of Government of India, State Governments, Union Territories, Government Undertakings, and Autonomous Bodies are collected, processed and preserved separately. A separate division for this purpose was established in 1972. The Library owns a very rich collection of Indian official documents from the days of East India Company to the present day. The collection also includes the documents published by the Government of Great Britain relating to India. A good collection of Burmese documents and few documents of Aden, Ceylon, Persian Gulf Political Residency are also part of this collection. At present the division has 4,90,000 documents.

Foreign Official Documents

The National Library is one of the repository libraries for United Nations organisation and its agencies. Thus, all the publications of U.N.O. and its agencies are received by the library free of cost. These documents are processed and stacked separately. The library also receives publications of the Governments of United States of America, Great Britain, Canada, Commonwealth Nations, and the publications of European Economic Committee. Almost all the volumes of the sectional sets of British Parliamentary papers since the beginning of the 19th century are also available. Apart from the depositary copies, the Library also acquires selected foreign publications through purchase. At present the Library has 400,000 foreign official documents.

Newspapers and Periodicals

All the newspapers and periodicals of Indian languages are received and processed in their respective language divisions. But English newspapers and periodicals—both the Indian and foreign, are acquired and processed separately. Separate Serials division is responsible for acquiring and processing of English Newspapers and periodicals. Library has a rich collection of late 19th and early 20th century newspapers and periodicals, but almost all of them are incomplete. The catalogue of periodicals, newspapers and gazettes available in the library up to 1953 is available.

Manuscripts

National Library has about 3600 rare and historically important manuscripts in different languages. These manuscripts are preserved separately along with other important and rare books in the Rare Books Division. The xylographs presented by H.E. the Dalai Lama are also preserved in this collection.

Maps and Prints

The library has a rich collection of maps. The collection ranges from 17th century onwards. Indian topographical sheets of earlier days (at scale of one inch, half inch and quarter inch to a mile) and maps of natural resources, population, transport and communication systems, agricultural production, Soil, Vegetation and Geology of India form the major part of the collection. At present the library has 85,000 printed maps, 54 cartographic manuscripts and 280 atlases.

Microforms

The Library has 500 rolls of Microfilms and 1000 Microfiches. These are preserved in the Rare Books division. Census of India (1872-1951) is one of the most important and rare document available in the form of Microfiches.

Modernization Activities

The Computer Division is the youngest division in the Library. It was established in 1988 to augment the modernisation activities in the Library. It started with a Mini Computer—HP 3000. MINISIS, a RDBMS software was installed for bibliographic control activities. In 2001 the Library switched over to Client-Server Environment with SUN E450 as the server. At present a Campus Wide Network is being developed with 98 HP Pentium III PCs as nodes.

Digitisation

The scanning and archiving or rare and brittle books and other documents on compact disc is undertaken. English books and documents published before 1900 and Indian publications of pre-1920 are considered for digitisation. So far 6,600 selected books in Indian and English languages have already been scanned and stored on 548 CDs— a total of over 25,00,000 pages.

Administration

The National Library is an institution by itself. It has its own separate administrative wing. Garden and the Security divisions are also part of it. The Director is the head of the institution. The Librarian is called the Principal Library and Information Officer (P.L.I.O.).

Membership

There are four types of members:

- Reading Room Member
- Lending Member
- Daily Card Member
- Outstation Membership

Services Inter-Library Loan

Selected libraries of the country and abroad may borrow the books for their readers from the National Library through inter-library loan facility. Four books are lent out for a period of 21 days for Indian libraries and two months for foreign libraries. Both ways postage is to be borne by the borrowing library. The National Library also borrows books from other libraries on reader's request, if the book is not available in the Library.

Bibliographic Services

Research scholars, Government agencies, universities and national level institutions may avail this facility. Selected list of reading materials or bibliographies are prepared by the library on request. Special bibliographies are prepared to augment the exhibitions, which the National Library holds. Compilation of exhaustive bibliographies on special topics, like Indology, are under way. The library provides bibliographies and/or bibliographic statistics to the national and international organisations. The Library provides supports the Central Reference Library, Kolkata in compiling the Indian National Bibliography.

Reprographic Services

Members of both the reading room and lending division may avail reprographic facilities against payment. The photocopies, microfilms and microfilms printout/photocopy will be provided within the limits of the International Copy Rights Act.

Services for Children

The National Library has a separate division for the children. Equipped with English, Indian and few foreign languages books, the division caters the information as well as recreational needs of the children. No formal membership is required to use this section. Any child can enter the Children's section, sign in a register and use the books in the division. The children's divisions' collection is not lent out. At present the Children's Library hold about 28,000 books and many periodicals.

Training and Guidance

The library provides training and guidance in conservation of library materials and in modernisation activities of the libraries to the different institutions on request. Regular courses are conducted in the National Library premises and in different parts of India, to impart knowledge in these fields.

The national library occupies the highest position in the national library system of a country. Yet, the national library still functions like a big public library.

ACADEMIC LIBRARY SYSTEM

The system of formal education consists of three stages:

1. School
2. College
3. University

A library attached to any of these academic institutions is called an academic library. Academic libraries differ from public library and special library in scope, collection and services. The main function of academic library is to function as an auxiliary of the parent institution in carrying out its teaching programme effectively. The primary characteristic of a good academic library is its complete identification with its own institution. The measure of its excellence is the extent to which its resources and services support its institution's objectives. Academic library is the most important intellectual resource of the academic community and helps the members of the institution individually as well as collectively for:

- Self-development,
- Fulfilment of curriculum requirements, and
- promotion of study and research.

SCHOOL LIBRARY

School is the primary centre for good citizenship. It is the foundation for any higher education. The formulation of the reading habit in students has to commence right from the day they step into the school. Every child with an average intelligence and ability starts taking keen interest in knowing things with curiosity. Right from the schooling he is on the way to acquire and enrich knowledge. The school library as a part of the school helps in achieving this goal.

Objectives

School library being a part of educational set-up does have aims and objectives as those of the school itself and the aims of the school are not too far from the aims of education in general. Whatever may be the level of school library, it aims to provide—

(1) materials for the use of pupils and teachers,
(2) develop and promote reading interest;
(3) encourage research and study from many sources; and
(4) teach the use of books and libraries, and provide recreational and leisure time reading.

Purposes

School library is the cradle of the intellectual conditioning of the child. It awakens and fosters reading habits among children and enlightens the immature minds. The growth and development of boys and girls is of paramount importance in school education. Hence the school library must be designed to fulfil the specific purposes such as—

- To participate in the school programme as it strives to meet the needs of pupils, teachers, parents and other community members.
- To provide boys and girls with the library materials and services most appropriate and most meaningful in their growth and development as individuals.
- To stimulate and guide pupils in all phases of their reading so that they may find increasing enjoyment and satisfaction and may grow in critical judgment and appreciation.
- To provide an opportunity through library experiences for boys and girls to develop helpful interests, to make satisfactory personal adjustments and to acquire desirable social attitudes.
- To help children and people to become skilful and discriminating users of libraries and audio-visual materials.

- To work with teachers in the selection and use of all types of library materials which contribute to the teaching programme.
- To participate with teachers and administrators in programmes for continuing professional and cultural growth of the school staff.

Functions

The educational pattern should be such that they orient the student's attitudes more towards the usage of library. For this kind of motivation, the parent, teacher and librarian all the three are responsible. From the institutional point of view the following are the essential functions of any school library, be primary, secondary;

(1) To support and supplement the objective of the parent body;
(2) To inculcated in the students the reading habit and to develop interest in library;
(3) To initiate the students to visit and further use the library;
(4) To create awareness in the students of the availability of different types of information sources; and
(5) To assist them in choosing the right document and to use the reference sources.

The primary function of a school library would be to orient and initiate the students to encourage and expand their library interests and usage. Dr. S.R. Ranganathan advocates library hour in the school's regular time table. This stimulates the teachers and students to find a definite means of library use. The cordial relation between the Librarian *vs.* Students and Librarian *vs.* Staff could be strengthened and personalized. Thus the school library functions as a—

- Service agency,
- A teaching agency,
- A resource centre, and
- Knowledge disseminating centre.

Collection

The nature and size of the library may vary from school to school depending upon the level, programme of instruction, student's needs, finance, etc. The collection of school library includes—

- Books
- Magazines
- Pictures
- Models
- Exhibits
- A.V. aids
- Instructional materials

All collection should be organized so that it is easily accessible to the students and teachers for effective use.

Clientele

Usually school library serves students and teachers and the other people are not permitted. In absence of a developed public library system it would be desirable for a school library to throw open its collection and services to the public as well particularly in villages.

Services

The school library provides the following services:

- Lending service
- Reference service
- Reprographic service
- Extension services

COLLEGE LIBRARY

The students, when they move from school to college level, needless to say their information needs too change and widen. A level it is more a process of learning than listening to classroom lectures, self-efforts gain significance. As true of any other academic library, college library's objectives too are based and in line with objectives of the college/parent body. The college libraries should primarily support the teaching programmes, in addition to other services warranted of a college library.

Objectives

The following are to objectives of college library as laid down by American Library Association (ALA):

(1) To assist in carrying out the instructional programmer of the college;
(2) To secure and organize service, books, periodicals and other library materials;
(3) To provide the physical facilities and equipment that will assist in the using of library resource;
(4) To train and guide students in the efficient use of the library and reference material;
(5) To encourage students to develop the habit of self-education;
(6) To encourage extra-curricular use of library materials;
(7) To assist and cooperate with faculty members in their instructional programmes;
(8) To fulfil the needs of research scholars, if any; and
(9) To co-operate with other libraries in the area and elsewhere.

Functions

If it is taken for granted that the college library thought to be an instrument of self-education, then the primary function of the college library is to create awareness and initiate the students to feel library as an integral part of their career. This presupposes necessarily the following functions of a college library:

(1) To provide sufficient library materials—textbooks, reference books, periodicals, etc. the institutional programmers;
(2) Organize and process the reading materials in a helpful way to make them easily available and accessible to the students and staff;
(3) Informing the users the arrivals of new additions to the library and other facilities available for the convenience and usefulness of the readers;
(4) Organizing initiation of freshman and user orientation programs in a gradual process and features of the college library activity;

(5) Offering reference service especially ready service;
(6) Extending bibliographical services on dement especially from the staff;
(7) Guiding and assisting the students in their extra-curricular activities; and
(8) Organizing programmers like Library Week Celebrations, one day Seminars, discussions to increase library consciousness in the minds of staff and students.

On the whole a college should enable the students and staff to seek and cultivate reading habit new knowledge to engage vigorously and fearlessly in the pursuit of truth and to interpret old knowledge and beliefs in the light of new needs discoveries.

Clientele

The clientele of the college library comprise of—

- Students,
- Faculty members,
- Staff, and
- Scholars.

Services

The services offered by the College library are—

- Lending service,
- Reference service,
- Inter-library loan,
- Referral service, and
- Reprographic service, etc.

UNIVERSITY LIBRARY

University is center of learning for higher education. It imparts instruction at graduate and postgraduate levels and provides facilities for research and specialisation. Each University has a central library attached to it and may have many constituent libraries attached to various departments. The University Library considered as the pulsing heart around which all the other academic activities function or it is the sun, around which teaching, learning and research revolve around.

Objectives

All the commissions on education in all the countries aptly describe the place of library in higher education. And the primary objective the University library is to promote and support the academic community in five stages. According to Dr. R.S. Ranganathan,

(1) *Preparatory study*—To gather and organize reading materials on all subjects of study for preparatory study before the class lectures;
(2) *Parallel study*—To provide another set of reading materials for parallel study after class lecture;
(3) *Follow-up study*—To provide a still another with entertaining and elevating books for use during leisure hours;
(4) *Leisure study*—To conserves the research potential for the services to advanced students, the scholars and teachers; and
(5) *Conservation*—To feed the stands with entertaining and elevation books for use during leisure hours.

The basic functions of a University Library are—

(i) To acquire and accumulate varied types of use material for meeting the needs of different levels of users;
(ii) To arrange the essential reading material and other library facilities for the smooth running of all formal programmes of learning;
(iii) To guide research scholars and provide them the resources useful for enhancement of research projects;
(iv) To keep the faculty members informed of the latest nascent thoughts in their fields of specialization;
(v) To establish an instruction centre in the library and render reader's advisory services so as to enable them to make maximum use of library resources; and
(vi) To create an atmosphere which brings the users and

use materials together so as to encourage reading for personality development, self-finance, pleasure and making the intellectual curiosity more acute and strong; and

(vii) To keep the authorities informed of the achievements and literary output of the university, to seek support and financial assistance for the development of the library.

Collection

University library has to cater to the diverse needs of undergraduates, postgraduates, research scholars and faculty members. It renders useful services like indexing, abstracting, bibliographical, reprographic, translation and other similar services. The collection in a university library is built up by taking into account the requirements of the students pursuing various formal courses, the researchers and teachers in all areas of higher learning.

The collection of a university library includes books of common interests to the students such as those prescribed in the curriculum of text-books and for supplementary reading; books for research and faculty members for their study, teaching and research. These may include old as well as the recent editions for detailed and specialized study, general as well as specialized subject reference books; newspapers, magazines and periodicals – general as well as in various subject areas, indexing and abstracting journals for research needs of the scholars, government publications, serials, pamphlets, patents, monographs, thesis, dissertations, archive material, etc., non-book material and their readers.

Generally, undue emphasis is placed on the acquisition of multiple copies of the text-books. Many university libraries have established 'Text-book banks', allocating large amounts for the purchase of text books. Such a policy hampers the use of other good books as the majority of the students hardly feel interested in looking beyond textbooks.

Functions

University library should keep it self in close touch with the progress of work at class room, staff room as its duty to students and staff. Wilson and Tuber assign six functions to the University library—

(1) Conversation of knowledge and ideas;
(2) Teaching;
(3) Research;
(4) Publication;
(5) Extension services; and
(6) Interpretation.

However, it must be noted that these functions are generalized and they vary from country to country.

Provision of effective library service conductive to academic environment calls for two major factors; viz. Orientation and Stimulation of Reading Librarian through the library services and activities is the prime motivation. The third major function of a university library could be said as References, Compilation of Bibliographies, Indexing and Abstracting Services, Translation and Reprographic Services, Current Awareness and SDI (Selective Dissemination of Information) Services, etc.

To conclude, the words of U.G.C. (UK, 1921) can be quoted here. It said, "The character and efficiency of a University of a University may be gauged by its treatment of its central organ, the library."

SPECIAL LIBRARY

Special libraries in the form they are known today, began to emerge and develop in the beginnings of the 20th century, in response to the increased tempo of industrial, scientific and technological advances. The term special library means a library which is concerned almost exclusively with the literature of a particular subject or group of subjects. It is viewed differently by different people as to the usage of the term in a particular way. To quote L.M. Harrod it is a collection of books and other printed graphic of recorded material relating with a limited field of knowledge and provided by a learned society, research organization, industrial or commercial undertaking, government departments or even educational institutions. It may also be special branch of a public library serving certain interests or occupational grounds such as a technical library or special subject library meeting the needs of all enquiries on that given subject such as music library.

Definition

The meaning of the special libraries can be conceived on the basis of its six basis factors, namely,

- Special collection,
- Special objectives,
- Special readers/users,
- Special location,
- Special information work, and
- Special service/offered.

According to L.H. Morley, special library is that unit in the organization responsible for locating and supplying whatever knowledge and experience that may advance its activities.

The renowned library scientist D.J. Foskett defines special library as one serving a group, having an extra-library existence, whose members direct at least some of their activities towards a common purpose. This excludes academic libraries as their users pursue their individual ends and are in no sense united by common purpose.

Dr. S.R. Ranganathan prefers call it the "Specialist Library", to supply detailed information regarding some specific fields—scientific, technological or otherwise. The resources are specialized and the users are specialists.

Why Special Libraries

The important factors that gave rise to the origin of special libraries are:

- Tremendous growth in specialized literatures;
- Pinpointed and intensive approach to specific information; and
- Application of the research results for further growth of subject areas.

Objectives

As regards the ultimate goal of special libraries there is no basic difference between a special library and the academic libraries. The basic objectives of a special library are:

- To implement the policies of the organization or concern to which they are attached.
- To impart facts and information rather than recreation.
- To feed the latest and up-to-date information to the researchers, managers, others concerned who are engaged in promoting the interests of the organization.
- To meet all the information needs of the organization and its members.

Functions

The functions of a special library are based on the objectives set-forth by the organization with which it is attached. The main functions of acquisition, organization and dissemination of materials and information remain the same in special libraries as in other libraries. But there is difference in approach, performance and techniques as well as materials collected. The special library performs the following functions:

(1) Collects, maintain, stores and retrieves data and information in view of the its goal;
(2) Analyses, synthesizes, evaluates and repackages the information;
(3) Providing critical reviews, reports, etc.;
(4) Provides consultation to queries, solutions to problems, guidance and advisory services on demand;
(5) Provides current awareness service and SDI (in anticipation of course);
(6) Provides indexes, abstracts, summaries and extracts;
(7) Performs literature searches and reference services;
(8) Offers inter-library loan to provide additionally needed materials;
(9) Organizes publication, seminar, discussion and other publicity programmes; and
(10) Provides bibliographic service both on dement and in anticipation and compiles union catalogues,

These functions call upon well-trained library personnel with distinctive qualities and qualifications to the tremendous responsibilities.

Collection

A special library lays marked emphasis on special collection—collection in specific field. The collection is built up on keeping in view the objectives and policies of the parent organization. The collection may also fulfil research requirements of the organization, but does not aim at collecting documents relating to formal education.

Clientele

A special library has specialist clientele with common interest, i.e. all the clientele's interest and requirements evolve around achieving the goals and objectives of the organization. The clientele normally have no individual interests or requirements.

Services

Each special library is a unique library. An information need of each special library is special and different from other libraries. Services of special library should be specially designed. Emphasis is to be made on information services which may be provided through documentation, current awareness service, SDI. These services require advanced techniques of information storage and retrieval.

FIVE LAWS OF LIBRARY SCIENCE

Laws of Library Science are subject laws and their jurisdiction is the subject of Library and Information Science. These laws are recognized and accepted as binding on all the branches of Library science such as classification, cataloguing, reference service, book selection, administration, etc. When we say laws of library science we refer to the five laws enunciated by Dr. S.R. Ranganathan, though conceived in 1924, the five laws of library science were published in 1931. The five laws are:

(1) Books are for use
(2) Every reader his/her book

(3) Every book its reader
(4) Save the time of the reader
(5) Library is a growing organism.

These five laws look very trivial, but embody deep thought. These laws give philosophical base, guaranteeing an everlasting future to the subject of Library and Information Science, library profession and library users. Let us now examine the implication of these five laws in detail.

First Law: Books are for Use

The first of Law of Library Science is "Books are for use." No one will question the correctness of this law. But in actual practice this is deplorably neglected by the authorities in its implementation. Books are the creation of God via the human beings. A book is a guide, a friend and a philosopher. The primary purpose of writing a book is the thoughts it contain should be communicated to all. To do so it is necessary to put the book to use. The first law demands that all efforts should be made to ensure that every book kept in the library used, because it is created for use. The first law has its implications on the following factors;

(1) Location
(2) Arrangement
(3) Building
(4) Book Selection
(5) Finance
(6) Fitting and furniture
(7) Working Hours
(8) Readers
(9) Rules and Regulation
(10) Staff.

Location

The location of a library may in general, be taken as an Index of the degree of faith the library authorities have in the first law. Distance must not stand in the way of the free and full use of books. If the resources of the library are to be fully exploited; if the library is to play a vital role of the community's intellectual centre, it must be located in the midst of the users. The common tendency among users is 'Principle of Least Effort'. A centrally located library will immensely help in increasing the use and becoming the hub of the institution's intellectual attainments.

Arrangement

The term 'arrangement' includes arrangement of various sections in the library and further arrangement within each of these sections, for instance, self-arrangement in the stock room. The library has to provide sufficient 'path-finders' such as Bay-Guides Name plates and Boards, etc. to enable the user to have easier and self-dependent access to varies units of the library. The positioning of various units likes New Arrival 'Stand' Circulation Desk, Property Counters, and Catalogue Cabinet. Reference Desk, Section Unit, Stack Room and Reading Room all should be sufficient and one leading to another. The gangways between rooms of bookshelves should be sufficient so also the pathway between reading tables. The height of the stack room shelves needs attention as the reader is unable to reach it, books may not be put into use.

Building

The library building needs careful planning by a team including librarian, architect and engineer. The exterior and interior of the building should be very inviting and functional. The various sections of the library should be well-articulated. There should be also space for lectures, seminars, reading circles and every other form of extension service. Above all, the building should be located in an easily and readily accessible part of the locality.

Book Selection

Every library has an unique user population and the library collection has to be user-based. Hence, the needs and demands are to be assessed before book selection is made. An unwarranted book collection defeats the very purpose of the library. In the process of selection, other factors to be taken care of include the edition, physical features of the book, viz. size, shape, style of printing, etc., dates of publications and such others. The first law envisages that books should be user's choice and continuously read enjoyed and understood.

Finance

The most important factor is the budget. The library usage can be increased only with sufficient reading materials and staff to serve the user population. Money can assure adequate materials and men library personnel. Thanks to library legislation, the libraries in those regions where library Acts are enacted finance is assured. Academic and special libraries are dependent on their institution that has to be magnanimous enough to allot better library budget to enhance the library usage.

Fitting and Furniture

The furniture requirements and specification differ from one library section to another. A working table in a technical section do not suit the purpose of a reading room. The book racks should be reachable to all users. The furniture should be functional to all users. The furniture should be functional, comfortable and durable. Lighting and ventilation should enable the user to sit for long continuous hours without irritation and disturbance.

Working Hours

The influence of the first law has no less profound on library hours. In view of users' habit and convenience, the working hours should be carefully planned. It is indeed considered criminal to close a library at any time when people can conveniently use it. Any money spent on library functions is to be well any legitimately spent. This calls for response from academic, special and public libraries and the common concept is the ideal arrangement would be that libraries always should be open suitable to users' population.

Readers

Library users are responsible enough in proper handing and behaviour inside as well as outside the library. Observation of silence and proper handing of library furniture and reading materials, prompt return of the discharged documents. Proper placement, correct shelving avoidance of hiding and stealing of books are all expected of users for maximum usage of library by one and all.

Rules and Regulations

Library's rules and regulations should be flexible and helpful rather than threatening. It should be framed as to the users' convenience and advantage. Rigid policies obstruct free access to any library. Instead should be warm, cardinal, guiding, and assisting and clear, with less ambiguity.

Staff

The advent of the First Law has had the most vital effect on the library staff. It is the staff who make or mar the library ultimately. The qualities and qualifications of library staff needs care while recruitment. The first law requires that to disseminate knowledge and to put the books to maximum use, the library must have qualified and professionally trained staff. The library staff should be given academic status and good scales of pay. Staff too should realize their professional responsibilities and ethics, attitudes towards their authorities, colleagues and readers, which could ensure better service and in turn maximum usage of the users.

Second Law: Every Reader His/Her Book

The second law is "Every Reader His/Her Book." Here the emphasis is on the reader or user of the Library. The basic requisites to satisfy the second law are as follows:

- The books should be selected according to the taste of the readers. If the books are procured according to the requirements and taste of the users then the librarian can provide them the right documents.
- If the documents are not available in the library then it has to procure on inter-library loan basis so that the right books will be connected with the right reader.
- The third preferable thing is open access system. In the open access system, the user will have better changes to select the right documents.
- The hidden contents of the documents should be brought to the knowledge of the users by giving cross-reference entries, i.e. subject analytical entries in the library catalogue. It will help the reader to select the right document.

The revolutionary cry of the Second Law is 'Books for all'. The Second Law stresses the democratization of the library where every reader has equal right to get the book of his interest. The Second Law magnifies the library into a nation-wide problem. If the First Law threw open the existing libraries the Second Law plants, new libraries and brings about the culture of new species if libraries. The Second Law with its revolutionary appeal dropped the seeds of the Library Movement all through the world.

The Second Law expects the Library Authorities to have careful scrutiny over Book Selection. Organization and Services to serve its collections for all, whose requirements are varied.

The question then that arises here is: What then are the obligations involved in an undertaking to provide every person his/her book? This is considered under four categories:

- The obligations of the state;
- The obligations of the Library Authority;
- The obligations of the Library Staff; and
- The obligations of the Reader.

Obligations of the State

The state has certain obligations to•its citizen and one of these is to provide equal opportunity to read. UNESCO declares in its manifesto that the right of access to information is one of the fundamental rights of every citizen. Concepts like universal availability of publications (UAP) also stress "books for all" phenomenon. State has to play a vital role to achieve it. Dr. S.R. Ranganathan has discussed the obligations of the state under three heads, namely,

- Finance;
- Legislation; and
- Co-ordination.

Adequate finance is the first requirement for running a chain of libraries to serve the needs of all. The state should provide finance in two ways by giving grant and by levying library cess. In a democratic society every citizen has the right to read and right of access to reading materials. The state should make available to all facilities for reading throughout their life. This can be achieved through library legislation. Further coordination among libraries ensure maximum utilization of available resources of a country or state. Coordination among libraries may become easy to implement if desired so by the state. The second law provides for the development and orderly functioning of a network of public libraries. The second law provides:

- State library act;
- State library authority;
- Local library authority;
- Local library committee and village library committee;
- State central library.

Obligations of the Library Authority

The second law has something to say to library authorities in respect of selection of books and staff. A library has very limited finance. It is therefore more desirable to assess the requirements of the users before selecting books for the library. The library should select books on all occupations of the actual and potential readers. For this purpose, the librarians need to know the subject scatter, standard scatter and language scatter of the books. With a reasonable collection of encyclopaedias and other reference books the problem of every reader his/her book will be solved to a greater extent.

Obligations of the Staff

The second law lays marked emphasis on the role and obligation of library staff. With their professional competence and missionary zeal they can satisfy the demand of the second law. When a reader enters the library, the staff should approach him with helping hand. Many new readers need initiation in the use of library.

Obligations of the Readers

The second law expects the readers also to discharge some responsibilities. Readers should be willing to observe library rules. Besides readers should restrain from cutting pages from books, hiding books, keeping books beyond due date, etc. All such acts amount to keeping other readers away from their books.

Third Law: Every Book its Reader

The First Law in a Sense is a complement to the Second Law and while the Second Law concerned itself with the task of finding for every reader his appropriate books. The Third Law would urge that an appropriate reader should be found for every book. The Third Law suggests that every book should get its reader. Books are mute and dumb entities. They cannot travel to find their readers. In order to make each and every book in a library used by readers, certain devices have to be adopted. The following factors are those, which the Third Law pleads for attention to fulfil its requirements;

- Book Selection;
- Catalogue;
- Extension Services;
- Open Access;
- Popular Departments;
- Publicity;
- Reference Service; and
- Shelf Arrangement.

Book Selection

An important bearing of this Law is Book Selection. One of the means for fulfilling the requirements of the third law is to give full weigh to the tastes and requirements of the clientele of the library. The book selection should be based on the following factors:

- The suggestions received directly from the users,
- The suggestions recorded by the assistants at the reference desk,
- The notes made from day-to-day observations by the reference staff,
- The prospective events of national and local importance, and
- The impressions gained in interviews with the leading members of the local community.

Catalogue

The library catalogue can be of immense help to set for

even book its reader. The different types of catalogue entries especially analytical entries do increase the use of books.

Extension Service

The object of extension is to convert the non-readers to readers, to create and stimulate the reading habits, to bring book and reader together and to turn the library into a social center whose function is the encouragement of reading. Thus those libraries that have come under the influence of the Third Law value these aims highly and take to extension service with great zeal.

Open Access System

In an open access library, the reader is permitted to wander among the books and lay his hands on any of them at his will and pleasure. The most prominent of the means used by libraries to satisfy the Third Law is the Open Access System. Open access increases the use of books. While making search for books, the readers are able to discover books which they did not know that the library had.

Popular Departments

One method by which potential readers could be converted into actual readers of the library is to provide the library with a Newspaper Room and a Magazine Room. It is a matter of common experience that these rooms attract a larger crowd than the library proper and the library staff could develop rapport with patrons easily and quickly here and try to lead few of them to the stack and reading rooms.

Reference Service

The mechanical devices like open access classified shelf arrangement and analytical cataloguing are seldom sufficient. The requirement always require the provision of human being as canvassing agents for books. The provision of such a staff—the reference staff as it is called—is one of the effective devices employed by modern libraries to carry out the mandate of the Third Law. The reference staff must know the qualities of the books thoroughly and act as a matchmaker between books and readers.

Publicity

Publicity is a powerful weapon to allure the readers to the library and thereby increase the chances for every book to find its reader. Continuous publicity is carried through annual reports, library bulletins, latest additions, special service folders, window displays, library week celebrations, etc. There are ample media to keep up the camping creating awareness amongst the public.

Shelf-Arrangement

Even in an open-access library, the chances for the rudiment of the Third Law can be made by the principle adopted for the shelf-arrangement. The third law emphasizes the need of arranging the books in a classified arrangement based on their thought content. Another important factor in shelf-arrangement which has a decided effect on the chance of a Book to get its reader is its easy accessibility to the readers of average height.

Fourth Law: Save the Time of the Reader

The fourth law "Save the time of the reader" demands that the reader should not be delayed unnecessarily. Delay causes frustration and dissatisfaction. A dissatisfied reader ceases to come to the library. It is therefore essential to keep the readers satisfied. A reader is satisfied to the most extent if he gets the services in a minimum possible time. Saving the time of the reader means saving his subjective time as well as objective time. Subjective time is the time which a reader feels he has spent in waiting for a service or a book. Objective time is the time actually spent is waiting for a service or a book. The following are the factors influencing the Fourth Law.

- Bibliography;
- Choice of books;
- Co-operation;
- Issue Method;
- Location;
- Pathfinders;
- Reference Service;
- Rules and Regulations;
- Shelf-Arrangement; and
- Time of the Staff.

Bibliography

The time involved in searching and listing together the required reading material available within the library and elsewhere is very large. It is not proper to divert the time of busy readers, especially researchers to the task of mere listing them. It would be economical to either have a fair and representative selection of bibliographical publications or prepare one such to suit the local needs. Due to information explosion numerous primary sources of information are scattered, especially Journal articles, which taxes the user's precious hours. Hence, indexing service can be of great help to readers.

Choice of Books

The main process that should be studied in the light of the Fourth Law is the choice of books. In a close access library the time involved in securing a book from the stack room is such that a reader runs away from going to such libraries. The system of maintenance at circulation desk keeping in track of books being on loan also influences the time spent by uses insides the library.

Cooperation

Another direction in which an attempt can be made to save the time of the staff and thereby reader is centralized acquisition and processing. The distribution of catalogue cards by the library of congress marks an epoch in the achievements of Fourth Law. Resource Sharing concept and library networks are other hallmarks in this direction.

Issue Method

Before the advent of the Fourth Law, the method of charging and discharging was very cumbersome and wasteful. But the recognition of the Fourth Law has led to the library profession to overhaul the charging system completely. It must be admitted that Library science owes the invention of the card system of charging and discharging to the sincere desire to satisfy the Fourth Law in all possible ways.

Location

The Fourth Law is also interested in the time taken by the reader to reach the library. The library should be located so as to be easily accessible.

Pathfinders

Assuming that the reader is admitted into the library and especially to the stockroom (open access system) he will be naturally be bewildered by the array of books and arrangement and may have to waste much time before reaching locating anything he requires for his purpose. It may be useful to place at the entrance the plan of the library and sign guides. And every shelf-plank be provided with necessary labels, shelf-guides, gangway guides to proceed in the stack-room. After that also it is essential that the spine of every has a tag marked with the call number enabling the reader identify and choose what he wants.

Reference Services

Beside the Mechanical tools some personal initiation will be essential to save the time of the reader. The reference staffs are sure to expedite the process of searching and distribution either the documents or the specific information required by readers. From the point of the fourth Law, the Reference service can be either Ready Reference/Short Range Reference Services and or Long Range Reference Services. Depending upon the nature of the user's query with experience and skillful reference staff can save the time of the reader to a larger extent.

Rules and Regulations

Rigid rules and regulations of a library can delay the service to the users. For instance, reprographic service is one which always consumes the users' time because of its lengthy procedure of filling application form and obtaining permission from the chief librarian. Such inconvenience and formalities can be as well avoided and made a routine to ensure a smooth flow of work within the library.

Shelf-Arrangement

The interest of the Fourth Law is not exhausted with all the above said factors. It has an equal interest in reforming the shelf-arrangement. In an open access library the nature of the shelf-arrangement can make or mar the mission of the Fourth Law. This law recommends proper shelf-arrangement according to some classification scheme.

Fifth Law: Library is a Growing Organism

Now, we come to the fifth and last law of Library Science. While the first four Laws deal with the functions of a library, the Fifth law tells us about the vital and lasting characteristics of the library as an institution. The elements of growth in a library are its size, (i.e collection and space), readers and staff. While the first four Laws indicated the spirit that should characterize the management and administration of libraries the Fifth Law enunciates a fundamental principle that should govern the planning and organization of libraries.

It is an accepted biological fact that a growing organism alone will survive. The Fifth law invites our attention to the fact that the library, as an institution, has all the attributes of a growing organism. The three main parts of the organism that are capable of growing in the concept of a library are the Books, Readers and Staff. It is well to repeat here that a modern library is a trinity of these factors. The library organization should plan its layout in such a way as to make it easy to keep with the necessary growth of the library. The organization of the library should plan in terms of—

- Growth in collection
- Growth in staff
- Growth in readers
- Growth in services

The implications of these five laws of Library Science have been profound, rich and revolution sings. These are all in conformity to the implications of every word in every Law. The implications suggest also some new practices yet to be implemented.

LIBRARY CO-OPERATION

In ancient times the bigness of collection was considered to be a significant factor in deciding the goodness of a library. A renounced library was supposed to have good number of manuscripts and other reading materials. This gave rise to the tendency of self-sufficiency among libraries. But the modern library has realized that the goal or aspiration of self-sufficiency is a delusion. The number of publications is growing in an exponential order and any library however large cannot procure all the publications with its limited resources. Today cooperation has become the lifestyle in all walks of human life.

Library cooperation signifies a symbol of good will, an intension to share resources, knowledge, bibliographical data, facilities and other fruits of technology, man's ingenuity and their results of accumulated wealth of knowledge.

Objectives

The basic objectives of library cooperation are:

- To reduce wasteful duplication of intellectual effort and the expense incurred in providing duplicate coverage of the same material.
- To provide an opportunity for the collaborating libraries to increase their resources to provide better services and more facilities without increase in their budget.
- To reduce the number of sources that a user must check in a given field and would assist in deciding whether services are appropriate or feasible.

The main objectives include the following:

(1) To increase available resources;
(2) To extend accessibility of resources;
(3) To diminish costs; and
(4) To promote exploitation of resources with the minimum expense in staff, time and tools.

Factors Necessitating Cooperation

Library cooperation as a means of extending the services and resources of libraries has its root in the socio-economic and technological changes being witnessed in the rapidly changing world. The factors that necessitate library cooperation are:

- Developments in the art of printing and in the field of paper technology;
- Bewildering discoveries in the field of science and technology;

- The growth in the types of publications;
- Explosion of knowledge and proliferation of subjects;
- Professionalisation of library science.

Ways and Means of Cooperation

The library cooperation can be achieved in the following areas of library activities:

(1) Administration and Organization.
(2) Acquisition and storage;
(3) Inter-Library Loan;
(4) Information Processing; and
(5) Information Services.

The major ways and means of library cooperation include Inter-library loan service—

1. Cooperative acquisition,
2. Centralised and cooperative cataloguing,
3. Union catalogue and bibliographical centres,
4. Documentation centres,
5. Union list of serials and bibliographies,
6. Cooperative reference and information services,
7. Cooperative storage, and
8. Cooperative photographic services.

Prerequisites for Cooperation and Resource Sharing

The pre-requisites for resource sharing among libraries are:

(1) Willingness to share for mutual benefit;
(2) Availability of resources to share; and
(3) Viable and realistic plan to achieve the objectives.

In brief resource sharing entails reciprocity implying a partnership in which each participant has something useful to contribute to other and which each is willing and able to make available, wherever needed. For effective resource sharing, the following are essential

(1) Board Agreement on-polices, procedures and programmers; areas of co-operation;
(2) Procedures laid down specially stated;

(3) Procedures need to be enforced;
(4) Time consciousness to speed up on the co-operative programmers; and
(5) Establishment of facilities for easy and faster accessibility and availability.

The success of any scheme of co-operation depends to a large extent upon the organization and administration.

EXTENSION SERVICES OF LIBRARY

It is now generally accepted that every member of a society ought to have access to the world of books. This means that education and literary awareness has well spread among the people of all civilization. In the process of this development, the library (public library) is in a special position to provide opportunity and the necessary materials for self-chosen and self-directed education. And a library is rated good or bad not by its staff strength, size of the library building and/or its collection but by its ability to put all its collection into fullest possible usage.

Decision relating to the range and quality of services provided by each library system will be matters of policy and as such should have the backing of the library authority and users' requirements. The librarian's task is to deploy the resources available efficiently and effectively. There are more users of public libraries today than at any time in the past. Yet unfortunately, misconceptions about the public library services are widespread. This is so even among the regular users. Partial use of a library is a waste. It is the principal duty of any public library to convert the non-users into users as they could grow larger in number if ignored or neglected.

There are still so many individuals, who exist both in urban and rural areas, experiencing difficulty to reach the library campus for varied reasons chiefly because of distance, cost and time. Few are of the category those could not and also not permitted to leave the premises of their stay such as hospitals and prisons, but the ones who would mostly need reading materials either to pass leisure time or as cure measures.

Emphasis in this instance will be that if the library is to occupy its proper and primary place in the society then public libraries must take efforts in dispelling these misconceptions and inconvenience prevalent among users. Their attention should be drawn to the value of libraries in contributing to the well-being of the individuals and the enrichment of the quality of life through encouragement of reading books, informal self-education and assistance in formal education. They should be shown how libraries can be of positive support to the cultural, educational, social, leisure professional, business and industrial activities. Herein arises the concept of 'Extension services' enabling the Public library and the community it has to serve to come much close to each other.

Extension Work—Definition

The Librarian's Glossary defines the term 'Extension work' as "Activities which are undertaken with the object of reaching growing of people who might otherwise be unaware of the library, such as lecture societies, rending circles, discussion groups, and the provision of books for prisons, clubs hospital and literary societies." Library Extension is also defined as "the provision lectures, film shows, etc. The library, arranging of talks, book display, etc. outside the library buildings in order to draw attention to the library book stock and services."

Extension Service is said to be a specialized form of activity reaching a particular group of people of reading community who are aware and/or unaware of availability or resources and services in a library.

Objective

A service institution does not serve only those who come to it, it also serves those who do not or cannot come to it. It does so by extending its services and thus by reaching those who do not or cannot reach it. The library is also a service institution and therefore it should also reach people by extending its services. By doing so, the library can convert many non-readers into readers. Objectives of extension work is to extend library services—

- By taking documents at the doorsteps of the people,
- To establish the library as the intellectual social and cultural centre, and
- To develop in people interest towards library by making available to them healthy, informative and recreational literature.

Need

The following factors emphasize the need for starting extension service by libraries:

- Limitation of would be readers
- Expectation of the third law
- Rights of citizens
- Social character of the library

Through extension programmes the librarians attempt to convert the library into a social centre. Their aim is—

- To convert non-users into users
- To create and stimulate the desire for good reading
- To act as a link between mind and idea
- To take effective part in the implementation of the cultural programme of the community
- To provide library services to schools not having their own libraries
- To participate in adult education programmes.

Forms of Extension Services

Extension activities will vary in type/from and in its extent from library to library. In general the extension services of a public library include the following:

1. Circulation of Library publication;
2. Cultural programmers;
3. Discussion groups;
4. Display and exhibition;
5. Film/Slide shows and other such AV aids use;
6. Library week celebrations;
7. Mass Media campaign;
8. Mobile system;
9. Reader's Circles clubs;
10. Reading programmer;
11. Story Hours;
12. Study Groups on Subject;
13. Talks and Lectures;
14. Village Contacts; and
15. Quizzes.

Circulation of Library Publications

Library publications include leaflets, pamphlets, bulletins, reports, handbooks, new arrivals list/recent additions list, and a whole range of such publications. A high standard of presentation both in libraries and through Library publications encourage the use of books and reading materials. This helps to publish the wide range of facilities and additional services available. The publications should be brief and to the point and care must be exercised in choosing a layout; type and papers and methods of printing so as to create maximum impact and economically as possible. Overlap in content needs to be avoided. However, this form of extension services could be adopted only for the literate user community.

Cultural Programmes

This type of extension service is as old as the concept of public library itself. Undoubtedly it is one of the best methods to attract the public, especially non-users and illiterate groups. This method also converts a public library into social and cultural center. The cultural programmes can be in the form of a musical score, drama, dance-drama, magic show, celebration of festival, kathakalasebam, etc. This kind of entrainment can attract more and more people towards the library and could be counted upon as a good source of inspiration, recreation and education.

Discussion Groups

This from of service can be extended to specialists on any topic of common group interest. It offers an opportunity to come together and share ideas and thoughts, ultimately promoting the desire to learn, read and bear more ideas. The feature of this form is its informal and general nature. So to say, it is one of the chief ways of bridging the gap between the literates and illiterates and lifting the rays of ignorance in the group.

Display and Exhibition

Some libraries in the west have even set-up their own publicity departments with full time qualified display artists. The effect of this method has been to improve the standard and quality of library services and thereby leading to an improved image of the library. This could be a daily routine feature or an occasional one. This form attracts both the regular users and occasional visitors attention. Two kinds of display illustrating the range of services offered and a career display may be used. In any kind of display, illustrative materials in the form of graphs, drawings, diagrams, poster charts, portraits and three dimensional objects will be take precedence over text. Text should be concise.

Film/Slide Shows Other Audio-Visual Aids

Another useful means which can be used as part of an extension activity is a tape slide presentation. A few library authorities have made documentary films about this library and illustrations of the library sources and services. Videocassettes may prove to be cheaper and more attractive ones.

Library Week Celebrations

Generally, libraries organize the library week from 14th November of every year. During this one week period lectures, talks, cultural programs, discussions are normally arranged bringing in the user community together. Nevertheless, library week serves to be one of the best publicity programmes devised by the libraries to expose it to the public it serves.

Mass Media Campaign

Mass Media—Press, Radio and Television offers opportunities to promote the desire for books and reading habits. Press releases, radio broadcast and TV Serials and episodes can publish library's collection and its services. Information via mass media reaches a large mass quickly, cheaply and with more impact on the target group.

Mobile Libraries

A mobile library is a library on wheels. It moves from one place to other on fixed timings and serves many localities. Therefore, it is one of the most effective and economical extension services. In America, the first library mobile service was started in horse-driven carriages. Later specially designed motor vans were built up to suit the requirements of the mobile library. The physical appearance and shape of the mobile van has been varying from time to time.

Reader's Circles/Clubs

'Friends of Libraries Group' is one kind of library-oriented activity, which does not necessarily involve library staff. This service chiefly relates to the literates. Readers of general and/or specific interest group meet regularly for discussion and sharing, based on library reading. This can be arranged and sponsored by the local authorities. This encourages the reading habit and increases the public awareness of various books and literature and of library services generally. Followed by the meeting, concerned documents are pursued for reading.

Reading Programmes

This kind of outreach activity is exclusively meant and useful for a specific group of users like blind people, illiterates and even children at times. Under this program, the library takes the responsibility to attend to this disadvantaged people, carry the reading materials to the rural areas and read them out either with the assistance of their own stall or local volunteers.

Story Hours

Libraries also arrange for story hours, plays, talks and other attractive forms of extension services to allure children to come to the library. The librarians also occasionally arrange for dramatic performance by amateur troops.

Study Groups

This form is meant for a special user group, namely, academicians and professionals. Students, staff, doctors, Lawyers can always be invited for a study group meet to exchange and share their skills and knowledge either from their experience and/or from library resource. This widens the interest to learn more, to take active part in the meeting and thus motivated to reach library for more reading materials.

Talks and Lectures

This is one of the earliest form of extension services. Generally experts in different fields are invited and regular talks are arranged weekly, fort-nightly or monthly. The talk can be on any chosen topic but pertaining to the documents collection in that particular library. Books reviews of the new addition to the library is also a part of this programme.

Village Contacts

This is a scheme that has been widely accepted as a means of advisory service available to very small and relatively isolated communities. Such services are also known as Village Link or Village representative schemes. Essentially they aim to provide within a small rural community an initial point of contact for any one requiring information or needing advice or assistance on any subject. Earliest of this kind was set-up in 1973 at U.K.

Quizzes

Competitions, quizzes and proficiency tests are ways of encouraging purposive reading and a means of introducing books as course of reference and information. This is particularly a valuable kind of services for students group and children. This is also a high motivator for better use and reliance on library literature and to acquire familiarity with different source for different information and to realize the richness of library's facilities in gathering and gaining skill and knowledge.

There is also another means of creating awareness by orienting the parents, teachers and senior citizens in a village by involving them in library programs and extension activities. They can be provide with excellent guides to introduce their wards to books and to encourage them to read, some library authorities provide back up collections of reading materials to local schools as well as materials for class projects. The profession could benefit considerably from a system, which informed it new developments in this field together with an agreed method of syndicating such publicity

A library can adopt anyone or one and/or more of the any forms of extension services discussed above simultaneously for its different groups. Almost all forms can be enhanced and made more effective by operating the audio-visual aids, especially in reaching the rural areas while dealing with illiterates. Thus, extension service is something additional to the library routine.

LIBRARY LEGISLATION

Library movement is a saga of organized growth and development. of libraries giving the details of establishment, maintenance and functioning of libraries in a geographical proximity. These aspects viz., establishment, maintenance and functioning make a library a growing organization. No country in the world can progress without providing free public library services to the citizens. It is imperative on the part of the democratic country like India to establish the service institutions like public libraries in order to strengthen the democratization of information and to promote the social, cultural, historical and scientific and technical knowledge in the public at large. Legislation differs from country to country. Hence the foremost consideration in the framing of legislation is the nature of the geographical area of jurisdiction. Local relevance must be taken care of.

The first ever draft of Public Library Bill is to be found in S.R. Ranganthan's 'Five Laws of Library Science' (1936). In the course of discussion on the second Law "Books are for all" the drafting of the modern library act emerged. In 1931, MALA (Madras Library Association) constituted a Three Man Committee consisting of K.V. Krishnaswamy, Iyer. T.R. Venkatrama Sastry and S.R. Ranganathan to draft a bill. Due to ill luck, the bill never got approved by the then government. A second attempt was made by Basheer Ahmed Sayyed in 1937 for its introduction, but when futile. Yet another to the other priorities the Bill had to wait till 1946, when S.R. Ranganathan presented it to Sri Avinashilingam Chettiar, the then education Minister. It was this weak Bill that ultimately emerged as the "Madras Public Libraries Act" (XXIV of 1948).

It is only after India's independence that, Dr. Ranganathan's dream of Public Library Act enactment was fulfilled. Through the good offices of the then Minister for Education, Avinashilingam Chettiar, a modified Bill was introduced in the state legislature which was passed as the Madras Public Libraries Act in 1948. Since then the following ten States have enacted library acts for their respective states:

1. Tamil Nadu (1948)
2. Andhra Pradesjh (1960)
3. Karnataka (1965)
4. Maharashtra (1967)
5. West Bengal (1979)
6. Manipur (1988)
7. Kerala (1989)
8. Haryana (1989)

9. Goa (1993)
10. Mizoram (1993)

MADRAS PUBLIC LIBRARIES ACT, 1948

An act to provide for the establishment of public libraries in the province of Madras and the organization of a comprehensive rural and urban library service therein.

Preliminaries

Short title, extent and commencent:

(1) This Act may be called the Madras Public Libraries Act, 1948.
(2) It extends to the whole of the state of Tamil Nadu.
(3) This section shall come into force at once; and the rest this Act shall come into force on such date as the Government may by notification appoint.

Definition

In this Act unless there is anything repugnant is the subject or context—

(1) "Aided library";
(2) "Director";
(3) "District";
(4) "Government";
(5) "Notification";
(6) "Prescribe":
(7) "State";
(8) "Public Library"; and
(9) "Year".

XXX State Library Committee

State Library Committee and its Functions

- A State Library Committee shall be constituted by the Government for the purpose of advising them on such matter relating to Libraries as they may refer to it.
- The Committee shall be constituted in such matter, and exercise and perform such other powers and duties as may be prescribed.

Director and his Duty

Appointment and Duties of Director

The Government shall appoint Director to public Libraries for the State and he shall subject to their control—

(a) Manage the Central Library being a library constituted by the Government as the Central Library or an existing Government Library recognized by them as the Central Library together with the branches of such library;
(b) Superintend and direct all matters relating to public libraries;
(c) Declare in accordance with the rules made under this Act, what libraries are eligible for and from the Government and superintend and direct all matters relating to such libraries;
(d) Superintend and control the work of all local Library Authorities under the Act;
(e) Submit to the Government every year a report on the work of libraries under this Act in the previous year; and
(f) Perform such other duties and exercise such other powers as are imposed or conferred by this Act or the rules made thereunder.

Local Library Authorities

Constitution of Local Library Authorities

(1) For the purpose of organizing and administrating public libraries in the State, there shall be constituted Local Library Authorities, one for the City of Madras and one for each district.
(2) The local Authority for the city of Madras shall consist of—
    (a) Three members elected by the Corporation of Madras,
    (b) Eight members nominated by the Government—
        (i) Three shall be office bearers of libraries

situated in the City of Madras and recognized in this behalf by the Government;

(ii) Two shall be headmaster or headmistresses of High Schools in the city of Madras; and

(iii) Once shall be the principle of a college in the city of Madras.

(c) The holder for the time being of an office, which the Government may, from time to time specify in this behalf.

(3) The local Library Authority for each district shall consist of—

(a) Eight members nominated by the Director of whom—

(i) Three shall be office bearers of libraries institute in the district and recognized in behalf.

(ii) Five shall be headmasters or headmistresses of high schools or principles of colleges in the district.

(b) One member elected by the district board and where there are two or more districts, one member elected by each such district boards.

(c) Such number of members as may be elected by the presidents of the panchayats in the district, the presidents of the panchayats in each talk election one number.

(d) Such number of members as may elected by the municipal councils in the district, each municipal council elect one or more members in accordance with the following scale:

Municipalities with a population	*Number of members*
(1) Not exceeding one lakh	One
(2) Exceeding one lakh but not exceeded two lakhs	Two
(3) Exceeding two lakhs	Three

(e) The holder for the time being of an office that the government may from time to time, specify in this behalf.

(4) The member referred to in clause (c) of sub-section (2) secretary of the (e) of sub-section (3) as the case may shall be the secretary of the Local Library Authority concerned.

(5) Every local authority shall elect one of members to be its Chairman.

(6) Subject to the provisions of sub-section (8), the term of office of a nominated or elected member of a Local Library authority shall be three years from the date his nomination of election, as the case may be.

(7) A vacancy in the office of a nominated or elected member of a Local library Authority occurring otherwise than by affix of time shall be filled by nomination or election in accordance with the provisions of sub-section (2) of sub-section (3), as the case may be, and the person nominated or elected to fill the vacancy shall, subject to the provisions of sub-section (8) hold office only for the reminded or elected.

(8) A member nominated in his capacity as the holder of a particular office, shall, if he ceases to be the holder of the office cease to be a member of the Local library Authority.

(9) No act of a Local library Authority shall be deemed to be invalid by reason only of the existence of any vacancy in, or any defects in the constitution of the Authority.

(10) Members of Local Library Authorities shall be eligible for renomination or re-election.

In Corporation of Local Library Authorities

Every Local Library Authority shall be a body, corporate by the name of the area for which it is constituted, shall have perpetual succession and a common seal and shall be vested with the capacity of using or suing or being sued in its corporate name of acquiring, holding or transferring property, movable or immovable, of entering contracts and of doing all things necessary, proper or expedient for the purpose for which it is constituted.

Executive Committees and Sub-Committees of Local Library Authorities

1. A Local Library Authority may appoint an executive committee consisting of such number of its members not exceeding seven, as it may deem fit, and delegate to such committee all or any of its powers of duties under this Act.
2. A Local Library Authority may also from time to time appoint sub-Committee to enquire into a report or advice on any matters which it may refer to them.

Schemes to be Submitted by Local Library Authorities

As soon as possible after a Local Library Authority is constituted and thereafter as often as may be required by the Director, every Local Library Authority may prepare a scheme for establishing libraries and for spreading library service within its area and submit it to Director for sanction. The Director may sanction it with such modifications and additions, if any, as he may think fit and the Local Library Authority shall give effect to the scheme as so sanctioned by him.

The Director may 'suo motu' or on application by Local Library Authority concerned modify any scheme sanctioned under sub-section (1) or replace it by a new scheme.

Power of Local Library Authority

A Local Library Authority may—

(a) Provide suitable lands and buildings for public libraries and also the furniture, fitting materials and conveniences requisite therefore.
(b) Stock such libraries with books, periodicals, newspapers, maps works and specimens of art and science, lantern slides, cinema reels and any other thing suitable for their purpose.
(c) Employ from time to time such as it considers necessary, for such libraries.
(d) With the previous sanction of the Government close or discontinue any public library or change the site thereof.

(e) Accept, with the previous sanction of the Director or the Government, any gift or books, or with the previous sanction or the Government, any other gift or endowment for any purpose connected with his activities.

(f) Provide for lecture and the holding of classes.

(g) In generals do everything necessary to carry out the provisions of this Act.

Vesting of Properties in Local Library Authorities

All property movable and immovable, acquired or held for the purpose of any public library is any area shall vest in the Local Library Authority of that areas.

Regulations by Local Library Authorities

(1) Subject to the provisions of this Act and the rules made thereunder, a Local Library Authority may make regulations generally to carry out the purposes of this act without prejudice to the generality of this power, such regulations may provide for—

(a) The admission of the public libraries in areas on such fees as it may specify;

(b) Requiring from persons desiring to use such libraries any guarantee or security against injury to, or misuse, destruction or loss of, the property of such libraries;

(c) The manner in which the property of such libraries may be used and the protection of property from injury misuse destruction or loss; and

(d) Authorizing its officers and persons who contravenes or fails to comply with the provision of this Act or the rules or regulations made thereunder.

(2) The Government may in their discretion, modify or cancel any regulation made by a local Library Authority under sub-section (1). Provided that before modifying or canceling any regulation the government shall give the Local Library Authority concerned is able opportunity to make its representations in the matter.

Finance and Accounts

Library Cess

1. (a) Every Local Library Authority shall levy in the area a library cess in the form of surcharge on the property tax or house tax levied in such area under the Madras City Municipalities Act, 1919 or the Madras District Municipalities Act, 1920, or the Madras Local Boards Act, 1920 as the case may be at the rate of plea for every whole rupee in the property tax or house tax so levied.
   (b) A Local Library Authority may, with the previous sanction of the Government and shall, if so desired by them, increase the rate specified in clause (a).
2. The cess levied under sub-section (i) shall be collected:
   (a) In the city of Madras, by the Corporation of Madras.
   (b) In an area within the jurisdiction of municipal council by the municipal council.
   (c) In an area within the jurisdiction of a punchayat.
   (d) In an area in a district not included within the jurisdiction of a municipal council on a panchayat, but the District Board.

As if the cess were a property tax or house tax payable under the Madras City Municipal Act, 1919, or the Madras District Municipalities Act, 1920, or the Madras Local Boards Act, 1920, as the case may be, and all the relevant provisions of the said acts, apply accordingly:

> Provincial that the Government may, by notification direct that for the purpose of the collection of the cess aforesaid the provisions of the Madras City Municipal Act, 1920 or the Madras Local Boards Act, 1926 as the case may be, shall apply subject to such modifications as may be specified.

3. The cess collected under sub-section (2) shall be paid to the Local Library Authority concerned by the Corporation of Madras Municipal Council, the panchayat or the district boards as the case may be.

Library Fund

1. Every Library Authority shall maintain a fund called the 'Library fund' from which all the expenses under this Act shall be met.
2. There shall be credited to the Library fund the following sums namely—
   (a) The cess collected under section 12, sub-section (2);
   (b) Contribution, gifts, and income from endowments made for the benefit of public libraries;
   (c) Special grants which the Government may make for any specific purpose connected with libraries; and
   (d) Fees, fine and other amount collected by Law Local Library Authority under any rules or regulations made under this Act.
3. The government shall contribute to the Library fund maintained by every local library Authority other than the Local Library Authority for the City of Madras, a sum not less than the cess collected under section 12, sub-section (2).

Maintenance of Accounts

- An account shall be open to such inspections, shall be subject to such aid, disallowance and surcharge and shall be (disallowance and surcharge and shall be) dealt within all other respects in such manner, as may be prescribed.
- The account shall be open to such inspections, shall be subject to such audit, disallowance and surcharge and shall be dealt with in all other respects in such manner, as may be prescribed.

Authorities

Notwithstanding any provision in the Act, the Government may, in cases where these think it necessary to do so. Supersede or reconstitute any Library Authority constituted under the Act.

Provided however, the Government all give notice to the Authority concerned together with the grounds on which they propose to supersede or reconstitute and shall consider any explanations that may be offered by such Authority.

Reports, Returns and Instruction Reports and Returns

Every Local Library Authority and every person in charge of a public or aided library shall submit such reports and returns and furnish such information to the Director of any person authorized by him as the Director or the person authorized may from time to time require.

Inspection of Libraries

The Director or any person authorized by him may inspect any public or aided library or any institution attached thereto for the purpose of satisfying himself that the provisions this Act and the rules and regulation thereunder are duty carried out.

Rules

Power to Make Rules

1. The Government may, by notification, make rules consistent with this Act to carry out the purpose therefore.
2. In particular and without prejudice to the generality of the forgoing power, such rules may provide for—
   (a) All matters required or allowed to be prescribed under the Act;
   (b) The method of conducting the election of members to Local Library Authority and all matters connected therewith;
   (c) The matters to be included in the scheme referred to is section 8;
   (d) The maintenance of the minutes of the proceedings of Local Library Authority;

(e) The publication of audited statements of the accounts of such Authorities and of the reports of the auditors; and

(f) A Library Graft-in-aid to, and the deceleration, inspection and co-ordination by the Director of aided libraries and the standards to be maintained by such libraries.

Miscellaneous

Amendment of the Press and Registration of Books Act, 1867 in its Application to the State.

The Press and Registration of Books Act, 1867, shall in its application to the State be amended as follows:

(i) In section 9, first paragraph clause (a), which relates to the delivery to Government of copies of books by the printer of a press for the words 'one such copy' the words "five such copies" shall be substituted.

(ii) In the section, in the last paragraph clause (i) for the words "A copy of the first or some preceding editing of which book has been delivered" the words five copies of the first or so the proceeding edition of which books have been delivered shall be substituted.

(iii) In section if, for the first sentence, the following sentence shall be substituted, namely:

"Out of the five copies delivered pursuit to clause (at the first paragraph of Section 9 of this Act, four copies shall be sent to the central Library referred to in Section 4, Clause (a) of the Madras Public Libraries Act, 1949, and the fifth copy shall be disposed of in such manner as the (state) Government may, from time to time determine."

LIBRARY MANAGEMENT

GENERAL PRINCIPLES OF MANAGEMENT

Management is a mental process. Right from the dawn of civilization man has been acquiring and sharpening the principle of management for better understanding of nature, better exploitation of resource, better human relations, better organization and governance. Scientific management though is of fairly recent origin, it has caught the attention of scientists; planners and policy-framers; officers and decision-makers, and in fact every one in every field.

Management is essential for all kinds of organizations, whether they be business organizations or non-business organizations, because every organization requires the making of decisions, the coordination of works, the handling of people or personnel, and evaluating the output of work. This managerial task is performed by the officer called Manager. Every organization, therefore, appoints managers. They may be called by different designations such as supervisors, directors, superintendents, etc.

In a library also we find so many designations as librarian, chief librarian, director, superintendent, etc. The management takes place at all levels in the organizational set-up. Every manager performs essentially the same function whether he belongs to the top, or middle or first line management. The only difference is the scope, quality and degree of authority. Qualified managers, therefore, are boon to their firms and to the society. Similarly in a library we find top level, middle level and lower level management. The librarian with the help of middle level and lower level staff manages a library. Therefore, a qualified and professional librarian is an asset to the library as well as to the society.

Meaning and Definition of Management

In an enterprise, there is a group of people having certain goals and objectives to achieve. They try to achieve the goal with the help of physical factors of money, machines, materials, etc. Similarly in a library, the librarian tries to achieve the goal with the help of physical factors of money, mechanical tools, men and materials. In general usage, the word management means a special group of people who direct effort towards common objectives through the activities of the people.

Management—Definition

Before describing the library management, it is essential to know the general term of "management" which is variously defined by different scientists. Some of important ones are:

- *Henry Fayol*: "To Manage is to forecast and to plan, to organize, to command, to coordinate and to control."
- Kimball and Kimball: "Management is the art of applying economic principles that underly the control of man and materials in the enterprise under consideration."
- *F.W. Taylor*: "Management is a distinct process consisting of planning, organizing, actualing and controlling, performed to determine and accomplish the objectives by the use of people and resources."
- Management is those persons in an organization with primary responsibility for executing the process of management. (The ALA Glossary of Library and Information Science)

On analyzing the above definitions and discussions we

come to the conclusion that good management achieves a social objective with the best use of human and material, energy and time and with satisfaction for all. Hence management is significant to every organization, public or private, governmental or business, because it deals with a natural function of human society, namely, the fundamental endeavour of achieving objects.

Management principles are not rigid. They are flexible. They change with the change in the environment. The complexity of human behaviour has affected the progress of management principles.

SCHOOLS OF MANAGEMENT THOUGHT

The schools of management thought are theoretical frameworks for the study of management. Each of the schools of management thought are based on somewhat different assumptions about human beings and the organizations for which they work. Since the formal study of management began late in the 19th century, the study of management has progressed through several stages as scholars and practitioners working in different eras focused on what they believed to be important aspects of good management practice. Over time, management thinkers have sought ways to organize and classify the voluminous information about management that has been collected and disseminated. These attempts at classification have resulted in the identification of management schools.

Disagreement exists as to the exact number of management schools. Different writers have identified as few as three and as many as twelve. Those discussed below include (1) the Classical school or Traditional School, (2) the Behavioural or Neo-Classical School, (3) the Quantitative or Management Science School, (4) the Systems School, and (5) the Contingency School. The formal study of management is largely a twentieth-century phenomenon, and to some degree the relatively large number of management schools of thought reflect a lack of consensus among management scholars about basic questions of theory and practice.

The following table provides a brief summary of five major schools of management thought, their approximate dates of origin, and their relative areas of emphasis.

MANAGEMENT SCHOOLS	*Beginning Dates*	*Emphasis*
CLASSICAL OR TRADITIONAL SCHOOL		Managing workers and organizations more efficiently.
Scientific Management	1880s	Systematic study of work methods in order to improve efficiency
Administrative Management	1940s	
Bureaucratic Management	1920s	
BEHAVIOURAL OR NEO-CLASSICAL SCHOOL		Understanding human behaviour in the organization
Human Relations	1930s	Advocates of human relation approach strongly believed that there should be no conflicts or classes in organization. In order to motivate individual em ployee, his desire should be ascertained in terms of his emotions beliefs, attitudes and habits.
Behavioural Science	1950s	Studying human behaviour consisting of psychology
QUANTITATIVE SCHOOL		Increasing quality of managerial decision-making through the application of mathematical and statistical methods.
Management Science	1940s	
Operations Management	1940s	
Management Information Systems	1950s-1970s	
SYSTEMS SCHOOL	1950s	Understanding the organization as a system that transforms inputs into outputs while in constant interaction with its' environment.
CONTINGENCY SCHOOL	1960s	Applying management principles and processes as dictated by the unique characteristics of each situation.

Schools in more detail. In addition, three contemporary management perspectives are discussed.

THE CLASSICAL SCHOOL

The classical school is the oldest formal school of management thought. Its roots pre-date the twentieth century. The classical school of thought generally concerns ways to manage work and organizations more efficiently. Three areas of study that can be grouped under the classical school are scientific management, administrative management, and bureaucratic management.

Scientific Management

In the late 19th century, management decisions were often arbitrary and workers often worked at an intentionally slow pace. There was little in the way of systematic management and workers and management were often in conflict. Scientific management was introduced in an attempt to create a mental revolution in the workplace. It can be defined as the systematic study of work methods in order to improve efficiency. Frederick W. Taylor was its main proponent. Other major contributors were Frank Gilbreth, Lillian Gilbreth, and Henry Gantt.

Scientific management has several major principles. First, it calls for the application of the scientific method to work in order to determine the best method for accomplishing each task. Second, scientific management suggests that workers should be scientifically selected based on their qualifications and trained to perform their jobs in the optimal manner. Third, scientific management advocates genuine cooperation between workers and management based on mutual self-interest. Finally, scientific management suggests that management should take complete responsibility for planning the work and that workers' primary responsibility should be implementing management's plans. Other important characteristics of scientific management include the scientific development of difficult but fair performance standards and the implementation of a pay-for-performance incentive plan based on work standards. Scientific management had a tremendous influence on management practice in the early twentieth century. Although it does not represent a complete theory of management, it has contributed to the study of management and organizations in many areas, including human resource management and industrial engineering. Many of the tenets of scientific management are still valid today.

Scientific management was a theory of management that analyzed and synthesized workflows. Its main objective was improving economic efficiency, especially labour productivity. The core ideas of the theory were developed by Frederick Winslow Taylor in the 1880s and 1890s, and were first published in his monographs Shop Management (1903) and The Principles of Scientific Management (1911). While working as a lathe operator and foreman, Taylor noticed the natural differences in productivity between workers, which were driven by various causes, including differences in talent, intelligence, or motivations. He was one of the first people to try to apply science to this application, that is, understanding why and how these differences existed and how best practices could be analyzed and synthesized, then propagated to the other workers via standardization of process steps. He believed that decisions based upon tradition and rules of thumb should be replaced by precise procedures developed after careful study of an individual at work, including via time and motion studies. Scientific management's application was contingent on a high level of managerial control over employee work practices. This necessitated a higher ratio of managerial workers to labourers than previous management methods. It also caused interpersonal friction between workers and managers, and social tensions between the blue-collar and white-collar classes.

Scientific management is often called Taylorism; the terms are often considered synonymous. A discerning view considers Taylorism as the first form of scientific management, which was followed by new iterations. Thus in today's management theory Taylorism is sometimes called (or considered a subset of) the classical perspective. Taylor's own early names for his approach included "shop management" and "process management." When Louis Brandeis coined the term "scientific management", Taylor recognized it as another good name for the concept, and he used it himself in his 1911 monograph. The field comprised the work of Taylor; his disciples (such as Henry Gantt); other engineers and managers (such as Benjamin S. Graham); and other theorists, such as Max Weber. It is compared and contrasted with other efforts, including those of Henri Fayol and of Frank Gilbreth, Sr. and Lillian Moller Gilbreth (whose views originally shared much with Taylor's but later evolved divergently in response to Taylorism's inadequate handling of human relations). Taylorism proper became obsolete by the 1930s, and by the 1960s the term "scientific management" had fallen out of favour for describing current management theories. However, many aspects of scientific management have never stopped being part of later management efforts called by other names.

Scientific management is a variation on the theme of economic efficiency; it is a late 19th and early 20th century instance of the larger recurring theme in human life of increasing efficiency, decreasing waste, and using empirical methods to decide what matters, rather than uncritically accepting pre-existing ideas of what matters. Thus, it is a chapter in a larger narrative that includes many ideas and fields, from the folk wisdom of thrift to a profusion of applied-science successors, including time and motion study, the Efficiency Movement (which was the broader cultural echo of scientific management's impact on business managers specifically), Fordism, operations management, operations research, industrial engineering, manufacturing engineering, logistics, business process management, business process reengineering, lean manufacturing, and Six Sigma. There is a fluid continuum linking scientific management by that name with the later fields, and there is often no mutual exclusiveness when discussing the details of any one of these topics.

In management literature today, the greatest use of the term "scientific management" is with reference to the work of Taylor and his disciples ("classical", implying "no longer current, but still respected for its seminal value") in contrast to newer, improved iterations of efficiency-seeking methods. In political and sociological terms, Taylorism can be seen as the division of labour pushed to its logical extreme, with a consequent de-skilling of the worker and dehumanisation of the workplace. Taylorism is often mentioned along with Fordism, because it was closely associated with mass production methods in factories, which was its earliest application. Today, task-oriented optimization of work tasks is nearly ubiquitous in industry. The theory behind it has evolved greatly since Taylor's day, reducing the ill effects, although in the wrong hands it is sometimes implemented poorly even now.

Ranganathan's Contribution to Scientific Management of Libraries

Generally, when the name of Ranganathan is mentioned, one is reminded of Colon Classification and his passion for intellectual analysis. But deep down, essentially he was a pragmatic personality as can be seen from his "Five Laws of Library Science." This has unified the innumerable details involved in Library management. In this context, it is worthwhile to say that book "Library Administration (1935) was a result of experience gained by him during his service in the administration of the Madras University Library for seven years as well as in teaching the subject. It is interesting here to note that modern management, concepts, such as rationalization of work" simplification of routines, streamlining of administration, standardization, productivity, etc., were very much evident from his writings. His observation that Library Administration has to be so planned and adjusted that the highest accuracy and the greatest promptness and economy are achieved is valid even today.

His systematic outlook as well as the breadth and depth of his contribution to the field of library management can be visualized as envisaged in the proper perspective when one pursues his "Library Administration." In his book, he has discussed:

- The theory of administration
- Distinctive facets of library administration
- Facets of general administration

In relation to each function, he has considered following points:

- Factors in Planning
- Job Analysis
- Routine for each Job
- Special points in order to eliminate waste and secure efficiency

- Correlation of work pertaining to function with work of other sections
- Time scheme for the performance of different jobs in the section
- Forms and registers required
- Files to be maintained by the section.

The writings reveal that the library administration has been transformed from traditional approach to a pattern of scientific planning. While Ranganathan's contributions in the field of library management are many, three of them are highlighted in this presentation. They are:

- Five Laws as Management Principles;
- Job Analysis and Routines; and
- Staff formula.

Five Laws as Management Principles

The Five Laws enunciate philosophy of librarianship which is universal in application as can be seen from Shera's observation that they are harmonical with the American concept of service. These laws can be considered as Management principles from which various activities pertaining to Library Management can be derived.

Job Analysis and Routines

Job analysis which serves a very useful purpose to Management while making appointments, assessments, promotions as well as while delegating responsibility and authority to individuals seems to have attracted the attention of Ranganathan. On the basis of an intensive analytical study at the Madras University Library, he had isolated nearly 1000 different jobs involved in the management of libraries and for each job the routines to be followed have been succinctly described by him.

The activities pertaining to the different factors in planning of each section is the deep insight he had in identifying the different activities as well as the problems encountered. It is remarkable that apart from mentioning the periodicity pertaining to each activity, he had emphasized on Correlation of the work of the section with the work of other sections. In other words, the methodology he had suggested for job analysis seemed to have anticipated many of the points discussed in the modern techniques of personal management.

Staff Formula

One of the outstanding contributions of Dr. S.R. Ranganathan was the staff formula to determine the manpower requirements based on the total quantum of work. The formula was based on the experience gained by him at the Madras University. It has since been tested at many of the libraries and has been accepted by the University Grants Commission. The same formula with a few modifications has been successfully adopted in determining the manpower requirement for various National Information System such as NICFOS, NICLAI, NICMAP, etc.

It can be said to the credit of Ranganathan that his staff formula is the best known today which deals with manpower to the different units of a library/information center, backed up by analysis of different functional activities. Manpower standards prevalent in U.K., U.S.A., Canada, etc. are general in nature not as specific as Ranganathan's staff formula.

Administrative Theory of Management

Administrative management focuses on the management process and principles of management. In contrast to scientific management, which deals largely with jobs and work at the individual level of analysis, administrative management provides a more general theory of management. Henri Fayol is the major contributor to this school of management thought.

Fayol was a management practitioner who brought his experience to bear on the subject of management functions and principles. He argued that management was a universal process consisting of functions, which he termed planning, organizing, commanding, coordinating, and controlling. Fayol believed that all managers performed these functions and that the functions distinguished management as a separate discipline of study apart from accounting, finance, and production. Fayol also presented fourteen principles of management, which included maxims related to the division of work, authority and responsibility, unity of command and direction, centralization, subordinate initiative, and team spirit.

Although administrative management has been criticized as being rigid and inflexible and the validity of the functional approach to management has been questioned, this school of thought still influences management theory and practice. The functional approach to management is still the dominant way of organizing management knowledge, and many of Fayol's principles of management, when applied with the flexibility that he advocated, are still considered relevant.

The classical approach can be examined on the basis of two perspectives—scientific management and classical organization theory. The most influential figures in classical organization theory are Max Weber and Henri Fayol. Henri Fayol emphasized that "the soundness and good working order of the body corporate depend on a certain number of conditions termed indiscriminately as principles, laws, and rules. He stressed that principles are flexible and capable of adaptation to every need. He listed fourteen principles of management on the following aspects, namely:

1. *Division of Work*: Work should be divided among individuals and groups to ensure that effort and attention are focused on special portions of the task. Fayol presented work specialization as the best way to use the human resources of the organization.
2. *Authority*: The concepts of Authority and responsibility are closely related. Authority was defined by Fayol as the right to give orders and the power to exact obedience. Responsibility involves being accountable, and is therefore naturally associated with authority. Whoever assumes authority also assumes responsibility.
3. *Discipline*: A successful organization requires the common effort of workers. Penalties should be applied judiciously to encourage this common effort.
4. *Unity of Command*: Workers should receive orders from only one manager.
5. *Unity of Direction*: The entire organization should be moving towards a common objective in a common direction.
6. *Subordination of Individual Interests to the General*

Interests: The interests of one person should not take priority over the interests of the organization as a whole.

7. *Remuneration*: Many variables, such as cost of living, supply of qualified personnel, general business conditions, and success of the business, should be considered in determining a worker's rate of pay.
8. *Centralization*: Fayol defined centralization as lowering the importance of the subordinate role. Decentralization is increasing the importance. The degree to which centralization or decentralization should be adopted depends on the specific organization in which the manager is working.
9. *Scalar Chain*: Managers in hierarchies are part of a chain like authority scale. Each manager, from the first line supervisor to the president, possess certain amounts of authority. The President possesses the most authority; the first line supervisor the least. Lower level managers should always keep upper level managers informed of their work activities. The existence of a scalar chain and adherence to it are necessary if the organization is to be successful.
10. *Order*: For the sake of efficiency and coordination, all materials and people related to a specific kind of work should be treated as equally as possible.
11. *Equity*: All employees should be treated as equally as possible.
12. *Stability of Tenure of Personnel*: Retaining productive employees should always be a high priority of management. Recruitment and Selection Costs, as well as increased product-reject rates are usually associated with hiring new workers.
13. *Initiative*: Management should take steps to encourage worker initiative, which is defined as new or additional work activity undertaken through self-direction.
14. *Esprit de Corps*: Management should encourage harmony and general good feelings among employees.

Bureaucratic Management

Bureaucratic management focuses on the ideal form of organization. Max Weber was the major contributor to bureaucratic management. Based on observation, Weber concluded that many early organizations were inefficiently managed, with decisions based on personal relationships and loyalty. He proposed that a form of organization, called a bureaucracy, characterized by division of labour, hierarchy, formalized rules, impersonality, and the selection and promotion of employees based on ability, would lead to more efficient management. Weber also contended that managers' authority in an organization should be based not on tradition or charisma but on the position held by managers in the organizational hierarchy.

Bureaucracy has come to stand for inflexibility and waste, but Weber did not advocate or favour the excesses found in many bureaucratic organizations today. Weber's ideas formed the basis for modern organization theory and are still descriptive of some organizations.

THE BEHAVIOURAL SCHOOL

The behavioural school of management thought developed, in part, because of perceived weaknesses in the assumptions of the classical school. The classical school emphasized efficiency, process, and principles. Some felt that this emphasis disregarded important aspects of organizational life, particularly as it related to human behaviour. Thus, the behavioural school focused on trying to understand the factors that affect human behaviour at work.

Human Relations

The Hawthorne Experiments began in 1924 and continued through the early 1930s. A variety of researchers participated in the studies, including Clair Turner, Fritz J. Roethlisberger, and Elton Mayo, whose respective books on the studies are perhaps the best known. One of the major conclusions of the Hawthorne studies was that workers' attitudes are associated with productivity. Another was that the workplace is a social system and informal group influence could exert a powerful effect on individual behaviour. A third was that the style of supervision is an important factor in increasing workers' job satisfaction. The studies also found that organizations should take steps to assist employees in adjusting to organizational life by fostering collaborative systems between labour and management. Such conclusions sparked increasing interest in the human element at work; today, the Hawthorne studies are generally credited as the impetus for the human relations school.

According to the human relations school, the manager should possess skills for diagnosing the causes of human behaviour at work, interpersonal communication, and motivating and leading workers. The focus became satisfying worker needs. If worker needs were satisfied, wisdom held, the workers would in turn be more productive. Thus, the human relations school focuses on issues of communication, leadership, motivation, and group behaviour. The individuals who contributed to the school are too numerous to mention, but some of the best-known contributors include Mary Parker Follett, Chester Barnard, Abraham Maslow, Kurt Lewin, Renais Likert, and Keith Davis. The human relations school of thought still influences management theory and practice, as contemporary management focuses much attention on human resource management, organizational behaviour, and applied psychology in the workplace.

Behavioural Science

Behavioural science and the study of organizational behaviour emerged in the 1950s and 1960s. The behavioural science school was a natural progression of the human relations movement. It focused on applying conceptual and analytical tools to the problem of understanding and predicting behaviour in the workplace. However, the study of behavioural science and organizational behaviour was also a result of criticism of the human relations approach as simplistic and manipulative in its assumptions about the relationship between worker attitudes and productivity. The study of behavioural science in business schools was given increased credence by the 1959 Gordon and Howell report on higher education, which emphasized the importance to management practitioners of understanding human behaviour.

The behavioural science school has contributed to the

study of management through its focus on personality, attitudes, values, motivation, group behaviour, leadership, communication, and conflict, among other issues. Some of the major contributors to this school include Douglas McGregor, Chris Argyris, Frederick Herzberg, Renais Likert, and Ralph Stogdill, although there are many others.

THE QUANTITATIVE SCHOOL

The quantitative school focuses on improving decision making via the application of quantitative techniques. Its roots can be traced back to scientific management.

Management Science and MIS

Management science (also called operations research) uses mathematical and statistical approaches to solve management problems. It developed during World War II as strategists tried to apply scientific knowledge and methods to the complex problems of war. Industry began to apply management science after the war. George Dantzig developed linear programming, an algebraic method to determine the optimal allocation of scarce resources. Other tools used in industry include inventory control theory, goal programming, queuing models, and simulation. The advent of the computer made many management science tools and concepts more practical for industry. Increasingly, management science and management information systems (MIS) are intertwined. MIS focuses on providing needed information to managers in a useful format and at the proper time. Decision support systems (DSS) attempt to integrate decision models, data, and the decision-maker into a system that supports better management decisions.

Production and Operations Management

This school focuses on the operation and control of the production process that transforms resources into finished goods and services. It has its roots in scientific management but became an identifiable area of management study after World War II. It uses many of the tools of management science.

Operations management emphasizes productivity and quality of both manufacturing and service organizations. W. Edwards Deming exerted a tremendous influence in shaping modern ideas about improving productivity and quality. Major areas of study within operations management include capacity planning, facilities location, facilities layout, materials requirement planning, scheduling, purchasing and inventory control, quality control, computer integrated manufacturing, just-in-time inventory systems, and flexible manufacturing systems.

SYSTEMS SCHOOL

The systems school focuses on understanding the organization as an open system that transforms inputs into outputs. This school is based on the work of a biologist, Ludwig von Bertalanffy, who believed that a general systems model could be used to unite science. Early contributors to this school included Kenneth Boulding, Richard Johnson, Fremont Kast, and James Rosenzweig.

The systems school began to have a strong impact on management thought in the 1960s as a way of thinking about managing techniques that would allow managers to relate different specialties and parts of the company to one another, as well as to external environmental factors. The systems school focuses on the organization as a whole, its interaction with the environment, and its need to achieve equilibrium. General systems theory received a great deal of attention in the 1960s, but its influence on management thought has diminished somewhat. It has been criticized as too abstract and too complex. However, many of the ideas inherent in the systems school formed the basis for the contingency school of management.

CONTINGENCY SCHOOL

The contingency school focuses on applying management principles and processes as dictated by the unique characteristics of each situation. It emphasizes that there is no one best way to manage and that it depends on various situational factors, such as the external environment, technology, organizational characteristics, characteristics of the manager, and characteristics of the subordinates. Contingency theorists often implicitly or explicitly criticize the classical school for its emphasis on the universality of management principles; however, most classical writers recognized the need to consider aspects of the situation when applying management principles.

The contingency school originated in the 1960s. It has been applied primarily to management issues such as organizational design, job design, motivation, and leadership style. For example, optimal organizational structure has been theorized to depend upon organizational size, technology, and environmental uncertainty; optimal leadership style, meanwhile, has been theorized to depend upon a variety of factors, including task structure, position power, characteristics of the work group, characteristics of individual subordinates, quality requirements, and problem structure, to name a few. A few of the major contributors to this school of management thought include Joan Woodward, Paul Lawrence, Jay Lorsch, and Fred Fiedler, among many others.

CONTEMPORARY SCHOOLS OF MANAGEMENT THOUGHT

Management research and practice continues to evolve and new approaches to the study of management continue to be advanced. This section briefly reviews two contemporary approaches: total quality management (TQM) and the learning organization. While neither of these management approaches offers a complete theory of management, they do offer additional insights into the management field.

Total Quality Management

Total quality management (TQM) is a philosophy or approach to management that focuses on managing the entire organization to deliver quality goods and services to customers. This approach to management was implemented in Japan after World War II and was a major factor in their economic renaissance. TQM has at least four major elements. Employee involvement is essential in preventing quality problems before they occur. A customer focus means that the organization must attempt to determine customer needs and wants and deliver products and services that address them.

Benchmarking means that the organization is always seeking out other organizations that perform a function or process more effectively and using them as a standard, or benchmark, to judge their own performance. The organization will also attempt to adapt or improve the processes used by other companies. Finally, a philosophy of continuous improvement means that the organization is committed to incremental changes and improvements over time in all areas of the organization. TQM has been implemented by many companies worldwide and appears to have fostered performance improvements in many organizations. Perhaps the best-known proponent of this school of management was W. Edwards Deming.

ELEMENTS OF MANAGEMENT

Libraries are generally a part of big organization. The operations of libraries are based on the guidelines, rules and regulations framed by their parent body. If it is a public library in that case the rules are framed by some committees. To ensure better functioning and smooth running of an organization, Luther Gullick propounded some basic elements of management on the pattern of Fayol's principles of management. These are known as 'POSDCORB' which stands for the following seven elements:

1. Planning
2. Organizing
3. Staffing
4. Directing
5. Coordinating
6. Reporting
7. Budgeting

Planning

Planning is a process which involves the determination of future course of action. To achieve better and desired objectives from an institution, the administrator should first plan and forecast the goals of an institution.

It is very closely associated with the goals or objectives of the organization. The goals may be expressed, implied, however, well-defined goals lead to efficiency in planning. Planning presupposes the stock taking of the existing conditions and the relevant causes. The solutions are suggested for removing the defects by a phased systematic programme.

Economic planning is concerned with the production of maximum input. In planning, entire wastage is avoided and every constituent factor is made to contribute its own share. The efforts are made to remove the basic defects and their future implications are taken care of.

The special features of planning can be identified as follows:

1. Planning is the process rather than behaviour at a given point of time.
2. Planning is primarily concerned with looking into future.
3. Planning involves selection of suitable course of action.
4. Planning is undertaken at all levels of the organization because all levels of management are concerned with the determination of future course of action.
5. Planning is flexible.

Planning requires wide knowledge and experience of works. It is the most basic of all managerial functions and is considered as a rational approach to pre-selected objectives. A systematic planning involves the following steps:

1. The problem exists and need for action is recognized.
2. Collect all the available information regarding the problem.
3. Assess the possible alternative solutions and method to solve the problems.
4. Take decision to act.
5. Put decision into action.
6. The evaluation on the basis of experience.

Organizing

Organizing means establishing of a formal structure of authority, which is well defined and coordinated towards the attainment of specific objective. The structure of formal organization denotes a system of well defined jobs, each bearing a definite measure of authority, responsibility, and accountability, and the organization to work most effectively together in accomplishing their objectives. It is an important process which starts after the planning is completed. Its objectives are achieved by the combined efforts of different specialists belonging to the organization.

After finalizing the creative phase of planning, the next step comes before them is who will do it. Since the work of library is done by a number of persons working together, librarians have to define who will do what and what will be relationship among them appropriate authority so that they are able to carry on their work effectively.

What pattern of organization should be adopted in the library is another important aspect. The pattern of organization varies from library to library depending upon the objectives, nature of users, type of staff, kinds of documents available in the library, financing, building and more important thing is the attitude of higher authorities.

Generally there are two types of administration, viz. centralized administration and decentralized administration so in the choice of a pattern these two points should be considered first. Since an organization is a man-based structure, therefore, flexibility must be considered as the alteration should be possible when it is required. The library is a growing organism so the organizational structure will become large and more people will join it and the structure will become complex.

Staffing

Like other organizations, library requires the services of a large number of technical and non-technical personnels to perform the works of different sections. The persons posted in the different sections of the library must have sufficient ability to meet its requirements. Staffing basically involves matching jobs and individuals.

The management function of staffing involves managing the organization structure through proper and effective selection, appraisal and development of personnel to fill the roles designated into the structure. The managerial function of staffing is defined as filling requirements, inventorying the people available, recruitment, selection, placement and promotion, appraisal, compensation and training of needed people.

Staffing is an essential element of management process. It is the process of acquiring, developing, employing, appraising, remunerating, and retaining people so that right type of people are available at right position and right time in the organization. Within each function, there are various sub-functions. For example, acquiring of reading materials personnel are involves in ordering the books section of reading materials and process of books and its bills for the payment.

An organization for its efficient working is totally dependent upon proper staffing and recruitment policies. The staff appointed in the library should have the special aptitudes and capabilities for doing the particular job. With the introduction of electronic machines, computers and other sophisticated instruments in the library operation, the personnel must be acquainted of these equipments. The practical experience of various jobs at the credit of applicants for various posts should be taken into consideration at the time of their appointment.

Directing

Every one of us, perhaps, may be aware about the concepts of directing and role of director or manager when the works of a big organization is in progress. The manager direct their subordinates how to they should do the work for achieving organizational objectives. A superior directs his subordinates as to how and when they have to perform various duties assigned to him.

Once planning, organizing and staffing have been achieved, and then action is required. To execute the action successfully, the direction is involved. Direction is defined as the continuous task of taking decisions and incorporating them in specific and general orders and serving these orders. New man and Warren have defined directing in the form of activating as "Activity deals with the steps a manager taking to get subordinates and others to carry out plans." Direction has some special features which are as under:

1. It is an important managerial function.
2. Its function is performed at every level of management.
3. It is a continuous process and it continues throughout the life of the organization.
4. It initiates at the top level in the organization and follows to bottom through the hierarchy.
5. It has dual objectives.

In a library, the harmony and efficiency of the staff depends upon the personal qualities of the Librarian. He should be capable of performing his duties as a leader. Besides, he should be able to boost up their morale. He should also be an example to be followed by his subordinates. In other words, he should not be frustrated with his job leather; he should do his job with zeal. He should be ready to sacrifice his personal comforts for the sake of library work and library staff. He should prove an ideal leader by dint of his hard work and sincerity for the staff welfare.

Coordinating

Coordinating is an important function of a manager, which deals with task of blending efforts in order to insure successful attainment of an objective. Though some writers do not regard coordination as a separate activity of the manager, but some have the opposite views and they considers 'Coordination' as a separate function of management. Haimann considers coordination as the part of all the managerial functions of planning, organizing, staffing, directing and controlling.

Coordinating may be defined as an on-going process whereby manager develops an integrated, orderly and synchronized pattern of group effort among the sub-ordinates and tries to attain unity of effort in the pursuit of common purpose. It is a harmonious combination or interaction. It is concerned with interrelating of the various parts of an organization.

The coordination can be achieved if the head knows well all the jobs and effects such automatic administrative machinery that be feels practically no necessity to interfere. It depends upon the kind of organization which has been brought into bring, i.e. as to whether he introduces Line Type or Line and Staff Type of structure or Functional type of organization. In other words, there should be delegation of powers but the staff members in whom the powers are vested should also be made responsible for their jobs. They should be answerable to the chief. An automatic procedure should be affected by means of introducing a practice of getting periodical reports from the various section heads. He should allow these Heads to use their initiative but whenever there is some difficulty or misunderstanding, the chief should thrash out the problem in periodical staff meetings.

Reporting

Reporting means keeping the authorities informed about the progress or regress of work and also keep them abreast. To perform this duty efficiently, the executive head has to keep him and his subordinates informed about their jobs and performances through research, records and inspection. It is a sound principle of organization that a periodical report is asked from a head of an enterprise. Such report will base on factual and real statistics. The librarian has to submit the annual report to the executive committee for this librarian issue a direction to the subordinates to prepare the report of their concerned section. On the basis of report received from different sections of the library, the librarian is able to prepare a comprehensive report. Report is the only authentic device for evaluation of library procedures and service. Librarian often use it because it is a continuous process and its costs are not apparent being hidden under general expenses of library.

Budgeting

Budgeting is an effective management tool in the hand of librarian or manager. Budget means formation of plans for a given future period in numerical terms. It includes fiscal planning, accounting and control. No organization can function properly without adequate finance. But it is very difficult to get adequate finance or funds for all kind of organizations, especially libraries which are fully depend on the parent's institution or government aid. Libraries do not earn any revenues in the physical sense. Their services, though essential for the well-being of the individual, the society and the government, are not considered apparently indispensable. Consequently, the legislators and bureaucrats alike reject the demands of libraries on one or the other pretext. The libraries are given almost the lowest priority in matter of allocation of funds. The librarian has to muster strength and acquire necessary skill and tact for securing adequate funds.

A library, in order to flourish to ensure maximum use or its resources and to work successfully needs to know and apply the general principles and functions of management.

PLANNING

Planning is a vital and necessary management function. The other functions of management like organizing, leading, controlling all carry out the objectives and goals are determined through planning.

Planning is deciding in advance what to do, when to do, how to do and who is to do it. Koontz and O' Donnell describe planning as "the selection from among alternatives of future courses of action for the enterprise as a whole and each department within it.

Planning is thus the first step in the management process concerned with the establishment of objectives and goals to be attained in the future in the light of an analysis of present limitations for attaining such goals with a view to their removal or reduction, anticipation of the future environmental factors and their impact, and designing the course of action and programmes for attaining such pre-selected goals. It involves both thought and communication.

George Terry defines planning as—Planning is the selecting and relating of facts and the making and using of assumptions regarding the future in the visualization and formulation of proposed activities believed necessary to achieve desired results.

Advantages of Planning

Before doing something, it is better to be clear as to what is to be done and how it should be done. Despite the obvious importance of planning, in practice it is often neglected and managers allow things to happen to them instead of making things happen. Sometimes excuses are made on the ground that the time required for planning is not available and immediate action is required. The advantages of planning are:

- Planning increases the organization's ability to adapt to future eventualities.
- Planning helps crystallize objectives.
- Planning ensures a relatedness among decisions.
- Planning helps the company to remain more competitive in its industry.

- Adequate Planning reduces unnecessary pressures of immediacy.
- Planning reduces mistakes and oversights.
- Planning ensures a more productive use of organization's resources.
- Planning makes control easier.
- Planning enables the identification of future problems.
- Planning can help the organization secure a better position or standing.
- Planning enables the organization to progress in the manner considered most suitable by its management.
- Planning increases the effectiveness of a manager.

Limitations of Planning

The following are some of the limitations claimed for planning: •

- The effectiveness of the plans depends upon the correctness of assumptions.
- Planning is expensive.
- Planning delay actions.
- Planning encourages a false sense of security.

To avoid such limitations and to make planning more effective, the objectives must be clearly defined. The plan should be simple and capable of being understood by those who have to effectuate it. The plan should be flexible to provide for unforeseen eventualities. It must be feasible and reasonable of attainment as unattainable objectives would lead to frustration.

Types of Plans

Planning bridges the gap from where we are to where we want to go. It makes things possible for things to happen which would not otherwise happen. Planning is an intellectual activity. Depending upon the complexity, plans can be of eight types, namely,

- *Purposes and missions*—identifies the basic function or task of an enterprise or agency or a part of it.
- *Objectives*—are the end towards which the activity is aimed—they are the results to be achieved.

- *Strategies*—general programs of action and deployment of resources to attain comprehensive objectives.
- *Policies—major and minor*—are general statements or understandings which guide or channel thinking in decision-making.
- *Procedures*—plans that establish a required method of handling future activities.
- *Rules*—Spell out specific required actions or non-actions allowing no discretion.
- *Programs*—are complex of goals, policies, procedures, rules, tasks, assignments, steps to be taken, resources to be employed, and other elements necessary to carry out a given course of action.
- *Budgets*—is a statement of expected results expressed in numerical terms. It may be referred to as a numberised program.

Steps in Planning

The following are briefly some of the steps claimed for planning:

- Being aware of opportunities
- Establishing Objectives
- Developing premises
- Determining alternative courses
- Evaluating alternative courses
- Selecting a course
- Formulating Derivative plans
- Numberizing plans by budgeting

Being Aware of Opportunities

Although it precedes actual planning and is therefore not strictly a part of the planning process, an awareness of opportunities in the external environment as well as within the organization is the real starting point for planning. It is important to take a preliminary look at possible future opportunities and see them clearly and completely. All managers should know where they stand in the light of their strengths and weaknesses, understand what problems they wish to solve and why, and know what they expect to gain.

Establishing Objectives

The second step is to establish objectives for the entire enterprise and then for each subordinate work unit. This is to be done for the long-term as well as for the short range. Objectives specify the expected results and indicate the points of what is to be done, where the primary emphasis is to be placed, and what is to be accomplished by the network of strategies, policies, procedures, rules, budgets, and programs.

Developing Premises

A third logical step in planning is to establish, circulate, and obtain agreement to utilize critical planning premises such as forecasts, applicable basic policies and existing company plans. They are assumptions about the environment which the plan is to be carried out. It is important for all the mangers involve in planning to agree on the premises. In fact, the major principle of planning premises is this: The more thoroughly individuals charged with planning, understanding and agree to utilize consistent premises, the more coordinated enterprise planning will be.

Determining Alternative Courses

The fourth step in planning is to search for and examine alternative courses of action, especially those not immediately apparent. There is seldom a plan for which is reasonable alternatives do not exist, and quite often an alternative that is not obvious to be the best.

Evaluating Alternative Courses

After seeking out alternative courses and examining their strong and weak points the next step is evaluating the alternatives by weighing them in the light of premises and goals. One course may appear to be the most profitable, but it may require a large cash outlay and have a slow payback; another may look less profitable but may involves less risk; still another may better suit the company's long-range objectives.

Selecting a Course

This is the point at which the plan is adopted—the real point of decision-making. Occasionally, an analysis and evaluation of alternative courses will disclose that two or more are advisable and the manager may decide to follow several courses rather than the one best course.

Formulating Derivative Plans

When a decision is made, planning is seldom complete, and a seventh step is indicated. Derivative plans are almost invariably required to support the basic plan.

Numberizing Plans by Budgeting

After decisions are made and plans are set, the final step in giving them meaning as was indicated in the discussion of types of plans is to numberize them by converting them to budgets. The overall budgets of an enterprise represent the sum total of income and expenses, with resultant profit or surplus, and budgets of major balance sheet items such as cash and capital expenditures. Each department or program of a business or other enterprise can have its own budgets, usually of expenses and capital expenditures, which tie into the overall budget.

If done well, budgets become a means of adding together the various plans and also set important standards against which planning progress can be measured.

ROUTINES OF LIBRARY—BOOK SELECTION SECTION

The Library work may be broadly categorized into two kinds of jobs, namely, work behind the scene and work with the readers. The work behind the scene refers to all sorts of in-house operations like book selection, acquisition, technical processing and maintenance of reading materials. The work with the readers refers to the actual service to the readers. The former work includes book selection, acquisition, classification, cataloguing, binding and other mechanical methods of reproduction.

Information Sources Development involves the two processes of Selection and Acquisition. The requirements for them are given below:

Selection Requires

- A Selection Policy (involving statement about users

and needs; subject , topic, or mission to be dealt with and type of information sources and materials to be covered).

- Selection Aids and Tools which will give help in selection and verification.
- Specification of a Selection Process (involving decisions on who selects; procedures for judging intrinsic value of information in sources and procedures for judging demand and user appropriateness.

Acquisition Requires

Procedures for procurement of necessary information sources in cases of no outright procurement , procedures for access to sources e.g. getting on loan , photocopying pertinent sections, getting permission to use them in another information center/system, etc.

The role of a library or an information center is to provide the right information to the right reader at the right time in a right personal way. The laws of library science preach that books should be used to the maximum extent and each and every reader should be provided with his required information or books. Any library however large cannot procure all the books that are published. In order to satisfy the needs of the clientele the library should have a suitable book selection policy.

Book Selection

Book selection procedures differ from library to library according to the policies and management of the Library. The financial resources, the readers, their reading needs and tastes vary from library to library. Smaller libraries will be contented by simply drawing up a list of books for purchase once a year whereas for bigger libraries this is a continuous job. Book selection is a very responsible job. Intelligent book selection for library use is based on definite principles and carried out with tools planned for the purpose.

Book Selection Policy

Some of the basic principles and policies from the view of Five Laws of library science taking into consideration the barrier of publication in large numbers and inadequate finance in developing countries like India are given below:

(a) Procure as exhaustively as possible only selective/ representative documents in the area of umbral region of interest of the library.
(b) Enter into an agreement of coordination/cooperation in acquisition with institution sharing similar interests.
(c) Depend as much as possible on inter-library cooperation to meet the information needs in the penumbral region of interest of the library.
(d) Depend entirely on inter-library cooperation to meet the information needs in the alien region of interest of the library.
(e) For the purpose of procurement, whenever feasible, adopt the modes in the following order of preference: Gratis, Exchange and Purchase.
(f) Whenever a part of the document serves the purpose, prefer it to the whole document.

Need for Book Selection Policy

Drury states, "The best reading for the largest number at the least cost. As per this principle, the library should select, within the financial resources available, the best documents which may satisfy the information needs of a majority of users. In this principle, three concepts relevant to selection, namely, satisfaction, majority of users, and economy are embedded.

Book Selection —How?

Based on the principle enunciated by Ranganathan, Dewey and others, one can formulate the Collection Development objectives of a library. The objectives, for example, that may be considered are:

- To identify the programmes or user needs to be supported (research, instructional, general information, reference, etc.)
- To identify the general subjects boundaries of the collection.

- To identify the general subjects priorities and limitations governing selection, including:
  - Degree of continuing support for strong collections.
  - Forms of material collected or excluded.
  - Languages, geographical areas, collected or excluded.
  - Chronological periods covered or excluded.
  - Other duplications.
  - Extent of duplication, if any.
- To formulate cooperative collection agreements, if any, with other organization which complement or otherwise affect the policy of the library.
- To identify the sources of selection and the selection and acquisition procedures to be adopted.

For a good collection development and book selection the following Policies must be based on the following:

- Existing strength of collection
- Actual current level of collection activity
- Desirable level of collection to meet programme
- Languages
- Chronological periods covered
- Geographic areas covered
- Forms of material to be collected
- The unit in the Library or selector with primary selection responsibility for the field.

Selection of Information Resources

Once the scope has been defined, one of the most important tasks of the library is to maintain control over the information at resources by first accumulating a collection of the pertinent reference materials and deciding how to include current papers, reports, books and other items of interest. This is so because the literature on a narrow subject field is dispersed in a wide variety and a large number of documents. It may be uneconomical and impracticable to acquire all the relevant documents. It would be more useful to build up a core collection based on well formulated selection and acquisition policies and programmes. The policies and programmes should:

(a) Enable the library to receive regularly the books, periodicals, reports, etc. published all over the world as quickly as possible; and

(b) Facilitate timely access to the users of the original documents required and also enable them to be continuously aware and knowledgeable about the developments in their respective areas of interest.

Sources of Information Helpful in Building a Collection

There are a number of sources of information, which considered individually or together, inspire selection. They may consist of:

- Reader's suggestions;
- Review columns in newspapers and periodicals; and
- Bibliographies.

Bibliographies as Book Selection Tools

From the point of view of book-selection value, the sequence of preference may be as follows:

1. Copy right lists;
2. Publisher's catalogues;
3. Bookseller's catalogues;
4. Book-selection lists;
5. Library catalogues;
6. Subject bibliographies;
7. Reading lists;
8. Author's bibliographies;
9. Bibliophilic bibliographies;
10. Printer's bibliographies;
11. Binder's bibliographies; and
12. National Bibliographies.

Other Book Selection Tools

Government Documents

The location of government documents issued by national state and municipal bodies requires special knowledge of special compilation that serves as guides to them, as well as awareness of organization producing them. A few examples of sources are given below:

(a) Monthly catalogue of U.S. Government Publications. U.S. Superintendent of Documents, 1895.
(b) British National Bibliography and British Books in Print, HMSO Publications.
(c) Monthly Catalogue Controller of Publications, Delhi, Indian National Bibliography.

Patents

Patents are an important source of information. Various primary and secondary journals publish information regarding current patents in specific subject fields. Official Gazetteers of patent offices of various countries are valuable sources of patent information. A few examples of sources of patent information are:

- Official Gazetre of U.S. Patent Offices.
- *Chemical Abstracts*—Cites important patents granted in all countries pertaining to chemical industry.
- *Houghton (Bernard)*—Technical information sources—A guide to patent standards and technical report literature.

Standards and Specifications

Standards and specifications are documents which state how materials produced should be manufactured defined, measure or tested. They are 'documents which lay down sets on conditions which should be fulfilled. An example of sources of information pertaining to standards is given below:

- *Catalogue of American Standards*: American Standards Association.

- *British Standard Year Book*: British Standards Institution. Most national standardizing publish an annual list of their standards in a year book or a catalogue.

Translations

There is a growing need for translation of articles and books from foreign languages into English in the field of fundamental and applied research. Therefore, various commercial and non-governmental organizations undertake translation work. Some of the sources of translations are listed below:

- *Technical Translations*: Published U.S. Dept. of Commerce.
- *Science Translations*: A guide to sources and services published by U.S. Dept. of Health Education and Welfare.
- *Index Translation*: International Bibliography of Translation, UNESCO.

Dissertation and Theses

A lot of valuable information is contained in doctoral theses and other dissertations and this untapped since they are not published. A few sources of information regarding dissertation and these are given below:

- Dissertation Abstracts University Microfilms.
- Directory of Graduate Research. American Chemical Society.

Factors in Planning Book Selection

Ranganathan suggests that the distinctive work of the Book Selection Section is to be planned with reference to the following factors:

- Sources
- Selection
- Indent
- Finance

Job Analysis

The work of the Book Selection relating to the factors mentioned in the previous section consists of the following items:

Sources

- o Sources Acquiring Work
- o Sources Arranging Work

Selection

- o Book Selection Work
- o Book Selection Carding Work
- o Book Selection Consultation Work

Indents

- o Indents Scrutinizing Work
- o Indents Passing Work

Finance

- o Allotment Work
- o Allotment Watching Work

In turn, each of the items consists of jobs which may be hourly, daily, weekly, fortnightly, monthly, etc. Details regarding each of the jobs are dealt with in Ranganathan's *magnum opus* Library Administration. It would be interesting to note that he has not only given a Table of Correlation showing the jobs that bring the section into contact with other sections but also has given an Illustrative time Scheme for the different jobs.

ROUTINES OF LIBRARY—TECHNICAL SECTION

One of the important section in a library is the Technical Section as it occupies a pivotal position round which all other activities take place. It is called by other names, such as, Processing Department, Technical Processing Section, Cataloguing Department, Technical Department, etc. Irrespective of the name by which it is called, the objective and functions of this section remain same. While the acquisition is responsible for the building up of good collection of documents into serviceable entities. This is achieved mainly by two functions, namely, technical processing which includes classification and cataloguing, and physical preparation of the documents for circulation and use by the readers.

Need for Technical Processing

The need for technical processing has been brought out by a number of reasons/factors. They are:

- Accelerated growth of information resulting in the production of a large number of documents and consequent, user of problems of inadequate time for reading and assimilation;
- Complexity in subject specialization coupled with interdisciplinary nature of information; and
- Demand from readers for better services., etc.

In addition, the pressure of the Five Laws of Library of Library Science especially the second and third laws have forced librarians to seek new procedures in the arrangement, and management of the collection.

Some of the uses of Technical Processing are:

(i) Helps in the systematic arrangements of documents/ information and thereby facilitates storage and retrieval whenever necessary.
(ii) Facilitates analysis of queries put by users.
(iii) Helps in the preparation of information services and products.

Organisational Structure

Technical Section of a library, especially a University Library may consist of various units such as Classification unit, Cataloguing Unit, Book Processing Unit, etc. to carry out the routine work of technical processing. In the case of a small library, such a demarcation into different units may not be there. Irrespective of the size of the library, it is necessary that this section be headed by a dynamic person with sufficient professional expertise and also be provided with staff to carry out the processing work. In addition, cooperation from other sections of the library is vital.

Planning

In this section, the major items of work are classification and cataloguing. They are of a highly technical nature and accuracy is the very essence of all technical processing work. It has been suggested by Ranganathan that in libraries, especially large libraries, it will be a good policy to prepare at least two copies of the catalogue to facilitate use by the readers on the one hand and by the classifier and the cataloguer on the other. In other words, one set of the catalogue should be in the technical section. This catalogue is described by some as "Official Catalogue."

Factors in Planning

The distinctive work of the Technical Section is to be planned with reference to the following factors:

- Classification
- Cataloguing
- Preparation of the volumes for public use
- Correction of Numbers and Catalogue entries
- Binding
- Classification and Cataloguing Codes
- Catalogue Cabinet

In the context of Planning of the Technical Section it is necessary to take certain decisions. These relate to:

- Choice of Classification Scheme.
- Choice of Catalogue Code.
- Choice of From—Internal and Physical—of the Catalogue.
- Classification and Cataloguing Policy.

Choice of Classification Scheme

A scheme of classification is but a tool in the hands of the library to organize subjects and to serve them out in an efficient way. Therefore, it is necessary that a lot of care and thinking should go while making a choice of a classification scheme for a library. Ranganathan has suggested the following points for consideration while choosing the classification scheme:

- Scope of Classification.
- Sequence of Basic/Main Subjects.
- Provision for new Basic/Main Subjects.
- Provision for "Systems of exposition of a Basic Subject."
- Crip words to denote ideas.
- Sameness of patterns in the sequence of subjects going with different Basic Subjects.
- Objectively used postulates and principles.
- Systematic procedure for practical classification.
- Avoidance of fault of alternative places for one and the same subject.
- Inner mechanism to find a helpful piece to new compound subject.
- Length of base of notational system.
- Provision of Connecting Digits.
- Hospitality in chain.
- Hospitality in array including extrapolation and interpolation.
- Agency for promoting use.
- Permanent organization for development.

Choice of Catalogue Code

Similar to the Classification Schemes, there are different types of Catalogue Codes, the more prominent ones being the Classified Catalogue Code of Ranganathan and the Anglo-American Cataloguing Rules (AACR-2). While CCC is a classified code AACR-2 is a Descriptive Catalogue Code and is mainly meant for a Dictionary Catalogue. Depending upon the need of the library, the extent of bibliographical description needed, etc. the appropriate code is to be chosen.

Choice of Form of Catalogue

By form is meant both internal and physical form of catalogue and possible, namely, classified and dictionary catalogue. The choice between the two will depend, on the type of the library and the clientele. While the Dictionary Catalogue is preferable in Public Libraries, the Classified Catalogue is preferable in Special and Specialist Libraries as it facilitates both classified and an alphabetical approach.

Job Analysis

Classification

The work of the Technical Section relating to Classification is to consist of the following items:

(a) Making a preliminary survey of volumes received from the accession section, which may be referred as Preliminary work;
(b) Assigning Call Numbering Work;
(c) Detecting duplication, defects, etc. in the volumes, and informing the accession section, which may be referred to as Detection Work; and
(d) Checking the assigned Call Numbers, which may be referred to as Checking Work.

Cataloguing

The work relating to cataloguing consists of the following items:

(a) Sorting the volumes according to cataloguing peculiarities and referred to as Preliminary Work;
(b) Writing out the necessary fresh catalogue cards and referred as Fresh Card Writing Work;
(c) Making the necessary entries in the catalogue cards already existing and referred as Card Consolidation Work;
(d) Dealing with the volumes raising difficulties in cataloging and referred Card Consolidation Work;
(e) Checking the catalogue cards and referred as Checking Work; and
(f) Typing catalogue slips is referred as Typing Work.

Preparation of the Volumes

The work relating to the preparation of volumes for public use may consist of the following items:

(a) Noting the accession number or the call number as the case may be, i.e., Card Numbering Work,
(b) Making the volumes fit for use by stamping fixing the data label, tag, etc., i.e. Preparation Work,
(c) Noting the Call number and accession number in the different parts of the columns, i.e., Volumes Numbering Work, and
(d) Sorting the prepared volumes into sequences and arranging them, i.e., Prepared Volumes Arranging Work.

Correction of Call Numbers and Catalogue Entries

The work consists of the following items:

(a) Collecting the volumes to be corrected and their main card and their first impression main slips, i.e. Preliminary Work;
(b) Reclassifying the volumes, i.e., Reclassification Work;
(c) Carrying out the corrections in the first impression slips, i.e. First Impression Slips Work;
(d) Carrying out the corrections in all other cards and slips, i.e., Correction Completing Work; and
(e) Reinserting the corrected main cards and the first impression slips, i.e., Reinsertion Work.

Binding

The binding work is to consist of—

(a) Examining the Call numbers of the volumes selected for binding to see if they require any revision, i.e. Call Number Examining.
(b) Preparing the instruction for tooling, i.e. Binding Slip Preparing; and
(c) Transmitting the volumes and slips to the Binding Section, i.e. Binding Books Transmitting.

Procedure

The procedures to be followed in relation to work in Technical section are given in detail in Ranganathan's Library Administration. They are enumerated below and are self-explanatory.

Classification

Preliminary work:

- Tallying the volumes with accession cards; and
- Preliminary Sorting of the volumes by main classes

Call Numbering work:

- Normal Volumes Call Numbering
- Deferred Volumes Call Numbering
- Classification Consulting
- Difficult Volumes Call Numbering
- Source Noting
- New Classes Noting
- Detection Work
- Detection Notifying

Checking work:

- Call Numbering
- Cross Reference Checking
- New Placing Checking

Cataloguing

Preliminary work

- Sorting Volumes on the basis of their cataloguing peculiarities
- Fresh Card Writing
- Main Card Writing
- Cross Reference Cards Writing
- Index Cards Writing
- Back of Main Card Writing
- Shelf Register Card Writing

Card Consolidation work

- Consolidation Cards Picking
- Consolidating

Reference Cases work

- Refractory Cases Consulting with the liberation
- Sources Noting
- Amendments noting

Checking work

- Fresh Cards Checking
- Consolidated Cards Checking
- Amendments

Typing work

- Fresh Slips Typing
- Consolidation Slips Picking
- Slips Consolidating
- Slips Checking.

Preparation of the Volumes

- card Numbering Work
- Accession Number Noting
- Call Number Noting
- Book Carding

ROUTINES OF LIBRARY—CIRCULATION SECTION

The term circulation has been defined by the ALA Glossary of Library Terms as the activity of a library in lending books to borrowers and keeping the record of the library. This activity is in conformity with the Five Laws of Library Science which states that in libraries book are collected for Use, kept for use and served for Use. Circulation Section is in complete charge of the mechanics of the use of the books by the readers and hence is in direct contact with the readers.

To be efficient and effective Ranganathan opines that the Circulation Section should be a courteous sentinel, i.e., it should know how to be courteous without being base, to be strict without being offensive, and to be friendly without being chatty For this purpose, it is necessary that the counter equipment required for ensuring the safety of the resources of the Library should be provided for by the authorities concerned.

Functions of Circulation Section

The following are the functions;

(a) Maintenance of records relating to each one of the users.
(b) Admitting users are members of the library and dealing with their with draw:
(c) Maintenance of records relating to loan of book:
(d) Taking charge of all the books returned after consultation by users; and
(e) All the work connected with reservation of book by user'

Circulation—Charging Systems

One of the important functions of a library is promote the use of the collection by the users/readers. This is achieved by providing accessibility to books for reading in the library itself or by lending them for home-reading. This latter activity is referred to as circulation and the system of issuing books is called as charging. If this has to be functionally effective it should be so designed to capture and manipulate three kinds of information.

(a) Information about the borrower (such as name and adders telephone number, identification number ,borrower Category)
(b) Information about the document (such as, call number identification number, author, title, date of publication): and
(c) Information about the transaction (such as, due date of loan, in some case the time or period of loan)

Charging System have evolved over time from the simple register Systems through Card System to the modern Automated Circulation System.

Register Systems

To begin with, the Day Book System was in vague; it kept a record of all daily transactions and provided information about the name and address of the borrower, bibliographical details of book issued like author, title and other information considered to be relevant. This system presented no difficulties as the number of borrowers were few and one could trace particulars and transaction without any problem whatsoever. Whenever a book was returned, the date of receipt with the initials of the librarian was recorded against the concerned entry. As the number of borrowers increased overtime, this simple system could not be functionally effective as the Day Book transactions were chronological. Consequently, it was difficult to answer questions like—

What are the books borrowed by a particular reader?
What is the due date of a particular book?
Who borrowed which book?

As an important ever this system came the ledger System where in one or more pages were assigned to each borrower. System provided for information about the borrower, book and the transaction. An index of borrowers was provided so that one could find the page number(s) where the transactions of a particular book and the number of books overdue without nerving the entire register. It was also not possible to identify the borrower of particular book.

Dummy System

To overcome this difficulty partially came the Dummy system a modified version of the Ledger System. In addition to the ledger, a wooden dummy containing information about the book borrower, and the transaction replaced the issued book on the shelf. Thus the need to go through the list of names, and titles for locating a particular book was eliminated.

Temporary Slip System

At this next stage came the Temporary Slip where in a slip containing all the information was prepared at the time of issue of a book. These slips were arranged data-wise or name of the borrower or by the identification alphabetically by the number of the borrower. When the books were returned, these temporary slips were either destroyed or given back to the users as a token of receipt of books returned. This system thus had the advantage of maintaining the circulation records at the counters itself for reference by the staff. Whenever it was necessary, these temporary slips may be considered as the fore-runners of the Card System.

Card System

The Card System may be considered as a sophisticated version of the Temporary Slip System. While the card replaced the slip in the One Card System. There was one card each for the book.

Two Card System

Browne System and Newark System were the most popular among two card Systems. The forms was devised by Browne towards the end of the nineteenth century and consisted of a book card containing information about the book and borrower's ticket with a pocket containing information about the borrower. Therefore, whenever a book was to be issued, the book card was removed and kept in the borrower's pocket or ticket and field either by call number, author or title of the book. This system was easy and convenient as it involved only one operation. However, one disadvantage was that there was no permanent record of the loan.

Network System was developed in 1900. When a reader presents a book at the counter along with the membership card, the counter assistant puts the due date on the membership card and the date slip of the book and the book card. He then puts the membership number on the book card against the due date marked. Then while the book and the membership card are given to the reader, the book cards are arranged by call numbers behind the date guide in a charging tray. When the books are returned after use by the render along with the membership card at the counter. The counter assistant books at the due date on the date slip of the book and picks out the book card filed behind the appropriate date guide. He then affixes the date of return stamp on the membership card and returns it to the reader and simultaneously puts the book card into the book pocket of the book concerned.

Mechanized and Automated Circulation Systems

Circulation, as a function of a library, is very specified definable and allied to common business activities such as material handing and inventory control. Circulation control is an operation mainly concerned with a clerical function of keeping tract of documents taken out of the library by the user. Circulation System is concerned with the procedures of charging, discharging, overdue control reserves, and associated through file maintenance activities. So, it has been one of the important functions to be automated.

Functions of Automated Circulation Systems

Automated circulation system can be either traditional or broad in scope depending upon the design goals and objectives established by the library. Thus, one of the basic considerations in the design and selection of a circulation system is the definition of the role and objectives of circulation in the library. The present day automated circulation systems usually perform some or all of the following functions:

(1) Provision of information on the location of circulation items or only those items on loan of else where, i.e., at the on reserve, being recatalogued', etc.
(2) Identification of items on loan to a particular borrower of class of borrowers (namely, off campus users).
(3) Recording of holds or personal reserves for items on loan but desired by another borrower, often with additional provision for notifying the library staff when the item is returned and printing a book available notice for mailing to the person who requested the item.
(4) Printing recall notices for items on long-term loan;
(5) Renewal of loans.
(6) Notification to the library staff of overdue items and printing of overdue notices.
(7) Notification to the library staff or delinquent borrowers (i.e. those with unpaid fines, or overdue books) either at the time of an attempted loan, or at the time a borrower is leaving the institution or on request from the library.

(8) Calculation of fines, printing of fine notices, recording receipt of fines, and sometimes printing of the receipts.
(9) Calculation and printing of statistics of various types.
(10) Analysis of both summary statistics and statistics for the circulation of particular items for use in acquisition.
(11) Provision for handing special categories of borrower and special types of materials.
(12) Provision for printing due date slips, automatically generating orders for lost books or need additional copies and printing mailing labels for remote borrowers.

STOCK VERIFICATION AND SHELF RECTIFICATION

Documents in libraries were considered to be store items. Consequently, as in the case of stores, which were subject to audit control, stock verification was insisted upon as an annual ritual for the libraries. This contention was an audit requirement. This, however, did not pose problems in earlier times when books were chained or when libraries adopted 'closed access' as the chances of loss were remote. But when libraries adopted 'open access' loss of books was inevitable, and librarians were made responsible for the losses.

Need for Stock Verification

While the librarians may have their own reservations in the matter of stock taking a certain degree of accounting becomes essential. Further, detection of loss is possible only by stock verification. It depends on the size and policies of the library. Another factor to be considered is whether a library should be closed during stock taking or whether some services should be curtailed keeping the essential service intact during stock taking.

Definition and Objective

Stock verification implies physical check up of articles on record. Stock verification in libraries implies the physical checking up of the presence or absence of documents in the records of these documents such as circulation records, shelf list cards, catalogue cards and accession register. The main objective is to assess the efficiency of library management particularly in respect of the maintenance work. The overall objective of stock verification should be to assess the quality of library work and service.

Advantages and Limitations of Stock Verification

The following are the advantages and limitations of stock verification:

Advantages

- Reveals the extent of loss of book in a library and thereby enables replacement of lost books and withdrawl of lost books from accession registers.
- Enables preparation of an in inventory of worm-out books and thus facilitates mending, repair and binding.
- Enables the library authorities to judge the popularity or otherwise of particular subjects in the collection.
- Provides an opportunity to the staff to acquaint themselves with the stock of the library.
- Facilitate shelf-rectification and weeding of titles over used and or not used.
- Ensure through dusting, cleaning and rearrangement.
- Helps updating the library catalogue and other records.
- Enables the library authorities to judge the efficiency or otherwise of library staff with reference to vigilance and carefulness in maintaining the collection.

Limitations

- Stock verification is costly, time-consuming, difficult and cumbersome.
- Disturbs the routines of the library and thereby increasing backing.
- Inconvenience to users and disruption of library services.
- Cost involves is sometimes more than the cost of book lost.

- Additional manpower may have been employed for stock verification, which may not reveal much.

Methods of Stock Verification

The following are some of the methods of stock verification:

- By Accession Register
- Numerical Counting
- Shelf List Method
- Sampling Technique

Stock Verification by Accession Register

In this approach while one calls out the accession number of the books on the shelves, another person tick marks the corresponding number in the accession register. This procedure of checking is repeated with the circulation record of the library. When the entire operation is completed, those entries in the accession register which have not been tick marked constitute the list of lost books. While this method looks simple, it is both time consuming and cumbersome. Further, frequent scanning in search of accession numbers and tick marking spoil the accession register physically.

So a suggestion is to have a duplicate accession register. But this is also a cumbersome procedure and involves a lot of time; money and energy. An alternative method is suggested by which a stock taking register with only the accession numbers and the corresponding years is prepared. The procedure mentioned earlier is repeated with this stock taking register and the unmarked accession number would be from the list of books lost. A variant of this latter method is to use slips with the accession numbers and the year written on them.

Numerical Counting

In this approach, counting of books on the shelves charged trays, and books arranged in other sequences is done and tallied with the total number indicate the number of books lost. This method is useful to that extent that it gives one an idea of the extent of loss as it does not give particulars of lost books.

Shelf List Method

In this approach, the Shelf List maintained in Card form is used. One advantage of a Shelf register is that the sequence of books parallels with the sequence of books on the shelves and hence verification becomes simple when compared with that of an accession register. Perhaps, a Shelf List in Card form is advantageous as it is flexible and ensures speedy stock verification of course, these methods of stock verification presuppose the maintenance of an up-to-date and accurate shelf list whether in book or card from. An added advantage if the shelf list is in card form is that stock verification can be done simultaneously by many persons.

Sampling Technique

To overcome some of the problems of stock verification, one can use some of the modern techniques used in material management and inventory control. One such technique is sampling technique. In this methodology, one may adopt any one of four methods of sampling namely: Simple Random Sampling, Stratified sampling, Systematic sampling, Cluster sampling. It has been found that stratified Sampling Methods are most appropriate for stock verification work.

Sampling Size

Sampling denotes the collection of typical units from the universe. In respect of Libraries, it is the collection of typical documents depending upon the methods of sampling to be adopted. The total number of units to be studied in a sampling is called sampling size. Sampling size depends upon the degree of precision require the variability of spread of the data being sampled, the sampling method used and the type of estimating employed.

Procedure

In applying sampling technique for stock verification in college or University Library the following procedure can be adopted:

Step I

This step involves grouping of the books in the library

according to their price. The price of a book can be obtained from the accession register. The pattern of grouping thus obtained should conform to the 'exponential distribution curve'

Step 2

Divide the universe of books into two groups, namely, low price books and high price books. For this purpose, fix a price (frication point), say X_0 which is the highest value of the low price books and the least value of the high books.

Step 3

A complete enumeration of the books high price group is made that is all the books in the high price group are to be physically verified and the missing books with the price are noted.

Step 4

For low price group determine the sample size, say, in make a physical verification of the books in the sample with the help of the accession register, and note the details regarding price with reference to the missing books.

Step 5

Cumulate the cost of the lost books by adding the cost of text books in the high value group with that in the low value group. The significance of this loss in relation to the total number of books circulated, during the year, it may be calculated using statistical methods.

Problems in Stock Verification

The main problem in efficient stock verification work arises due to the larger number and variety of document stock in the college and university libraries. The work of stock verification in all large libraries will take more than six months. Further, stock verification work usually affects the library routine in respect of library work and service to reader. There are cases of some college libraries closing down the access to the library for the readers. During this period; library atmosphere looks dull like that of a storehouse.

Overcoming Some of the Problems

Most of the problems of stock verification may be due to the lack of proper rapport in communication between the stock verification staff and the library staff. Only periodical meetings between the stock verification staff and the library staff can establish this. Many of the problems in stock verification could be overcome if the library staff adopted a periodical shelf rectification and recording the findings.

Who should do Stock Verifications

As per audit requirement, stock verification should be done by persons those connected with the store items, namely here documents. By implication, it would mean that it should be done by an outside agency. But, verification by outsiders of non-professionals who are not familiar with the library and its practices may create problems. Hence, it is suggested that library professionals undertake stock verification. It is fact that there may be scope for malpractice if done by professionals of the library concerned, professionals from outside may be asked to perform this task.

Another factor to be considered is time and cost involved when an outside agency conducts stock verification. In addition, follow-up action is, generally difficult when an outside agency is employed.

Hence, it is desirable that if stock verification is considered necessary and inevitable professionals within the organization may be asked to perform it. Perhaps, safeguards against bias and malpractices possible, if any, may yield the best results.

Loss of Books

Dr. S.R. Ranganathan observes, even with the best of safe-guards the most human treatment possible, and vigilance of a high order, there will be some loss. The authorities of the library should be prepared for it. The cause of loss may be due to either the criminal nature to steal; of some users or due to poor vigilance arrangements in the library. It has been argued that reasonable loss in an open access library is inevitable and unavoidable due to human failure, misplacement and various other socio-economic factors and the moral behaviour of the society. Therefore, some norms are adopted for writing the loss of books.

Responsibility for Loss of Books

Librarians are not held responsible for loss of books in foreign countries. But, in India, librarians are made responsible for the loss and penalized for the same. This trend is however, changing with the Management accepting a reasonable loss as inevitable in an open access library. Dr. Ranganathan views are:

1. Mutilation of books is the result of inherent criminal impulse in a few readers. This is exactly as stealing is an inherent criminal impulse in a few people in a society.
2. It is as improper to make the librarian pay the cost of all mutilated books as to the policeman to pay the cost at property stolen.
3. It is the college authorities—particularly, the principal and the member of the teaching staff—to away the student population from this criminal tendency.
4. Neither equity not social justice, nor any kind of property can make it the librarian's duty to be sole agent in a college to reform the conduct of students.

Steps to Minimize Losses

The following are some of the steps that can be followed for minimizing loss of books:

(1) Stock room should be well protected and all windows need to be wire meshed.
(2) Entry and Exit to the library may be through one single entrance.
(3) No, personal belongings should be allowed into the library. However, space has to be provided for depositing personal belongings before the users of the library.
(4) The maintenance staff should be careful vigilant perform their duties efficiently.
(5) Checking of books issued at the check gate should be properly done.
(6) Installation of mirrors, close-circuit television, electronic detectors, etc. may be used to deter. The usuries from taking away books unlawfully.

(7) Since, soon accessibility of required books tempts users to adopt malpractices provision of photocopies at subsidized charge will go along way in preventing multination of taking away of books.

(8) Orientation programmer to users should be given periodically so that the libraries are used properly.

Shelf Rectification

In an open access library, readers tent to replace books on the shelves after use through they are requested/directed not to do so. This results in misplacement of books. A misplaced book is as good as lost. Sometimes readers hide books on a particular subject by placing them alone with books in some other subject. Some readers to resort to this malpractice as to have exclusive access to the books whenever they want on the one hand and to deny access to other readers on the other. Such misplacement either accidental or deliberate results in the violation of the second and third laws of library science. Hence, restoring order among the books on the shelves becomes an absolute necessity. This work of restoring order is called Shelf Rectification. One of the by products of shelf rectification is that the maintained staff would be able to identify books that need to be mended, repaired, rebound, etc. Dr. Ranganathan suggests that shelf rectification and stock verification process should be combined to get beat results.

PERSONNEL MANAGEMENT

Personnel management is concerned with the effective use of the skills of people. They may be salespeople in a store, clerks in an office, operators in a factory, or technicians in a research laboratory. In a business, personnel management starts with the recruiting and hiring of qualified people and continues with directing and encouraging their growth as they encounter problems and tensions that arise in working toward established goals.

In addition to recruiting and hiring, some of the responsibilities of a personnel manager are:

1. To classify jobs and prepare wage and salary scales.

2. To counsel employees.
3. To deal with disciplinary problems.
4. To negotiate with labour unions and service union contracts.
5. To develop safety standards and practices.
6. To manage benefit programs, such as group insurance, health, and retirement plans.
7. To provide for periodic reviews of the performance of each individual employee, and for recognition of his or her strengths and needs for further development.
8. To assist individuals in their efforts to develop and qualify for more advanced jobs.
9. To plan and supervise training programs.
10. To keep abreast of developments in personnel management.

To understand the personnel manager's job think of how you would deal with the following examples of challenging employee situations:

The firm's employees—especially the most qualified ones—can get comparable, if not better jobs with other employers. When a firm faces a scarcity of supervisory and specialized personnel with adequate experience and job capabilities, it has to train and develop its own people. This can be time consuming and expensive.

The cost of hiring and training employees at all levels is increasing, for instance, several thousand dollars for a salesperson. A mistake in hiring or in slow and inefficient methods of training can be costly. Personnel managers must comply with the law by employing, training and promoting women and persons from minority groups. The problem in doing so is that many of these employees have not had appropriate experience and education in the past.

Most employees, whether or not represented by labour unions, continue to seek improvements in direct compensation, employee benefits, and working conditions. All commitments must be based upon what the firm can afford, comply with current practices of other employers, and be understood and accepted by the employee. To do this, all employee policies and operating procedures should be developed and negotiated with great care.

Some employees may not perform satisfactorily simply because their firm offers competitive compensation, benefits, and working conditions. In addition to these financial or physical compensations, they want responsibility, the opportunity to develop, and recognition of accomplishment in their jobs. The law has established requirements for pension and other benefit plans, and also bar mandatory retirement at age 65. Complying with such changes presents real challenges.

Personnel management works to achieve practical solutions to such problems. In large firms, it generally provides support to line management. In this staff capacity, the personnel department has the responsibility to develop and implement policies, procedures, and programs for recruitment, selection, training, placement, safety, employee benefits and services, compensation, labour relations, organization planning, and employee development.

Often, the owner-manager of a firm also has to be the personnel manager. In such a case it is necessary to have an overview of current trends and practices in personnel management. All small businesses must staff their operations. This involves bringing new people into the business and making sure they are productive additions to the enterprise. Effective human resource management matches and develops the abilities of job candidates and employees with the needs of the firm. A responsive personnel system will assist you in this process and is a key ingredient for growth.

Human resource management is a balancing act. At one extreme, you hire only qualified people who are well suited to the firm's needs. At the other extreme, you train and develop employees to meet the firm's needs. Most expanding small businesses fall between the two extremes, i.e. they hire the best people they can find and afford, and they also recognize the need to train and develop both current and new employees as the firm grows.

One function of personnel management deals with how to hire and train the right people and addresses the characteristics of an effective personnel system, such as:

- Assessing personnel needs.
- Recruiting personnel.

- Screening personnel.
- Selecting and hiring personnel.
- Orienting new employees to the business.
- Deciding compensation issues.

Another function addresses the training and development side of human resource management. A third function deals with how the personnel system and the training and development functions come together to build employee trust and productivity. These three functions stress the importance of a good human resource management climate and provide specific guidelines for creating such a climate.

Definition

One of the best definitions, from which the objectives and functions can be inferred, is that given in the Management Dictionary.

That activity which directs human resources into a kind of dynamic organization which accomplishes its goals through provision of opportunities for maximum individual contribution under desirable working relationships and conditions; it includes selection, allocation, utilization and development of employees as well as improvement of working conditions to obtain maximum productivity and efficiency under specifically emphasized consideration for individual and human elements.

Thus, two components—personnel which means people and management which means responsibility for accomplishment—can be identified which together determine objectives of personnel management.

Personnel management is that phase of management which deals with the effective control and use of manpower as distinguished from other sources of power.

Objectives of Personnel Management

The objectives can be briefly described as:

- To attract and secure appropriate people capable of performing effectively the library's specific tasks.
- To utilize the human resources effectively.
- To generate maximum individual development of the people within the library.

Challenges of Modern Personnel Management

There are a number of problems in personnel management. These problems are caused by constant changes that occur both within the firm and outside the firm. Among the major changes that are occurring, the following are important

- Changing mix of the work force
- Changing personnel values of the work force
- Changing expectations of the citizen-employees
- Changing levels of productivity
- Changing demands of the Government

Functions of Personnel Management

The objectives mentioned earlier imply the following functions of personnel management:

- Selection and recruitment
- Placement
- Training and Development
- Wage and Salary administration
- Health safety and security
- Record maintenance

Library Staff

The efficiency and effectiveness of Libraries and Information Centers (L&IC) would largely depend on the competence/capacity of the staff employed and on the facilities and environment provided for their work and development. The L&IC's are expected to provide a variety of library/information services to readers in different subject fields. They have to interact with users who may be school going children, college and university students and faculty subject specialists, extension workers, public, etc. Hence the professional staff should have appropriate qualifications in the respective subject-fields and in library and information science. In addition, they should have adequate experience and training, innovative capability, proper attitude and pioneering spirit towards work so that there will be harmony among and mutual enrichment of the functional subject.

Categories of Staff

The different categories of personnel required in the L&LCs are:

- Professional
- Semi-professional
- Supporting Staff

The different levels, the number of persons in each level, their qualifications, cost of employing them, etc. will depend upon the type quality and quantity of work to be done in each unit or sub-unit. This, manpower/staff requirements for L & ICs should be examined from the point of view of:

- Type and categories of staff
- Skill requirements and levels and training of staff
- Availability of staff at different levels
- Selection and Recruitment of Staff
- Cost estimates and Salary structure.

Professionals

Libraries are no longer considered as mere storehouse of knowledge, but are treated as learning centers and information service organizations. Hence, information professionals who possess a education and have a broad understanding of the fields of knowledge and their organization are required to attend to the professional activities of the library. In addition to knowledge of traditional subjects taught in library schools, the modern library professionals should be familiar with concepts pertaining to micro-computing, marketing, information technology and its applicability, information seeking behaviour, information management, economics of information, etc.

Information professionals should also possess the following skills:

- Traditional skills of acquiring, organizing and disseminations of information.
- Skills in communication, systems analysis, interpersonal relations and financial planning.
- Managerial skill for—technology management and

application to library and information work, problems solving decision-making, etc.
- Skills to analyses, synthesis, interpret, consolidate, and evaluate information and knowledge.
- Advocacy skills, a greater sensitivity to social and political forces and an increased ability to define and articulate values and value systems.

Depending on the level, professionals would involve in overall management, policy making, planning, co-ordination, control, leadership, external relations (at senior levels), information services, etc. at other levels. The professionals in academic libraries are named as Librarian, Deputy Librarian, Assistant librarian, Professional Assistant. In special libraries designations are Information Systems Manager, Head, Information Scientists/Officer, Information Analyst, etc.

Semi-Professionals

On the other hand, there are a number of people who perform routine and repetitive jobs in a library. They are called as Semi-Professionals and possess undergraduate qualifications and library training at diploma or certificate level. The semi-professionals may also be provided "in-service-training at the organizations where they are employed. They perform jobs pertaining to book ordering, checking bibliographical details of documents, accessioning descriptive cataloguing, charging and discharging, sending reminders for non-receipt of documents, etc. They are designated as library assistants, technical assistants, record assistants, etc.

Supporting Staff

Information Technology (IT) is now commonly used to describe the result of merging of computer and telecommunication technologies. The influence of IT, especially the computer in our everyday life is evident as can be seen from the vending machines, computer games, digital telephones, remote control television sets, electronic gardens, etc., one comes across. This influence is expected to come in a big way, in the future, to the working of libraries and information centers as it is being used in libraries for many purposes.

- Supporting clerical functions associated with acquisition, technical processing, circulation work.
- Supporting information storage, retrieval and dissemination service, etc. (Library Automation).

In addition Reprographics have come to stay in libraries. Thus, it become necessary that the library has been supporting staff to handle the computer, communication and media technologies for providing library and information services.

Another category of supporting staff required is for handling purely administrative and financial matters. These include purchase of store and supplies maintenance of services, security general office administration, personnel administration, etc. The number and level of supporting staff would depend on the size and magnitude of operations.

Manpower Estimation

In estimating manpower requirements for libraries, some of the questions that need to be answered are:

- What is the workload in each unit of the library presently, what is the extent increase in the future?
- What is the type/quality of work to be performed in each unit?
- What type of staff are to be employed—professional, semi-professional, supporting staff?
- What should be the qualifications—academic professional—experience necessary for each job?
- What should be the salary for each of the staff at the different levels?

In other words, it is necessary to analysis each of the jobs to deperformed in the library. This procedure is called as job analysis activity or work analysis.

Job Analysis

Job analysis has been defined as the method of finding out is to be done and determines the best method of doing it and the qualifications required of a worker to be able to do the job satisfactorily.

In order to do a good job analysis, it is necessary to collect accurate, reliable and comprehensive data regarding each job. Data pertaining to specific activities, responsibilities, special information needed by the worker, how of the work to be performed working conditions and physical demands need to be obtained from the concerned employees, their supervisors, experts in the field through questionnaires, interviews and observation.

One of the best books discussing the concept of job analysis in libraries is Ranganathan's Library Administration, in which he has analysed the various activities to be performed in each section of the library.

Job Description

Based on job analysis, job description can be prepared. A job description should give details regarding the various activities and duties equipment, methods, working conditions, responsibilities relationship to work/job performed in other units/sections of the library, minimum qualifications, experience and other essential factors concerned with the job. Job description facilitates selection, recruitment, placement, and training and performance appraisal of individual workers or employees.

RANGANATHAN'S STAFF FORMULA

While there are different types of libraries—such as, Public, Academic, and Special—the pattern of activities, i.e. selection, acquisition, technical processing, circulation, documentation, etc. in them is more or less the same. As a consequence, pattern of staff requirements is also similar. However, the professionals employed should have the right aptitude and attitude and should work for the objectives of the respective libraries.

In determining the staff requirements, there is an university acceptable standard staff formula for all types of libraries. Even, the standards available are inadequate and not comprehensive, luckily, in India, Ranganathan's Staff formula can be used with necessary modifications to all types of libraries. The following table gives a standard, based on Ranganathan's Staff Formula, for different types of libraries.

Unit-wise Distribution of Professionals

In the unit-wise distribution of professionals, the main criterion to be considered are the quality and quality of work to be done in each unit. If, however, planning covers more than one phase, it is necessary that due weightage is given to factors such as promotion, pyramidal structure, etc.

In the context of staff deployment policy, the objective should be to allot appropriate work forces to meet the requirements of specific duties. Criterion by which the achievement of this aim can be measured are:

- Are the staff allocated in sufficient numbers?
- Are they of correct professional caliber?
- Are they able to cover the opening and closing duties involved?
- Are they able to man all the service points?

S. No.	*Work in sections with functions*	*Annual quantum of work per person*		
		Public Libraries	*Academic Libracies*	*Special Libraries*
1.	Books section: Selection ordering. accessioning of books	6000 documents annually added	Same as public libraries	Same as public libraries
2.	Periodtcals Section — ordering, receipt, display, and preparing for binding	1000 periodical titles received	100 periodical titles received	500 periodical titles received
3.	Technical processing section— classification, cataloguing	2000 documents	Same as public library	1500 books
4.	Circulation section— charging and discharging of books	1500 Gate hours	Same as public library	Same as public library
5.	Reference section	50 queries/ readers per day	Same as public library	Same as public library
6.	Maintenance section	One person for every 600 documents added	Same as public library	Same as poblic library
7.	Documentation section	One person for every 1000 entries prepared	Same as public library	Same as public library
8.	Supervisory staff	One for every 1500 hours the library is kept open	Same as public library	Same as public library

Qualification of Library Staff

University Library Staff: The minimum qualification for appointment to the post of Librarian, Deputy Librarian and Assistant Librarian/College Librarian according to UGC letter of 30th June 2010 are given below:

UNIVERSITY LIBRARIAN

(i) A Master's Degree in Library Science/Information Science/documentation with at least 55% marks or its equivalent grade of B in the UGC seven points scale and consistently good academic record set out in these Regulations.

(ii) At least thirteen years as a Deputy Librarian in a university library or eighteen years' experience as a College Librarian.

(iii) Evidence of innovative library service and organization of published work.

(iv) *Desirable*: A M.Phil./Ph.D. Degree in library science/ information science/documentation/achieves and manuscript-keeping.

DEPUTY LIBRARIAN

(i) A Master's Degree in library science/information science/documentation with at least 55% of the marks or its equivalent grade of B in the UGC seven point scale and a consistently good academic record.

(ii) Five years' experience as an Assistant University Librarian/College Librarian.

(iii) Evidence of innovative library service and organization of published work and professional commitment, computerization of library.

(iv) *Desirable*: A M.Phil./Ph.D. Degree in library science/ Information science/Documentation/Archives and manuscript-keeping/computerization of library.

UNIVERSITY ASSISTANT LIBRARIAN/COLLEGE LIBRARIAN

(i) A Master's Degree in Library Science/Information

Science/Documentation Science or an equivalent professional degree with at least 55% marks (or an equivalent grade in a point scale wherever grading system is followed) and a consistently good academic record with knowledge of computerization of library.

(ii) Qualifying in the national level test conducted for the purpose by the UGC or any other agency approved by the UGC.

(iii) However, candidates, who are, or have been awarded Ph.D. degree in accordance with the University Grants Commission (Minimum Standards and Procedure for Award of Ph.D. Degree), Regulations 2009, shall be exempted from the requirement of the minimum eligibility condition of NET/SLET/SET for recruitment and appointment of University Assistant Director of Physical Education/College Director of Physical Education and Sports.

Staff Recruitment and Orientation

Method of Recruitment

Recruitment is a process by which the right people are selected and placed in appropriate positions in the library. But, the question is where to find the right type of professional staff; one obvious place would be the library schools where courses in library and information science are conducted. Another would be by reference to other professionals in the field. More conventional channels would be placement offices of professional societies like IASLIC ILA, employment in newspapers professional journals and news letters. Of course, it goes without saying that advertisements should give full details regarding the job— the job title duties, responsibilities, the academic and professional qualifications, experience required, salary scale, last date for applying and relevant information.

This is followed by the constitution of selection committee who would interview the candidates and select best among them keeping in mind the requirements of job concerned.

Orientation

Once a person is selected and recruited in a library it is

necessary that he be given an orientation programme so that he fits into the new environment and also to motivate him to higher levels of performance. It has been found that poor or unsatisfactory performance staff conflicts, job dissatisfaction, etc, can be traced to inadequate orientation of an employee to his work. The minimum information to be provided for a new entrant should include—

- General Background
  - o *Information Service*—Objectives, organization special features, rules.
  - o Personnel information, position, classification system, promotions, salaries, rules, conduct.
  - o *Benefits*—Training, meeting, hospitalization, retirement leave.
  - o *Facilities*—Canteen, club, etc.
  - o Special Job Induction.
  - o Description of the employee's position.
  - o Relationship of the position to immediate coworkers.
  - o Organization and operation of the employee's department and its relationship to other functions.
  - o Equipment, personnel facilities, reporting procedures and other related facts.
- Individual Job Description
  - o Details of work
  - o Salary, how computed, deduction (Atherto, 1977).

It would be ideal if descriptive like brochures, booklets, etc. are sent to the new entrant before he reports for duty. Once he joins an orientation programme covering several days would go a long way in making the new surroundings. This programme can be through guided tours audio-visual presentations, in service training, etc.

Performance Appraisal

The objective of performance appraisal is primarily to assess the strengths and weaknesses of existing personnel of the library. However, there are other objectives/purposes for appraisal schemes adopted by different organizations. The following are some of the purposes:

- To monitor Performance
- To plan for future performance
- To identify potential
- To assess from ability
- To identify training needs
- To counsel and motivate
- To assist with career and succession planning.

Different organizations adopt different appraisal schemes. Annual confidential reports written by Supervisors of employees is a method of performance appraisal.

Motivation and Management

While everyone recognizes the importance of the axiom that get the best out of the staff one should understand the individual and the conditions of work, it is ironical that library administrators have not paid sufficient attention in this regard. Ward has listed the following reasons why people work:

- To earn money
- Social need to work among a community
- Dependency needs upon bosses and colleagues
- Psycho-needs, such as power and influence
- Incentive they get their daily work
- Financial reward, job satisfaction, contacts with other professionals, appreciation, etc.

These reasons are in conformity with the theories of motivation such as, Maslow's Theory, Mc Gregors 'Theory X and theory Y', Herzberg's Motivation—Hegiene Theory, etc. Therefore administration should make earnest efforts in applying these motivation theories in their respective libraries and information centers. Many of the problems encountered by personnel as well as the management will disappear. While problems encountered by personnel relate top salary/pay structure, job security control and supervision, working conditions, interpersonal relations, recognition, status, advancement, etc, the problems encountered by management are poor performance/low productivity absenteeism, tardiness, quitting, turnover, etc. Perhaps it would be relevant to mention here that problems of the personnel become the causal factors for the problems of the management.

Work Co-ordination

Staff Manual

A staff manual should be prepared in which the function of the library and the duties of each staff member may be prepared. The manual may be arranged logically under subjects and not as a description of each staff member's work because allocation of duties as the personnel changes will change. A good index should be provided for the manual as it would facilitate a new recruit to use the manual. One of the most important section of a staff manual is that it contains personnel policies affecting all staff members are recorded.

A manual is, obviously, very helpful in training new staff members. It is also useful to the administrative officers of the organization since it gives concrete evidence of the activities of the library.

Staff Meetings

In order to ensure smooth working of the library, staff meeting should be held periodically. These meetings should primarily be meant for discussing technical problems arising from library work in the different sub-units. It will be a good practice to make brief reports of these meetings for future reference. Such meetings would also help to foster a spirit of mutual understanding and cooperation among the staff member.

Thus, while man's relationship to the context or environment in which he works is important and necessary to give attention to Man's relationship to what he does. Gone are the days when people were satisfied with a mere pay packet. The order of the day is something more than the pay packet –, i.e., the challenges of the job, achievement, advancement, recognitions, etc. Therefore, in order to get the best out of the people some points to be borne in mind are:

- Selection and Recruitment of Personnel should be systematic and cursory.

- Placement to be appropriate .
- Give adequate training and orientation.
- Provide employees with definite and unique responsibilities a short administrative chain of command, adequate means to exhibit productivity to others, freedom from fear to failure, opportunities to merge fear of failure, opportunities to merge self-actualisation with normal responsibilities.
- Provide pay and other values (fringe benefits), communes rate with qualifications and experience necessary for the job.
- Control and supervision to be as is necessary.
- Give appreciation and recognition when it is due.
- Assessment/evaluation should be objective.
- Create an environment conductive to works as well as for the development of good inter-personal relationships.
- Develop satisfies and eliminate dissatisfies.

To conclude, as McGregor puts it, "The essential task of management is arrange organization conditional and methods of operations so that people can achieve their own goals best by directing their own efforts towards organizational objectives."

INFORMATION SOURCES

TYPES OF INFORMATION SOURCES

"Source" means the origin of something. An information source is a source of information for somebody, i.e. anything that might inform a person about something or provide knowledge to somebody. Information sources may be observations, people, speeches, documents, pictures, organizations, etc. They may be primary sources, secondary sources, and tertiary sources and so on. Literature of a subject is its foundation. It represents a record of achievement of human race. Literature is diverse, complex and multilingual in nature. It is becoming more and more interdisciplinary. It is growing in a fast pace. In sciences, it is almost doubling itself incoming five to ten year. In social sciences it is doubling at the rate every eight to twelve year. Literature serves the international needs of various kinds of users. It forms sources of information needs of various kinds of users.

We may recognize the following kinds of sources of information:

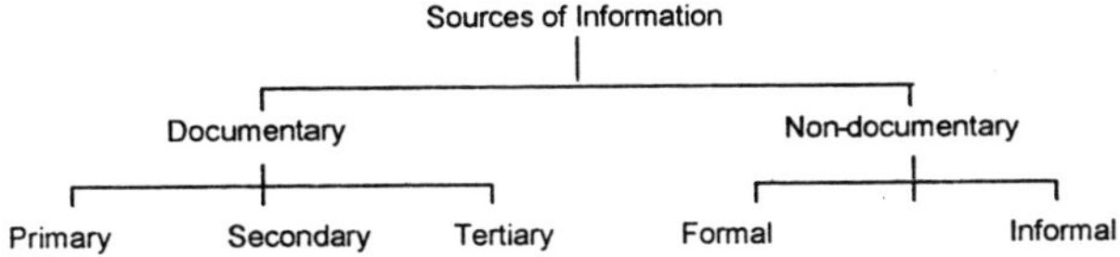

PRIMARY SOURCES

Primary sources of information are the first published records of original research and development or description of new application or new interpretation of an old theme or idea. They are original documents representing unfiltered original ideas. These constitute the latest available information. A research producing new information can make it available to the particular community through the primary sources. Often it may be the only source of information in existence.

Primary sources are unorganized sources, which are rather difficult to use by themselves. The secondary sources help us to use these. These are important sources of information. A subject becomes a discipline in its own light when independent primary sources begin to be produced more in that area. The rate of growth of a discipline to a large extent depends upon the amount of literature being produced in the form of primary sources reporting developments in the form of primary sources in the concerned filed.

Functions

These aid the researches to:

(a) Keep up-to-date and well informed of the new developments.
(b) Avoid publication in research.
(c) Help others to build on this by means of further work and thus generate more information.

Primary sources are published in varied forms. Normally, these take the form of a journal article, monograph report, patent, dissertation, etc. Some of them may be unpublished. These are described below.

A. Periodicals

Periodicals include journals, bulletins, transaction, proceeding or similar works which appear regularly and continuously in numbered sequence. However, the newspaper and annuals are excluded. The bulk of primary source literature appears in the form of periodicals. There are many periodical article is the main means of communication for the exchange of scientific information. The same can be said about many other areas of knowledge. It may be pointed out that an article in a journal would be considered primary source if it contains information representing original thinking or a report on a new discovery.

Information contained in periodicals are almost invariably more up-to-date than that appearing in books. Periodicals usually report the results of recent researches more quickly than books. Information on new processes and discoveries can appear in a periodical within the weeks of their formulation. However, the same might take to three years before the same can appear in book from.

If all the information appearing in periodicals was also covered in books, then libraries would no longer be expected to maintain long files of back volumes of periodicals. Experience shows that most of the materials reported in periodicals are never published in books.

Example:

Historical Journal, 1958; New York, Cambridge University Press, Quarterly.

Nature, 1899; London, MacMillan, Weekly.

Physics of Fluids, 1958; New York, American Institute of Physics, Monthly.

B. Research Reports

Research reports are reports regarding research and development projects. These are primitive form of literature, because these are produced earlier in a research programme. Often these take the form of progress reports which serve temporary reference. Due to the inadequacies of the periodicals, research reports issued as separate documents offer a successful alternative. These from vital part of primary sources, specially in the areas of aeronautics and applied atomic energy. This kind of literature is often called "unpublished" or "Semi-published" literature, because normally these are not available through regular book trade channels, but are made available to interested parties under certain kind of control.

Examples

Scientific and Technical Aerospace reports, National Aeronautics and Space Administration (NASA)

Government Report. Announcements and index (GRA & I)

C. Standards and Patents

Standards form primary source of information. The importance of standards can be gauged from the fact that progress of modern society would be difficult without standards. These lead to simplification of production and distribution of products produced by a manufacturer. These ensure reliability for the consumers. As a result of standardization, those items which do not follow prescribed standards get eliminated from the market.

A typical standard is a pamphlet covering definition, methods, properties, measurements, etc. It may be illustrated with tables and diagrams. In India Standard Institution is a major organization issuing standards. It brings out about 300 standards annually.

Example

International Standards Organization, Guidelines for the establishment and development of monolingual thesaurus for information retrieval, 1034E revises 3rd August, 1971.

British Standards Institution, Microfiche, BS 4187: 1975.

Patents

A patent is a government grant of exclusive privilege which allows making use or selling of a new invention for a term of years. A patent takes file form of an official document, having the seal of government attached to it, which confers an exclusive or right over a period of time to the proceeds of invention.

Patents are regarded as a part of the primary sources because an invention has to be new, only then it can patented. Very often, there may be no published description of the idea incorporated in a patent of its application. It may be mentioned that patents are special interest to chemists and engineers. In each country, there is one publishing agency and these are serially numbered. In India, Patent office is responsible for granting patents. At present over 3000 patent are granted every year. The patents are listed in official patent are office as bibliographical tools. Besides, regular indexing and abstracting services also cover patents.

Examples

Chemical Abstracts, 907, Boston, sap., American Chemical Society, 1907, Vol I, Weekly.

Indian Science Abstracts, Delhi, Indian National Scientific Documentation Centre, Vol. 1. 1965-, Monthly,

Physics Abstracts, Science abstracts series A. London, Institution of Electrical Engineers, 1898-, Fortnightly.

D. Trade Literature

Trade literature is an important source for getting information about particular products and their development. Often it may be the only source for such information. As such when the required information is not available elsewhere, then particular trade literature may become a primary source.

Trade literature aims to describe and also illustrate equipment or goods or processes of services relating to manufactures. The basic objective of such a literature is sell products produced by a manufacture or to advance the prestige. It is issued by manufacturer or dealers and is often very well produced. It is issued in a variety of forms. It may take the form of a technical bulletin, price lists, data sheets, etc. Trade literature lies usually outside the hope of usual trade channels. The booksellers are disinterested to handle this kind of literature.

E. Thesis and Dissertation

Universities normally require a candidate working towards a doctorate degree to write a dissertation under the supervision of a guide. It is sometimes called thesis. These are usually expected to show evidence of original research and are supposed to form an important category of documents for researchers in the concerned field. These should be considered primary sources of information. Much of what is worthwhile in dissertations is later published in the primary periodical or books, but frequently certain data relating to an important original work may never get included in traditional forms of literature.

F. Conference Proceedings

Conference range from small gatherings of the local branch or specialist section of a professional or learned society such as the Royal Institute of Chemistry or the Institution of the Rubber Industry to the Great international scientific progress with thousands of delegates from all over the world. Most commonly described as conference or conventions they may also be known as Symposium, Seminar's sessions, assemblies, workshop and round tables by institutes and colleges.

They play an important role in scientific and technological communication. Many of the papers presented often reports research work several months before publication in the periodical. Indeed a nature of conference is the large number of interim reports on incomplete work. Conference offers the range both in degree and number of opportunities for scientific communication.

G. Official Publication

Government publications are not official publications alone, because official publications cover not only national but local Governmental publications. They embrace all works of life and their presence is full by all people. Nationally the publishing activities of governments have increased with the expansion of their activities. They provide statistical data concerning the countries and also rarely publications concerning the history, culture, and social economical and political aspects of the life of their people. Government documents are often "Official" and authoritative sources of information concerning a country.

SECONDARY SOURCES

Secondary sources of information are those which are either compiled from or referred to primary sources of information. These contain information regarding primary information. The original information having been usually modified, selected or recognized so as to serve a definite purpose of groups of users. Such sources contain information arranged and organized on the basis of some definite plan. These contain organized repackaged knowledge rather than new knowledge. Information given in primary sources is made available in a more convenient form. Due to their nature secondary sources are more easily and widely available than primary sources. These not only provide digested information but also serve as a bibliographical key to primary source information. The primary sources are the first to appear. These are followed by secondary source. It is difficult to find information from primary sources directly. Therefore, one should consult the secondary source in the first instance, which will lead him to specific primary sources.

A. Secondary Periodicals

All periodicals do not report original work. There are a number of periodicals which specializes in interpreting and providing opinions on developments reported in primary sources of information. Such periodicals may be considered secondary sources.

Examples

New Scientist edited by Bernard Dixon, London, IPS Magazins 1956......, Weekly.

New Society, London Science Publications, 1962, Weekly.

B. Review Literature

A review is a survey of the primary literature. It aims to digest and correlate the literature over a given period. It also indicates the developments and trends in the field concerned. It may appear as a collection of papers on regular basis. (Annual or Quarterly or Monthly) or in the form of an article in a periodical. A review provides background information to a new problem in a suitable form and serves as a key to literature. List of references given in a review can as a first rate bibliography of the concerned subject for a period covered by it

Examples

Annual Review of Biochemistry, 1932, Palo Alto, Annual Review of Information Science and Technology, 1966, Vol 1, Washington D.C., American Society for Information.

C. Reference Books

Reference works, which contain the desired information itself are considered secondary source of information. These include encyclopaedias, dictionaries, hand books, tables, formularies and manuals. These are compiled, so that everyday information can be provided readily.

Dictionaries

A Dictionary is a book, which deals with words of a language or of some special subjects, author, etc. Thus a dictionary is a word book. Although a dictionary is supposed to deal with words but often it may go beyond this.

Examples

Random House Dictionary of the English Language, edited by Jess Stein, Unabridged edition, New York Random House, 60

Websters "Third New International Dictionary of the English Language, unabridged with seven language dictionary. Springfield, Mass, Merriam, 1961.

Encyclopaedias

An Encyclopaedia is a book giving information on all branches of knowledge or a specific subject. It is an ideal book, which deals with concepts. An encyclopaedia is a store-house of knowledge giving all information of significance. However, it is best used for finding answers to background questions related to general information and self-education. One often turns to encyclopaedias for one's every day information requirements. This is also true of scientists and technologists.

Examples

Encyclopaedia Americana, New York, Grelier, 1976, 30 vols. McGraw Hill Encyclopaedia of Science and Technology, 4th ed., New York, McGraw Hill 1977, 15 Vols.

Hand Books

A hand book is a compilation of miscellaneous information in a compact and handy form. It contains data, procedure, principles, etc. Tables, Graphs, Diagrams and illustration are provided. Scientists and technologists use handbook in their fields rather frequently.

Examples

Hand Book of Chemistry and Physics: A ready reference book of chemistry and physical data, 52nd ed., Cleveland Ohio, Chemical Rubber, 1971.

Machinery's Hand Book: A reference book for the mechanical engineer, draftsman toolmaker and machinist by E. Oberg and F.D. Jones, 19th ed., New York, Industrial Press.

Tables

Many of the hand books contain data in the form of tables. Some of the hand books devote substantial portion of the work to tables as compared with text. Tables are a convenient form to present data (e.g. extremely useful in science; especially physical sciences and technology.

Examples

International Critical Tables, New York, McGraw Hill, 1226-33, 7 Vols. annex.

Tables of contents and numerical data, Oxford, Pergramon Press, 1947 Vol.

Formulas

The practicing scientist or technologist turns more readily to and it is these that make up the bulk of titles in descriptive list such as W.R. Turnbull Scientific and Technical Dictionaries. It is common of such dictionaries to go beyond their basic function of defining works and examples. Abound of dictionaries are with substantial appendices of table, formulate and other non-dictionary data.

Pharamacopocias are drug Hand books. The British Pharmacopocias appears every five years on the recommendations of Medicine commission under Act of Parliament. Supplementing pharmacopocias are formularies such as British National Formulary which are usually receipt books. Formularies other than pharmaceutical make a category of reference books that could be well studied with hand.

Examples

The Chemical Formulary (N.Y.) Chemical Publishing, G, 1933.

Manuals

In the common practice, a manual is an instruction book which instructs how to do something by specific and clear directions.

Examples

Manual for writers of term papers, theses, dissertations, revered, Chicago University of Chicago Press, 1955.

Professional investor's manual, by R.S. Greenly, London, Greenly, 1974.

D. Monographs

A monograph is a short treatise on a specific subject. A monograph and a treaties serve the same purpose with the difference that a monograph is an attempt on a limited scale. Very often a monograph may be brought out as a part of a series.

Examples

Study in the history of ideas by E. Baldwin Smith Monographs in arts and archeology series, 25, Princeton, N.J. Princeton University Press, 1971.

E. Text Books

A text book is a book of information. Its primary aim is not to impart information about a specific subject but to enable one to develop proper understanding of the subject. Presentation is extremely important and it is prepared to serve a particular level of readership. It cannot be comprehensive. Often presentation is colorful and attractive giving plenty of illustrations and diagrams. A good text book takes into consideration the method of teaching and the level of readership. There is a difference of opinion about the place of text books as tertiary sources.

Examples

Theory of Cataloguing by Girja Kumar and Krishna Kumar, 2nd ed. Delhi, Vikas, 1977.

Text book of Cytology by Waiter V. Brown and Eldridge, M., 2nd ed., Berthe, St. Lovis Mosby, 1974.

F. Bibliographies

A bibliography is an organized list of primary or other sources relating to a given subject(s) or person. It is usually arranged alphabetically by author or chronologically or topic-wise. It may be comprehensive or selective. Sometimes, it may be provided with annotations. It may be published as a part of a larger work or as a separate work. The basic aim of a bibliography is to assist the users in locating the existence of or identifying a book or any other material which may be of interest to him. A well prepared bibliography provides a definitive coverage of documents over a period of time within specified limits. Thus, it also serves the purpose of retrospective searching of literature.

Examples

Dudley David Criffith, Bibliography of Chavcer, 1908-53, Scattle, University of Washington Press, 1955.

ASLIB book list, A monthly list of recommended scientific and technical books with annotations, London, ASLIB, Vol. 1, 1935, Monthly.

G. Translation

Translations are an important part of secondary source. Their characteristics are the same as those of primary or secondary or tertiary sources from which these are translated. Many of the authors of research papers used to cite original sources rather than translations.

TERTIARY SOURCES

Tertiary sources of information contain information distilled and collected from primary and secondary sources. The primary function of tertiary sources of information is to aid the searcher of information in the use of primary and secondary sources of information. Most of these sources do not contain subject knowledge. Due to increase in Literature, tertiary sources are becoming increasingly important. Out of various kinds of sources, tertiary sources are the last to appear.

Tertiary source is to aid the searcher in using the primary and secondary sources. They are unusual in that most of them do not carry subject knowledge at all.

(1) Bibliography of Bibliographies e.g. (a) List of books, (b) location lists of periodicals, (c) list of indexing and abstracting sources.
(2) Year books and directories.
(3) Guides to the literature.
(4) List of research in progress.
(5) Guides to libraries and sources of information.
(6) Guides to organizations.

Bibliography of Bibliographies

A bibliography of bibliographies lists bibliographies which direct readers to useful bibliography through subject name or an individual, place, institution, etc. The bibliographies referred to may be in the form of a separately published book or part of the book or part of a periodical article or some other type of document. As the number of bibliographies published every year is large, bibliographies of bibliographies are highly selective in nature.

Examples

Bibliographic index cumulative bibliography of bibliographies, 1937; New York, Wilson, 1938;

A world bibliography of bibliographies and bibliographies catalogues, calendars, abstracts, digests, indexes and the like, by Theodore Besterman, 4th ed., Geneva, Societies Bibliographica, 1965, 67, 5 vols.

Directories

A directory is a list of names and addresses of persons, organizations, manufacturers or periodicals. It may list information in a way which best serves the requirements of its users so as to enable them to get required information readily. The work "directory" may not appear in the title. The range of subjects dealt by directories is tremendous.

Examples

World Directory of Mathematicians, 4th ed., Stockholm, Almprist and Wiksell, 1970.

World guide to technical Information and Documentation Services, UNESCO, 1975.

World of learning, 1947-, London, Europe, annual.

Guide to Literature

A guide to literature assists a user to use literature of a specific subject. It helps to evaluate and introduce literature and lays emphasis on literature rather than the content of a specific subject. It mainly covers secondary and tertiary sources.

Examples

Reader's Guide to the Social Sciences, edited by Bert F. Hoselits, revised edition, New York, Free Press, 1970.

Guide to Historical Literature, by American Historical Association, New York, Macmillan, 1961.

Uses

It is obvious that scientists and technologists are in constant use of information and the average worker spends an estimated twenty percent of his time searching for it. Now there are at least four ways to find out a fact that needed. A worker may consult all types of sources. It is easier to understand the pattern of use, if one groups various kinds of consultations into a series of approaches, as has been demonstrated by Melvin J. Voridt.

Approaches

(1) The current approach
(2) Every day approach (background approach)
(3) Exhaustive approach
(4) Browsing approach

The above categorisation of sources of information is based on the characteristics of the documents. Categorization of documentary sources of information is useful. It takes into consideration relative currency and accuracy of sources of information. Primary sources are more current than secondary and tertiary. Primary sources are generally more accurate than secondary sources due to the fact that they represent original ideas.

In searching for information, a researcher usually starts with secondary sources and tertiary sources and ends the search with primary sources. Secondary and tertiary sources contain information in organized form and these serve as guides or indicators to detailed contents of primary literature. With increasing amount of literature being produced, it is becoming almost impossible to use primary sources directly. Hence secondary sources serve as an important tool to keep one up-to-date and well informed in his field of specialization.

NON-DOCUMENTARY SOURCES

Non-Documentary sources of information form a substantial part of communication especially in science and technology. Users' studies have underlined importance of such sources. These sources provide information, which other sources do not. There are two kinds of sources (formal and Informal). Formal sources include research organizations, societies, industries, government departments, universities, consultants, etc. Informal sources include conversation with colleagues, visitors, attendance at professional meetings, etc. Very often, the conversation or discussion would point out primary or secondary sources (documentary sources). Informal sources are live sources, which are extremely important in the process of communication. Very often, if a scientist working on an experiment needs some data, he would turn to his colleague working in the same laboratory rather than consult a printed page. Informal sources tend to be more convenient sources because it is certainly easier to have a dialogue with an expert than use a bibliography or index or card catalogue or even consultation of a reference librarian.

REFERENCE SOURCES

Different users require different types of information in various contexts. Such information is available in a variety of forms. The complexities in the information requirements of user communities and the availability of information in various forms both in volume and content, necessitates the customisation in the organization of sources of information to suit the information needs of users. For this purpose, it is necessary to be conversant with different types of users, information needs of users and also the sources of information. In many situations, the available sources may not be able to satisfy the readers completely. This may lead to package and repackage the information contained in the original sources to meet the situation.

However, looking at the existing structure of sources, generalization of different categories of sources are possible. There may be different types of sources, such as documentary, non-documentary, institutional, human, etc. which may be used to obtain information. Each of these sources has its own characteristics and peculiarities with regard to the nature of information content, form and mode of availability. Though there are varieties of sources, the documentary sources or books in various forms play a predominant role even today in making the information available.

Books are a conventional type of material known to everyone. They are different in kinds suiting varied levels of readers. They vary in treatment and the coverage of the subject. Based on such a grading they may be categorised as follows:

(1) Text books
(2) Treatises
(3) Monographs
(4) Classics
(5) Reference books

Text book

A text book is meant for the use of students in a specific branch of study. Generally, it is written in accordance with the Syllabus prescribed for a particular level in a course of study. Mostly it contains the tag text book in its title.

Example

Textbook of Physics.

Treatise

A treatise is a book which treats of some particular subject commonly containing a methodological discussion or expression of the principles of the subject.

Example

Laski's 'Grammar of Politics'.

Monograph

A monograph is a separate treatise on a single object or class of objects, in contradiction to general treatise in which this is dealt with, as part of a wider subject. It gives a complete account of anyone family-tribe or genus, nothing being neglected for a perfect knowledge of it.

Example

Brenen's "Literature of Spanish People."

Classic

A classic is a literary work of first rank and of acknowledged excellence.

Example

"Kamba Ramayanam."

From the point of use, book can be classified into two categories as given below:

(a) Books which are written so that these can be read consecutively for inspiration, enjoyment or information. An ordinary book has characters such as—
   (i) It is made of continuous exposition,
   (ii) It is developed, Para by Para, by chapter. There is a link at each stage. There is an element of continuity. Ordinary books can be read continuously from cover to cover. Ordinarily these are allowed to be lend out by libraries.

(b) Books which are designed to be consulted or referred to from time to time for a specific piece of information. Normally such books are not read continuously.

The first category is called ordinary books and the books of the second category are called reference books.

Reference Book

According to Barton, "A reference book, as generally understood is a book to be consulted for some definite information rather than for consecutive reading." A reference book collects and organizes known information in a way which it recall expeditions and exhaustive.

ALA Glossary defines a reference book as follows:

(1) A Book designed by its arrangement and treatment to be consulted for define items of information rather than to be read consecutively.
(2) A Book whose use is restricted to the library building, S.R.R. approaches the definition along six lines and they are:

Positive Function

A reference book is designed to be looked up for specific information.

Negative Function

A reference book do not need itself to continuous reading.

Definition of Internal Characteristics

A reference book usually possesses the following characteristics:

(1) It is not meant for continuous reading.
(2) It meant for consolidation of specific pieces of information.
(3) Very often, a reference book may contain disjointed entries.
(4) Information in a reference book is so organized that the arrangement differs from ordinary books.

Katz considers the two definitions of ALA as unsatisfactory. He states that there are many reference books which can be borrowed. Many reference books are having such literary value that they can be read continuously for pleasure. He prescribes certain qualities for reference books as—

(1) It is miscellany of information, organized for quick and convenient use.
(2) Arrangement of information usually, but not always follows some consistent plan.

(3) It usually gives only a bird's eye of a topic, rarely covering it in depth.
(4) It concentrates on facts.
(5) It answers reference questions.

The principles to be observed in building up a collection for reference are given by Hutchinson as follows:

(1) Provision should be made for meeting the reference book needs of the libraries, own clientele though discrimination in the kinds of material.
(2) The reference sources of the region should be taken into consideration.
(3) A good collection of bibliographical source should be built.
(4) The reference librarian should play his part in the selection and acquisition.
(5) Some funds should be set aside consistently for reference materials.
(6) Point of reference value should the considered of more importance for reference collection than literary style.
(7) The reference collection should be organized systematically in order to provide as many different kinds of approaches to information as possible.

Arrangement of Information

The arrangement of information in a reference book may be in anyone or combined format of the following:

(a) Alphabetical,
(b) Classified,
(c) Numerical,
(d) Conceptual, and
(e) Geographical.

Reference Books—Categories

The Categories of reference books include—

(1) Dictionaries,
(2) Encyclopaedia,

(3) Year books. Directories and Almanacs,
(4) Hand books and Manuals,
(5) Bibliographies,
(6) Geographical Sources,
(7) Bibliographical Sources, and
(8) News Summaries, etc.

DICTIONARIES

The word "Dictionary" has been derived from the Medieval Latin word 'dictionarius', originating from the term "Dictio" meaning, word. Dictionaries primarily deal with words of a language. The arrangement of words in any dictionary is alphabetical.

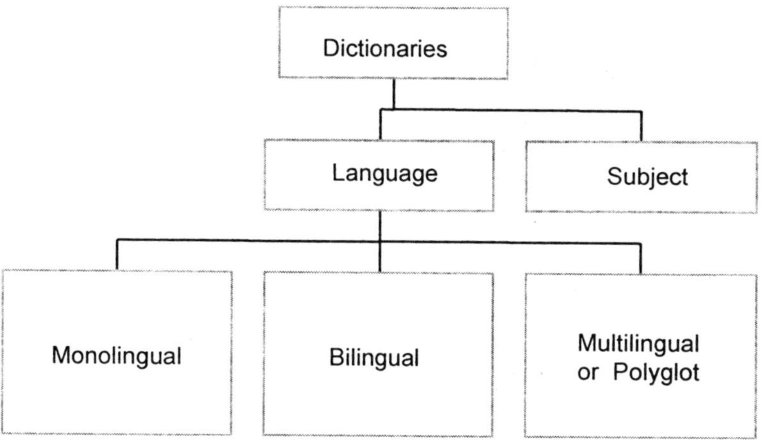

Dictionaries—Kinds

Depending upon the content, dictionaries can be broadly categorized into two namely Subject dictionaries and Language dictionaries.

Dictionaries—Reference Functions

While listing the words either in a language or in a subject in an alphabetical order, a dictionary usually provides.

(a) Spelling,
(b) Meaning,

(c) Etymology,
(d) Pronunciation,
(e) Usage,
(f) Syllabication,
(g) Parts of speech,
(h) Synonyms and antonyms,
(i) Abbreviations,
(j) Quotations, etc.

Dictionaries—Types

Depending upon the pattern of word treatment, dictionaries fall into different types as follows:

(1) *Glossary*: A list of dialect or explanations of Technical Terms in a special field or in a particular book.
(2) *Vocabulary*: A list of limited number of words belonging to a subject supplemented by explanations.
(3) *Lexicon*: is a dictionary of a foreign language.
(4) *Thesaurus*: A controlled vocabularies list conceptually arranged.
(5) *Concordance*: An alphabetical Index of Principal words in the Bible or Works of an author showing location in the text.

In addition to the above types there are.

(a) Dictionary of Synonyms,
(b) Dictionary of Antonyms,
(c) Dictionary of Quotations,
(d) Dictionary of Phrases,
(e) Dictionary of Slangs,
(f) Dictionary of Usage,
(g) Technical Dictionaries, and
(h) Subject Dictionaries.

Examples

(1) Webster's Third New International Dictionary of the English Language, 3 Vol.
(2) Oxford English Dictionary, 13 Vol. 2 supplements.

(3) Funk and Angel's Dictionary of the English Language.
(4) Cassell's Spanish-English, English-Spanish dictionary.
(5) ALA Librarian's Glossary.

ENCYCLOPAEDIAS

The word encyclopaedia was derived from the Greek words "enkyklios paideia" meaning, the "Circle of knowledge." An encyclopaedia is a compendium of knowledge. An encyclopaedia is a book giving information on all branches of knowledge or a specific subject. It is an ideal book which deals with concepts. An encyclopaedia is a storehouse of knowledge giving information of significance. Louis shores calls an encyclopaedia "The queen of reference sources", emphasizing "It is not only a summary knowledge, most significant to making, but the sum total of information system design followed in most basic reference books." An encyclopaedia contains articles on a variety of subjects. The articles are written by experts on each of the subjects. In addition to articles, encyclopaedias may include illustrations and diagrams, definitions of some words, and references to additional information. A general encyclopaedia includes overview articles on a wide range of topics. A subject encyclopaedia contains longer and more detailed articles on specific topics, events, or fields of study.

ALA Glossary defines an encyclopaedia as 'a work, containing informational articles on subject in every fields of knowledge usually arranged in alphabetical order, or a similar work limited to a special field or a subject'.

Basically an encyclopaedia describes, while a dictionary defines. Arrangement of information in an encyclopaedia may be alphabetical or classified.

Encyclopaedia—Kinds

They fall into two classes as follows:

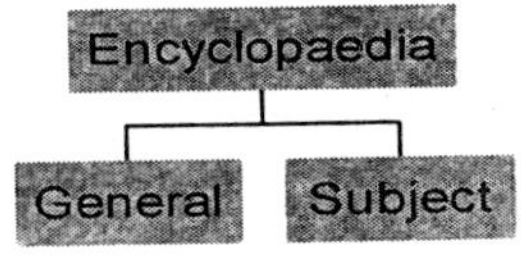

(A) Encyclopaedia—Reference Functions

It is a quick reference tool. It provides background information on every branch of Knowledge (general) or One specific field to knowledge (specialist).

A Selected List of Encyclopaedias

I.. General—Single volumed
 Ex:
 (1) Columbia Encyclopaedia
 (2) Pears cyclopedia.

II. General—Multivolumed
 Ex:
 (1) Chamber's Encyclopaedia
 (2) Encyclopaedia Britannica
 (3) Encyclopaedia Americana

III. General—For Juniors
 Ex:
 (1) Children's Britannica
 (2) Oxford junior Encyclopaedia
 (3) Work Book Encyclopaedia

IV. Specialist
 Ex:
 (1) Careers Encyclopaedia
 (2) McGraw Hill Encyclopaedia of Science and Technology.

Encyclopædia Britannica

The Encyclopædia Britannica was first published in 1768–1771 as Encyclopædia Britannica, or, a dictionary of arts and sciences, compiled upon a new plan. The Britannica was an important early English-language general encyclopaedia and is still regarded as one of the most important reference books in the English language. It is published today by Encyclopædia Britannica Inc., a privately held company.

From the late 18th century to the early 20th century, the Britannica's articles were often judged as the foremost authority on a topic, and sometimes included new research or theory intended for a scholarly audience. During this era, the Britannica gained its reputation and had a unique position in English-speaking culture.

The role of the encyclopaedia changed substantially in the early 20th century, and the Britannica reflected these changes, from the 1911 Encyclopædia Britannica, onward. One key change was a shift away from attempting to encompass the cutting edge of human knowledge, a goal made impractical by, among other things, the rapid expanding of scientific knowledge around the turn of the century. A second change reflected a changing readership. As the use of the encyclopaedia as a general reference grew, readers expected shorter, more readable articles, rather than the primary authoritative scholarship which had defined earlier versions.

Today, new reference sources, including academic journals, textbooks, specialized publications and electronic resources have redefined, and, more recently nearly eliminated, the demand for the print encyclopaedia. The Britannica has evolved primarily into electronic versions available on CD-ROM and via the World Wide Web, though a print edition is still available. It has survived fierce competition from an ever-increasing number of alternative information sources. The articles in the Britannica are commonly considered accurate, reliable, and well-written, and it continues to be widely consulted as a work of general reference.

Encyclopaedia Americana

The Encyclopaedia Americana is the second largest printed general encyclopaedia in the English language (after the Encyclopædia Britannica). As the name suggests it is produced in the United States and is aimed at the North American market. Thus, its coverage of American and Canadian geography and history is especially strong. It is also notable for the many glossaries it contains. Most articles are signed by their contributors.

As of 2004, the 175th anniversary edition has 45,000 articles containing 25 million words and was written by 6,500 contributors. It includes 9,000 bibliographies, 150,000 cross-references, 1,000+ tables, 1,200 maps, and almost 4,500 black-and-white line art and color images. It also has 680 fact boxes. However, because the work is revised volume-by-volume, some articles are considered to be out of date.

Currently, the encyclopaedia is produced by Scholastic

Library Publishing, a division of Scholastic Inc and Grolier Inc. An online version, requiring subscription, was introduced in 1997. Americana is aimed at middle school, high school, and college students. It is available to schools and libraries as one of the options in the Grolier Online reference service, which also includes the Grolier Multimedia Encyclopaedia, which is designed for middle and high school students, and the New Book of Knowledge, an encyclopaedia for elementary school students. Grolier Online also offers a Spanish language encyclopaedia and specialist reference works on science, lands and peoples, and the states of the United States and Mexico. Grolier Online is not available to individual subscribers.

DIRECTORIES

Directories form the largest category of reference sources. Directories provide information about organizations of different kinds covering learned bodies, scientific societies, professional bodies, trade associations, etc. A directory is a list of persons, organizations, professions, industries or trades. The list is systematically arranged, either in alphabetical or in classified order. Because the information in directories becomes out-of-date fairly rapidly they are published annually or new editions are brought out in every two three years.

Types of Directories

(1) Local directories

Usually for the large towns and cities only. These normally include,

(a) A list of private residents, arranged alphabetically by surname.
(b) An alphabetical list of streets, giving the name of the occupier of each property in each street.
(c) A classified list of trades—similar to the "Yellow pages" in a telephone directory.
(d) List of establishments such as places of worship, places of entertainment, etc. e.g. Kelly's Post-office London Directory.

(2) Professional directories

These are list of qualified practitioners in particular in professional, and include brief biographical details and sometimes information about the profession itself. For example:

(a) Crockfrod's Clerical Directory—published every other year,
(b) Law List—annual,
(c) Library Association Year Book—annual,
(d) Medical Directory—annual,

(3) Trade directories

(a) General and National—i.e. all trades and industries of a particular country. Arrangement is usually classified or alphabetical; by the type of trade or industry; with an additional alphabetical list of individual firms, e.g. Kelly's Directory of Manufactures and Merchants; Kompass, UK.
(b) Specialist and National—i.e., concerned with one field of industry in a particular country, e.g., British Plastics Year Book.

(4) Telephone directories

Each telephone directory covers the subscribers in a defined geographical area. The main list is alphabetical by name of subscriber, but the "yellow pages" section which is separately published contains classified list of subscribers arranged by type of industry or service.

Ulrich's International Periodicals Directory

The Ulrich's Family of Directories is maintained, updated and generated from the Bowker Serials Bibliography Data Base On-Line. This data base Provides current information on new titles, changes, merges, splits and cessations of titles. The Ulrich's Directory lists about 70,800 periodicals of all kin as from all over the world, covering 542 subjects' areas. This directory includes periodicals which are currently available. It covers only those periodicals which are issued more frequently than once a year and usually published at regular intervals, articles and irregular serials are not covered.

They include ISSN (International Standard Serial Number), subscription price, year first published, language of text advertising review, abstracting section, bibliography section, charts, illustrations where abstracted and indexed, formed, titles, key words, annotation, etc. Now this is available in the form of CD-ROM also which provides various search options.

This work consists of 4 main sections:

(1) *Classified List of Periodicals (A to Z)*: The main section is the Classified List of periodicals. It contains about 67,650 main entries under 542 subject headings with 17, 20 cross references.

(2) *Cessations Sections*: In this section, it gives a list of periodicals which have ceased/suspended publication since the 26th Edition. All are arranged alphabetically by title.

(3) *Index to Publications of International Organizations*: This index consists of four sections, namely, (1) International organizations, (2) International Congress proceedings, (3) European Communities, and (4) United Nations.

Special Features: (1) subject guide to abstracting and indexing. (2) Cross Index to subject. (3) In this telephone numbers of Canadian and United States publishers are provided along with the publisher information about given in the entries. This information is constantly updated. (4) In addition, information about micro form availability is given, with micro form publishers denoted by standardized abbreviations, (5) Coverage of abstracting and indexing information is updated regularly, (6) The Director follows a bi-annual policy of revisions and a supplement is published in between listing periodicals not mentioned in the previous base volume.

HANDBOOKS AND MANUALS

A handbook is a compilation of miscellaneous information in a compact and handy form. It may contain data, procedures, principles, etc. The dictionary meaning is "A small book or treaties, such as may conveniently be held in hand." Louis

Shores has defined this category as "A reference book of miscellaneous facts and figures on one or many subjects assembled for ready use, in response to popular interest or to a specific need for concise, handily information."

The two terms Handbooks and Manuals are almost identical in their meaning. They provide information on formulated procedures on "How to do", "How to make " or "How to perform", e.g. Britain: an Official Handbook, Library Manual, Mathematical Handbook for Scientists and Engineers, Teach Yourself and all such Teach Yourself Series.

BIOGRAPHICAL (DICTIONARY) SOURCES

A biography is defined as written life of a person. Biographical sources are ready reference sources that provide information about an individual. Louis shores have defined Biographical Dictionary as "Essentially directory of notable persons, usually arranged alphabetically by surnames, with biographical identifications that range from brief outline to extended narrative."

Biographical reference may be divided into three types, namely,

(a) International and general,
(b) National and general, and
(c) Specialists.

Biographical Dictionaries

(a) International and general, e.g. Webster's biographical dictionary (include living and deceased person) and The International Who's Who (living persons only).
(b) National and general, which can be subdivided into two kinds—
  - o Current, including only persons, e.g. who's who.
  - o Retrospective, including only deceased persons, e.g. Dictionary of National Biography, and who was who.
(c) Specialist, which cover persons concerned with particular professions, defined areas of knowledge of specified of society, e.g.,

(i) Kelly's Hand Book of Titled, Learned and Official Classes,
(ii) Who's Who in Librarianship, and
(iii) Who's Who in the Theatre.

GEOGRAPHICAL SOURCES

Geographical sources deals with the surface of the earth including the divisions of the world into continents and countries. The climate, plants, animals, natural resources, people and industries form part of the geographical studies. Geographical reference tools have become an important segment of basic reference collection for most libraries. The reference libraries are obliged to answer a number of questions seeking information about cities, towns, mountains, lakes, rivers, forest, etc., in connection with their description, location and other details.

Maps, Atlases and Globes

Maps, atlases and globes are the main sources of geographical information. A map is representation of certain boundaries of the earth. An atlas is collection of maps, tables, charts, etc., whereas a globe is a spherical representation of the earth.

Definition

Maps: According to ALA Glossary of library and information science (1983), "a map is a representation normally drawn to a scale and on a flat medium of a selection of material or abstract features on, or in relation to, the surface of the earth or another celestial body."

Examples

1. Hyderabad in Maps. Hyderabad: Bereau of Economics and Statistics, Govt. of Andhra Pradesh, 1953.
2. Maharashtra in Maps/by K.R. Dikshit; assisted by charulata Patil. Mumbai; Maharashtra State Board for Literature and Culture, 1986, 245p.

Atlas

According to ALA Glossary, an atlas is, "a volume of maps, plates, engravings, tables, etc., with or without descriptive letter press. It may be an independent publication or it may have been issued to accompany one or more volumes of that."

Examples

1. Basic Resource Atlas of Tamil Nadu/ed. By A. Ramesh and P.S. Tiwari. Madras: Dept. of Geography, University of Madras, 1981.
2. Planning Atlas of U.P., Lucknow: Govt. of U.P., 1987.

Globe: The difference between a map and globe is one of form. A map is any geographic image of the earth drawn to scale on a flat surface whereas a globe is spherical representation of the earth surface. It is hollow ball of metal, bearing a world map on its surface and is mount on an axle which permits its rotation. The term 'globe' is synonymously used for the earth.

Gazetteers

A Gazetteer is a directory of geographical places in addition to geographical location; it gives historical, statistical, cultural and other relevant information, such as pronunciation. Because they provide a variety of factual material about places, gazetteers are important reference sources. Recent editions describe a place as it is now; old editions give historical information about it. The economic growth or decline of gives historical information about it. The economic growth or decline of a town or city as indicated by data on population, type of industries, schools and so on; will often be shown by the brief facts given in gazetteers over a period of years. Some gazetteers include entries for rivers, capes and other geographical features.

In using a gazetteer, it is important to note the publication date as an indication of the regency of the material; the system of pronunciations and abbreviations used; the arrangement of the material and any additional material, such as maps and tables, which may be included in appendices.

Examples

1. Gazetteer of India, Govt. of India, Ministry of information and Broadcasting, center Gazetteer Unit.
2. Bihar District Gazetter/ed. by Roychaudhry
3. Orissa District Gazetteers/ed. by Nilamansenapti. Koraput, Cuttack: Govt. Press, 1966.

Travel Guides

The main purpose of any travel guide is to inform the traveler as what to see, where to stay and how to reach a particular place.

Glossary of Library and Information Science defines a travel guide "as a handbook for travelers that gives information about a city, region or a country or a similar handbook about a building, museum, etc."

These guides include useful information about specific place. Information included in the guidebooks also historical, economic and social aspects.

Example

Uttar Pradesh A-Z, Lucknow: Department of Tourism, Uttar Pradesh, 1996.

NEWS SUMMARIES AND NEWSPAPER INDEXES

Whenever reference queries on significant news or specific events, both current and retrospective are to be answered. "Index to Newspapers and News Summaries are used as dependable tools. They record incidents, events and facts from local, national and international Newspapers in a condensed form. Usually they are published in loose leaf form, so to be filed in libraries every week:

- Kissing's Contemporary Archives: Weekly Diary of World Events, 1931, Bristol, Keesing.
- Facts on File: The index of world events, 1940, New York.
- Africa Diary: Weekly record of events in Africa with Index. 1961, New Delhi, Africa Press.
- Asian Recorder: A weekly digest of outstanding Asian events with Index, 1955, Delhi Sankaran.

EVALUATION OF REFERENCE SOURCES

A reference librarian should know how good or bad a given reference book is. In order to achieve a thorough understanding of reference books, it becomes necessary to evaluate them. Evaluation means an assessment of various reference books. Reference book is one which consulted intermittently. It is not read from cover to cover. In order to achieve a thorough understanding of reference is books, it becomes essential to evaluate them. Reference books are different in their purpose from ordinary books. Therefore, a different approach is required for their study and evaluation. The check list for the evaluation of reference book should consist the following: of authority, scope, treatment, arrangement, special features, drawbacks and format.

Need for Evaluation

The following are the reasons for the evaluation:

Reference books are different in their purpose from ordinary books. There are a number of reference books published by various organizations. The Library despite of its type has to invest large amount of money for the procurement of reference books. Hence care should be taken for the selection of reference books. The following are the reasons for evaluating the reference books.

1. Cost of Publication

The general inflatory tends has effected the cost reference books. The cost is increasing in a steady rate in the modern world. The library is confronted with ever increasing demand and never satisfying budgets. So to spare money wisely the librarian should evaluate.

2. Quantum of Publication or Material available in the Market

There may be a lot of documents available on a given subjects in the market. But all of them are not equally important. A document which is good for some information may not be good for others. So the librarian must evaluate the document available according to the actual need, financial position of the librarian and procure the document which is most useful to the library.

3. Scope and Coverage

The document must have a wide scope and coverage. A librarian must be vigilant to check whether the events in a book are up to date or not covered almost all the possible information of the last year.

4. Needs and levels of users

Librarians should select books according to the age and level of users. The books for school children should be in simple language and must be explained with diagrams and colour plates.

Criteria of Evaluation

Louis Shores proposed six principles to evaluate the reference books:

They are,

1. Authority
2. Scope
3. Treatment
4. Arrangement
5. Format
6. Special Feature

Authority

The librarian has to evaluate the author's responsible for the reference books. (Authors include compilers, collaborators) For evaluating authorship one has to,

(a) Consider the experience and educational background of the author.
(b) Consider the reputation of the author as revealed in the pervious works.
(c) Consider the extent of responsibility of the authors.
(d) *Genealogy*—That is to consider whether the person, book is a revised edition or a reprint.

Scope

The scope of a reference book includes the purpose, coverage and the recency of the document.

(a) *Purpose*: Each book should have a purpose based on which it is written. The purpose must be stated in the preface. The librarian should notice whether the books fulfilled the purpose or not.
(b) *Coverage*: The librarian should have special knowledge to determine the quality of articles regard to up-to-dateness, accuracy reliability, it must cover more information possible.
(c) *Recency*: The documents must have some information which are new origin. To evaluate this the librarian must know the trend of subjects.

Treatment

Treatment includes accuracy, objectivity and style:

(a) *Accuracy*: The librarian should consider to what extend the information is accurate. Facts and figures, which are approximate, should not be considered.
(b) *Objectivity*: The information in a document should not be biased one. It must be a balanced one.
(c) *Style*: The style of writing or reporting should be noted. Diacritical marks help to pronounce the world correctly. But the diacritical marks are not necessary for junior dictionary.

Arrangement

Arrangement is of great importance. It is essential that one should be able to locate information quickly, good arrangement adds value to the reference book.

(a) *Sequence*: The arrangement of main text can be in alphabetical, chronological, conceptual or classified, tabular. It should identify broader terms, related terms and narrower terms.
(b) *Type of alphabetization*: There are two types of alphabetization. They are: (i) letter by letter as in the case of dictionary, and (ii) world by world as in the case catalogue.
(c) *Index*: Index to the main text is extremely important. The index must be reasonable and provide a number of approaches complemented by cross reference. Index may help in speedy location.

5. Format

Format refers to binding, quality of paper, type faces, page make up, illustration, plates, diagrams, map sets. The matter should not be presented in the consistent manner.

6. Special Features

List of personal names; sometimes even short biographical sketches may be given. List of place names, some times geographical or historical point of view may be added to the special features; may also include list maps, colour picture, graphs, diagrams, colour print, observation signs, samples foreign terms, etc.

We have discussed about the points governing the selection of books in the foregoing paragraphs. However, the selection of books has to be made by an overall judgement taking into consideration of all the above points as a whole.

REFERENCE SERVICES

REFERENCE SERVICE—DEFINITION

In the early days libraries were regarded as storehouses and books were meant for preservation only. Librarians were more custodians of library collections. The public was not permitted to have free access to books in libraries. Open access system was unknown then. Such conditions have been discussed under the UK Library Movement which is actually known as the first library movement on earth. The developments over time and the human appreciation for social values gave new dimension to the concept library and its services.

During the initial stages the librarian located and provided the required reading materials to the use from that library collection. He did not do more than that it was only a document finding service. Later the librarian began to interface with user needs and extended gradually the magnitude of this help aided by library tools and techniques. This course of action and assistance added a shape to the library services.

The extent of librarian's interaction in the form of service became a much debated topic. Both librarians and users wanted to know the limits and boundaries of demand for and provision of library service. When the picture became clear, experts termed this concept as reference service.

What is Reference Service?

You know every profession such as Legal, Medical, Postal, etc. renders a service characteristic of their profession. The service thus rendered bears a specific name in each profession. In the same way the service rendered by librarians has also a specific name and that is reference service.

In simple terms reference service is essentially the process of answering questions. This process differs from the question answering functions of many social organizations. They all answer questions relevant to their systems and their activities only. But a library only provides an answer whatever be the question, on whatever subject may it be. Therefore, it procures and preserves information in the form of reading materials. Remember the question may be on anything. Do you know how did library services reach this point of answering any question?

Melvil Dewey inaugurated the American Library Association in 1876 which is known as ALA; Dewey suggested that the acronym ALA also meant "Ask Library Anything." It becomes true in courses of time. While service organizations answer questions related to their activities only library is the only social organization which is equipped with course materials and hence is capable of answer any question on any subject as Dewey pointed out. In its principal function a library resembles a teacher.

Reference Service Definitions

Reference Service has been defined appropriately by a number of library scientists. Let us see some of them.

Hutchins, Margaret

"Reference Service included the direct personal aid within a library to person in search of information though their purposes may vary. It also denotes various activities especially aimed at making information as early available as possible."

Hutchins reflected the interpretations of Melvil Dewey saying that whatever be the purposes of the enquirer, reference service should provide the relevant answer.

ALA Glossary

The librarian's glossary published by the American

Library Association defined reference service as "That phase of the library work which is directly concerned with assistance to the readers in locating information and in using the resources of the library in study and research." ALA Glossary emphasizes the need for a personal assistance to the readers either for study and teaching or research at a higher level.

Ranganathan, S.R.

"Reference Service is the process of establishing a contact between a right reader and a right document at the right time in a right personal way."

The whole philosophy of librarianship is found encompassed in the above definition. He emphasized beyond any doubt that reference service is,

(1) A process
(2) A personal assistance
(3) Timely provision {of}
(4) Relevant information
(5) To the right user in the context of his needs

According to him reference service is a personal help to each reader to find the relevant document or information answering his interest or query in his mind. The service "Should be" pin pointed, exhaustive and expeditions. As D.J. Foskett puts it "Reference Service is essential humanism is practice, because the aim is to help in one way or the other, to secure greater happiness through the possession of knowledge." Thus the scope of reference service is definitely more than what a common man may have understood.

Before commencing service, a library undertakes a number of routine works. Let us see what all those routine works in a library are whether it is big or small and also the relative importance of those activities.

Reference Service: The Hub and Foundation

Now let us look into the Medical Service. A Doctor examines a patient. In addition he obtains the results of a patient's Blood Test, Urine Test, Sputum Test and such other tests as the case may warrant for. Obtaining the test results is not his ultimate aim. Instead he is going to use all such results to diagnosis the disease of the patient. Finally, he administers medicine to the patient in order to cure his ailment. A medical treatment is the Hub and Foundation of Medical Service. All Bio-Clinical activities are the hand maids to promote medical services. Similarly in library service a number of routine works are undertaken and they include,

(1) Book selection
(2) Book ordering
(3) Periodicals work
(4) Maintenance work
(5) Classification
(6) Cataloguing
(7) Compilation of Bibliography
(8) Documentation work, etc.

All the above items of work are means to end. The end is reference service. Hence, Ranganathan calls reference services as the Hub and Foundation of all library activities. Reference Service is a collective name representing many items of services.

Reference Service—Menu

Reference Service includes the following items:

(i) Initiation to freshman
(ii) Document finding service
(iii) Ready reference service
(iv) Current Awareness Service (CAS)
(v) Selective Dissemination of Information (SDI)
(vi) Documentation service
(vii) Reprographic service
(viii) Readers advisory service
(ix) Interlibrary loan
(x) Referral service
(xi) Translation service
(xii) Such other bibliographic services

Depending upon the nature of the library system the above listed items may be adopted in total or in part.

INITIATION TO FRESHMAN

There are many users who enter the Library. They are not aware of the functioning of the library. They do not know about the information sources kept in the library. It is necessary to make the newcomer aware of different departments, collections, techniques, rules and regulations and services rendered by the library, so that he may consult the library independently.

The aim of the modern library is to invite and attract the readers to come freely and make use of the library collection. No body can deny that library is a human institution, which shall attract itself all the citizens in its area. But readers who come to the library may vary in respect of their characteristic. To a freshman the library will be in the first instance bewildering. Hence, one of the first things to be done by the Reference staff is to relive the bewilderment, which confronts the readers who are meeting for the first time a large and highly organized library.

Taking them on hand and showing them round with sympathy and enthusiasm, which makes them to feel that library is place worth coming to be one kind of initiation. Since both of them enter the stack room, it is quite natural to the new comer to know something about the arrangement of books and it is the duty of the reference librarian to explain the system of classification and in what may the arrangement of books on the shelves is based on. The freshman should be gradually introduced to the necessity for the library arranging the books in different collections. Main collections, special various sections such as periodical section, back volume section, reprographic section, etc. At this stage the freshman may be in a position to be told about the use of the catalogue. He is to be told what the catalogue is, why it is provided and how he can spot out his books from whatever aspect, he approaches it.

Library users should be made to be familiar with the structure and the use of the library catalogue. The catalogue is artificial in many respects. The freshman has to be told all about the conventions followed in the catalogue, i.e. in the matter alphabetization, rendering of personal names cross reference entries, punctuation marks, etc.

Genially is the first requisite in the initiation of a freshman by the reference staff. A freshman has to be told of the working of circulation section, the physical location of catalogue, and the existence of information desk, the kind of service offered by it, and the right of readers to take service from it. In spite of the signboards, it is also necessary to tell the freshman the existence of newspaper room, periodicals room, research room, etc. It is necessary to explain the freshman even in his very first visit everything about the rules of the library, mechanics of issue of books, condition of loan, care of readers ticket, etc. A freshman should also be told about library ethics, library hygiene, etc.

In the public library initiation is casual and contingent on the voluntary coming in of a freshman. In college library, the initiation of fresh students can be planned and undertaken at stated time, in groups of stated strength. In this the co-operation of the teachers is necessary. The library must be made as the heart of the college and the students should be given practical instruction in the exploitation of the printed materials in the library.

Qualities of Good Librarian

A "good librarian" is someone whose existence is recognized by the reader/user/customer.

This is the most basic. Be it seen or heard, your presence must be made known to the customer, however vague. In short, the customer must know that the librarian exists. I know this point is debatable but I convinced myself eventually. Even if one is the greatest librarian in the world, if the customer doesn't recognise your existence (and therefore the value you add or create) sooner or later, they're going to ask, "What do I need you for?", even though they use the library.

A "Good librarian" is someone who is accessible. Librarianship is fundamentally about service. There is no service in the long-run (or at least not one with the librarian employed) if customers cannot reach the service provider—whether it's a face-to-face service, or correspondence via email, or whatever is the gizmo-of-the-day.

A "good librarian" is someone who produces results. The key word is "results." It implies the entire range of personal and technical competence of the librarian—search skills, book talking, facilitation, cataloguing, managing budgets, managing staff—whatever the tasks assigned. The results are in accordance to what the customer wants.

A "good librarian" is one who understands and applies Ranganathan's Five Laws of Library Science.

The Five Laws are:

Books are for use.
Every reader his or her book.
Every book its reader.
Save the time of the reader.
The Library is a growing organism.

A "good librarian" is someone who's passionate about their job "Passion" implies that a good librarian tries hard to go beyond the "mediocre" and "adequate." The job, ultimately, is about providing a service to customers. There can never be good/ excellent service without passion in what we do.

NEEDS AND PURPOSES OF REFERENCE SERVICE

The factors that necessitated reference service in a library are as follows:

(1) Information Explosion
(2) Bewildering Library Techniques
(3) Types of Readers
(4) Complexity in the physical forms of documents
(5) Complexity in the organization of information
(6) Time value of information
(7) Universal education
(8) Barriers to communication
(9) In observation of the Five Laws of Library Science

Information Explosion

The sum total of information produced each subject is called it Literature (Example: Economics Literature, Physics Literature, Medical Literature, Chemical Literature, etc.), Literature output in sciences (Natural and Physical Sciences) doubles once in five years and in Social Sciences double once in eight years. The volume of information output in each subjects it is enormous. This situation marked with the term "unprecedented proliferation of scientific literature" or

"Information Explosion." For example, chemical abstract was started in 1907. The first year's issues contained a total of 11,847 abstracts. It recorded a steady increase year after year. In 1950 the total was 59,098, in 1957 it crossed the mark of 1,00,000 and in 1967—2,42,527, in 1977 it crossed 4,10,137. The volume alone contained 4,60,569 abstracts and in 1987 volume alone one finds more than 5,00,000 abstracts.

Bewildering Library Techniques

A library adopts a number of tools and techniques before organizing the reading materials on the shelves. Many such techniques seem to be more artificial and they may bewilder the readers. It requires a human element to interpret such techniques to the users and make them feel at home.

Types of Reader (Psychology-based)

All the readers coming to a library may not straight away approach the library staff or books. Apart from the normal readers, Ranganathan identifies the following types of readers based on this individual psychology.

They are

1. Shy readers
2. Readers with inferiority complex
3. Readers with superiority complex and
4. Readers with traumatic complex.

Due to their abnormal or subnormal psychology they neither seek any help nor obtain information. The librarian or his staff has to come to the rescue of such people. They have to catch the readers in their mood and prepare them to read the books. Thus it becomes a social obligation for a librarian to study every user psychology and convert him into normal reader, then help him in familiarizing with the staff, services and documents.

Complexity in the Physical form Documents

This is electronic age. Its impact is heavy on the production of reading materials also. Many of us are very familiar with books which is a conventional form. But there are a number of non-book materials (NBM) which a library has begun to procure. Many of the NBM require electronic appliances to decode (read) the information in them. Someone possessing a through knowledge of their operation has to help the readers. Who else can be the right person other than a reference staff?

Complexity in the Organization of Information in Documents

Readers are familiar with books and their conventional arrangements of information in the form of—

(a) Chapters,
(b) Paragraphs,
(c) Sentences,
(d) Bibliography, and
(e) Index, etc.

There are sources of information in every library and the arrangement of information in term follow anyone of the sequences mentioned below: They are

(a) Alphabetical
(b) Classified
(c) Chronological
(d) Geographical and
(e) Conceptual

Whatever be the arrangement of information in reference sources, there is someone in libraries to make readers understand the sequence and help them to get their required information.

Time Value of Information

Anything not provided in time may not have any value at all information is no exception. The actual time required to retrieve a piece of information is called the objective time which is a varying factor. Any extra time taken more than the required actual time to do a job is called subjective time. Without proper assistance/service, a reader tends to waste more on subject (extra) time. "For want of a horse shoe a battle was lost" is a famous saying emphasizing timely attention of anything. Failure to provided information intimate may ultimately cause individual as well as normal waste in many aspects. Locating information, hence, cannot be left to an individual's task alone.

While information grows exponentially, the time available at the disposal of users remains almost the same. Hence, they cannot scan even a small fraction of the subject literature available in their own areas of specialization in time. A trained professional can help readers to avoid any waste of time while searching for information and make it a more meaningful and value-based process by his service.

Universal Education

Free access to information and a right to know have become fundamental human rights. In order to promote the above rights modern democracies aim at universal education. Distance education gas become popular educations have reached the nook and corner of rural areas too.

Given a basic standard of education, a library becomes a flexible instrument of self-education to the common man. If the Government's objectives are to be promoted someone has to motive the common man towards the resources of a library and that someone is the reference librarian.

Barriers to Communication

Professor A. Neelameghan has identified a set barrier to scientific communication that hasincluded time, language, economics, jargon, culture and politics.

Of course, reference service only can come to the rescue in connecting the reader with his required information by removing any possible barrier facilitate noise free communication.

Adherence to the Five Laws of Library Science

Five laws of library science have established their validity. A librarian true to his profession should practice reference service in strict adherence to the prescription on the five laws.

TYPES OF REFERENCE SERVICE

The most common duty of the reference section in a library is to answer queries. Reference section is that division which interprets the library's collection to the users. The staff in this section should be able to anticipate the nature of reference help that may be sought by the clientele. The staff will have to adopt an item of referen ce service according to user needs and hence he is required to know the different kinds of reference service that are in vogue.

Reference Service—Western Approach

The western library identified two kinds of reference services as follows:

(a) Direct Service, and
(b) Indirect Service.

(a) Direct Service

All the services, answering queries in a suitable form wherein the user and the staff come face to face are identified as direct (reference) service. It denotes the provision of exact information to users.

(b) Indirect Service

Book selection, Book ordering, Accessioning, Classification, Abstracting, Indexing, Cataloguing, Technical Processing, Shelving of documents and such other works are all means to an end. All these functions aim at reference service. Staff of such sections officially do not come into direct contact with the users. Yet they are contributing constantly to the work forming vital part of service. At such behind-the-screen activities of staff are enlisted under indirect reference service.

Indian Approach

According to Dr. S.R. Ranganathan, there are two kinds of reference service and they are,

1. Ready Reference Service, and
2. Long Range Reference Service.

READY REFERENCE SERVICE

This concept was termed as Short Range Reference service in the earlier works of Dr. S.R. RANGANATHAN. Later he replaced the term "Short" by "Ready." One should not be confused thinking that short and ready reference services are totally different concepts. No, they are not different but one and the same.

According to Dr. S.R. Ranganathan, "Ready Reference Service is the service finished in a very short time—in a moment if possible."

The characteristics of ready reference service is based on these factors, namely,

(a) Time,
(b) Sources consulted, and
(c) Natural of library.

(a) Time

Ready reference services should be able to provide an answer to a query immediately. It should be momentary or instantaneous. According to Ranganathan, answering a ready reference query should take only a few seconds and it cannot exceed thirty minutes in any case.

(b) Sources Consulted

Ready reference service is a fact finding service. We may have to provide small facts or a few figures as answers to a question. This category is ready reference services. They are:

1. Dictionaries
2. Encyclopaedia
3. Year Books and Directories
4. Head Books and Manuals
5. Almanacs
6. Bibliographical Sources
7. Geographical Sources
8. Bibliographies
9. News Summaries

We may have to use any one of the above sources to find the fact of figure (answer) to ready reference query. Thus ready reference service is restricted to ready reference sources only.

(c) Nature of Library

Ready reference service may be of utmost importance

especially in,

(a) Business Libraries
(b) Academic Libraries
(c) Public Libraries

From the user's standpoint, S.R. Ranganathan specified the libraries where ready reference service may be more warranted for. But yet there is no exception. Ready reference service is common to general functions of a library irrespective of its system affiliation.*

Ready reference service is highly appreciated by three types of users such as,

(a) Absentee enquirers,
(b) Casual visitors, and
(c) Regular customers.

Absentee enquirers may not come to the library in person but may approach the library over phone or by post. Some information, once retrieved should be recorded. When the same information is required by some other users, it can be provided from the record instead of searching again in the sources. For example, during the birth centenary year of Bharathidasan, many people may come to the library asking for bits of information on his biographical details such as his place, date of birth, parenthood, bibliography, etc.

On the first instance, you have to search for the information on biographical sources. Once you retrieve it, before providing the information to that first enquirer, you can keep a copy of the same with you. When a second and more enquiries come on the same matter, you can look into your record copies and provide the information, you can save time, energy and staff man-hours. Hence Dr. S.R. Ranganathan said that ready reference service in such a perfect manner leads to national economy.

Ready Reference Service Process

The process involves three aspects, namely,

(a) Preparation,
(b) Service, and
(c) Assimilation.

(a) Preparation

This is the fundamental aspect. A reference staff has to prepare himself with a through knowledge about—

(i) New Reference Books,
(ii) New Edition of Reference Books, and
(iii) Fugitive materials.

A librarian cannot provide up-to-date information without dated editions. He should keep a vigilant eye over the market for any new arrivals either revised or totally new editions. Fugitive to ephemeral here means any short-lived materials such as light reading magazines and newspaper. For example, what is the Gold medal status of India till yesterday in Asiad? Can be located in a daily newspaper only.

Where to locate the political development over the Ram Janma Bhoomi last month?

The answer may be the date and number of *India Today* or any other weekly magazine that carry the information.

A relevant working collection of ready reference sources and a through knowledge about them keeps a library staff ready to serve the users.

(b) Service

The second stage in the process of ready reference service falls into three types as,

(1) Providing the exact required information.
(2) Putting the enquirer on the right tract to find the information himself.
(3) Training the enquirer in fact finding.

In case of an absentee enquirer, (Phone or Postal enquires) the exact answer has to be provided.

Suppose a visitor tasks for the population statistics of cities and towns in Madurai District. You can take the visitor to the shelves where census volumes have been arranged. You can pick out the specific volumes and put in the hands of the visitor. He can locate and note down more particulars. This is exactly putting the enquirer on the right track.

A user who is likely to become a regular visitor for collection factual information may be chosen to be trained. He should be instructed properly.

(1) Fist to precisely enunciate his own information requirements,
(2) To chalk out the proper line of search, and
(3) To locate and record the information with bibliographical details of the document referred.

(c) Assimilation (Sharing once experience with colleagues)

After a days work the reference staff shall share one experience with his colleagues not only in the reference section but also with staff in various sections. This will help to evaluate the collection, tools and techniques and the overall functioning of the library system.

LONG RANGE REFERENCE SERVICE

We learnt that ready reference should be rendered—

(a) Within a few seconds,
(b) With the help of standard ready reference sources and fugitive materials, and
(c) Mainly to enquires and requiring facts and figures.

Here again for long range reference services S.R. Ranganathan prescribes their tests identify. They are,

(1) Time Test,
(2) Source Test, and
(3) Nature of Information (Required).

Time Test

Few long range reference questions may take more than half an hour. In general, they may be a continuous process and may take an hour, a day, a week or a few months. Time factor there is purely a dependent variable.

Source Test

Long range reference service may at times with standard reference sources but definitely do not end with them. You know that if the service starts and necessarily ends with ready reference source then it comes under ready reference service. Sometimes the sources from other outside libraries may have to be consulted. For example, a research worker in SITRA (South Indian Textile Research Association) may require an information from ATRIA (Ahamedabad Textile Industries Research Association) or from a Manchester Textile Research Institute in U.K.

Nature of Information

Facts and figures are required in ready reference service. Here in long range reference service it is not confide to fact finding alone. Mostly information scattered over a wide range of materials and geographic area are required. The information providing process may be continuous. It may be many a time mission/project or problem-oriented service. Librarians may have to scan worldwide publications to provide information to a scholars working on the "Alterative to Fuel Energy."

Long Range Reference Service: Process

Again the process here is the same as in ready reference, but with changing magnitudes. They are:

(1) Preparation,
(2) Service, and
(3) Assimilation.

1. Preparation

The library staffs prepare themselves by acquiring a through knowledge about—

(1) The subject/discipline they deal with,
(2) Kinds of information needs/approach,
(3) Various kinds of sources,
(4) Library/tools and techniques, and

(5) Types of long range reference services and methodologies.

Then only he can claim to be ready to meet the user and his needs.

2. Service

Dr. S.R. Ranganathan prescribes the following procedures to make long range reference service effective. They are:

(1) Precise enunciation of the user needs,
(2) Deciding the Search strategies,
(3) Providing the information in a suitable form.

Precise enunciation of the user needs is to identify the key words appropriately expression the scope. Indexing techniques will help to do so.

After deciding what to search for select sources and methods of search so that relevant information within the shortest possible time is located. User profiles and document records are of great help in this process.

Finally after location the information (sometimes interlibrary loan may be required) provide the same in a suitable form as desired by the user.

3. Assimilation (Sharing one's experience with colleagues)

This process resembles the one under ready reference service. In addition to the points mentioned earlier, here the librarian will have to interact more with the clientele in order to evaluate the services and information rendered to them. Accordingly the service may have to be altered.

Types of long range reference service are:

(1) CAS (Current Awareness Service),
(2) SDI (Selective Dissemination of information),
(3) Documentation,
(4) Reprographic Services,
(5) Interlibrary Loan, and
(6) Such other bibliographic services.

Sample: Reference Queries

1. What are the synonyms of the word "Love"?
2. Some background information on Test Tube Babies.
3. Year of establishment of Madurai Kamaraj Unversity.
4. The text of the National Anthem of India in English.
5. Name of the Noble Prize Winner for Peace in 1987.
6. Air distance from Chennai to Trivandrum.
7. Authors of the book Freedom at Midnight.
8. A list of Canadian Journals on Botany.
9. Address of D.R.T.C.
10. Medals position of India in Seoul Olympics.

USER NEEDS

Identification of the user needs is basic to any type of reference service. As there can be no medication without diagnosis, there can be no library service without identifying the user needs. The ultimate aim of any library is to satisfy its user needs.

Terminologies

In simple terms a 'user' is defined to be "a person who uses a library." In a broader context a user is one who is capable of using a specific library. This is how a perfect librarian counts his users. Who are all the users of a public library in a village or town? All the citizens residing in that area are to taken as the potential users. In Ranganathan's view, a library should attract all potential users and make them into habitual users.

Non-Users: Those who come within the purview of a library service, but yet don't use the library for various reasons are identified as Non-Users. But remember that with a library's effective programmes a non-user may turn into a user at any moment.

The reasons for a library not being used may be as follows:

1. The potential user is irritated over the non-availability of required information of the library.
2. The staffs of the library are not user-friendly.
3. The user may resort to compensate the non-availability by borrowing from teachers, friends or neighbors.

However, the library to prove its meaningful existence should attract the users into the system. The extent of the use of the library speaks for the efficiency of the service by the librarian and his staff. Hence, Dr. S.R. Ranganathan states that a librarian is the right persons to covert the potential energy in every man into kinetic energy by means of providing adequate and relevant documents/information at the right time, matching the user needs. Prior to identifying the user needs, it is fundamental to identify the user groups for any service programme.

Identification of Users

The manufacturing of any product commence only after a careful study of the market potential which is nothing but the consumes. This target potential user group only decides the product design. Similarly, here it is the user and his information needs play a vital role in deciding the service design in a library. Hence, the identification of the library user and his more essential.

Before any attempt is made to identify the information needs of the users of the library it is necessary to find out:

- (a) The potential users,
- (b) Their numbers,
- (c) Discernible groups, and
- (d) The organization of which they are members.

The wise system designer recognizes that the user of the information must be an active participant in the system whose needs direct the design. Let us discuss the users in various systems such as:

1. Schools,
2. Colleges,
3. Universities, Public libraries, and
4. Special libraries.

Users in School

The two main target groups in schools are obviously pupils and teachers. Under these two broad categories, there may be sub-groups. Basically these sub-groups can be grouped by year or standard, by ability and mostly at a later stage by subject.

However, irrespective of the sub-groups affiliation, pupils specially gifted with extraordinary intelligence and skills should be identified. This may be a small group but more efficient.

Within the broad range of teachers there may be specialists in areas like—

1. Reading skills,
2. Media skills,
3. Study skills, and
4. Communication skills, etc.

The librarian will have to identify such teachers and work closely with them as their cooperation is going to be of a greater value training the pupils to library use.

Users in Colleges

The main groups in Colleges are students and teachers. However, the students can be identified as separate groups—

(a) by year/class,
(b) by subject, and
(c) by courses if needed (part time/full time)

The teachers again may be Specialists, Guides, Research scholars themselves and so on. Besides the above two categories come from a wide range of cross section of the citizens. They are:

(a) Children,
(b) Women,
(c) Students and teachers,
(d) Workers and Professionals,
(e) Retried people,
(f) Physically handicapped people,
(g) Open University students, and
(h) Ethnic minorities.

In general, whoever does not find a library system in the working or studying institutions become a potential user of the public library. The users in a public library are of heterogeneous type.

Users in Special Library

For the purpose of identification of users in special libraries, Universities of various types such as Traditional Academic Universities, Professional Universities and Technological Universities may also be counted along with R & D institutions. Libraries affiliated to all the above categories may be treaded as special libraries. Their users may fall broadly into the following categories:

(a) Preachers and Practitioners engaged in R & D in the various fields of technology, industry, medicine, agriculture, communication, etc.
(b) Planners, managers and other decision-makers engaged in Coordination and development activities in Science and Technology at public and private sectors.
(c) Researcher in the basic and applied sciences.

Now, we have enumerated the users of the various library systems. Let us see the methods of identifying the user needs.

Methods of Collecting Information about User's Needs

Dr. Seetharama of DRTC states that in collecting information to design a system consonant with the user needs, several methods have to be used to complement, balance and minimize an individual bias. He has listed several methods. He suggests,

1. Survey of user's needs using questionnaire.
2. Interviewing users, their subordinates and superiors and colleagues.
3. Study of the user's literature output.
4. Study of the literatures use patterns of the users.
5. Meeting users periodically in small groups.
6. Liaison.

USER STUDIES

The term 'user studies' has been defined variously by different information scientists. According to Wysoki user studies or use studies could be concerned with studying information processing activities of the users. Empirical studies of the use of, the demand or need for information is usually called user studies. In fact, a study that is focused on users to understand directly or indirectly their information needs, use behaviour and use pattern is usually called a user study. For a meaningful user service, user study is a precondition.

User Studies—Genesis and Development

An early user study in the field was conducted in the late 1930s by Louis R Wilson. The study was an attempt to investigate the distribution and status of libraries in the United States. When we trace the development of user studies it will be seen that it was activated by two international conferences viz. The Royal Society's Conference held in London in 1948 and the Washington Conference of 1958.

A study entitled 'pilot study on the use of scientific literature by scientists' conducted by Ralph R. Shaw is considered another important pioneer study in this direction. During 1950s and 1960s there were comparatively only a limited number of studies. A comprehensive bibliography in user studies compiled by Davis and Bailey in 1964 contains only 438 studies. It is reported by Crawford that by 1977 more than 1000 important studies were conducted on user studies. A number of user studies including state of the art reports and review reports were also published.

User Studies and their Usefulness

The user studies, information-need studies, use studies; information-transfer studies, communication behaviour studies, information-behaviour studies, dissemination and utilization studies are closely related. When approached from the point of view of the scientist or technologist, these are studies of science communication—behaviour, when approached from the point of view of any communication medium they are use studies. When approached from the point of view of the science communication system, they are studies in the flow of information among scientists and technologists.

Hence the terminology depends much on the approach and the angle from which one sees. Some motives and purposes of users give rise to information needs and requirements. To satisfy such needs and requirements users adopt many ways and means of accessing and searching sources of information. Then they try to acquire necessary information both regularly and in an *ad hoc* way as necessary from these sources. In the act of acquiring information, the user uses or calls upon the sources of information and applies the information to the purposes as predetermined, thus leading to satisfaction or dissatisfaction in relation to purposes and needs. In reality these sequentially represented steps are neither discernible nor strictly linear.

Though information seeking behaviour in one sense deals with actual seeking information represented at the stage of means of searching various sources of information. It would be more appropriate to cover other earlier stages and later stages to get a clear picture of the entire sequence.

The factors/variables that affect information transfer process and user behaviour are innumerable and any empirical study has to make its own assumptions to simplify the situation (Old man). A model of information seeking activities of scientist and his research group presented by Orr provided a fairy exhaustive list factors that affect the scientist's information seeking behaviour. He asserts that any particular type of communication behaviour must be assessed in relation to all other communication behaviours.

In the past, there was no agreement about the scope of information seeking behaviour as well as user studies. Seeking is used interchangeably with gathering and using information. The terms communication behaviour and information transfer/flow are used almost synonymously with information seeking behaviour. However, a thin line of demarcation can be drawn. Information seeking behaviour studies continue to the point of view of user as receiver of message or information.

User studies are necessary not only for planning and designing information system but also for their efficient and effective operation. There are likely to be many surprises to even an experienced librarian about his own clientele as he would not have heard them all in a systematically planned set-up in his day-to-day work.

User studies helps to improve the relation of the library with users in an objective way provided it is done with the organization concerned. Accurate and objective knowledge about users and their information behaviour are the essential ingredients for designing an information system. The effectiveness of library and information system depends on the extent to which the system characteristics corresponds with the user and on how much the potential user is willing and able to make use of it. In fact, research in library and information science is more meaningful if the findings increase the efficiency and effectiveness of information flow to suit the interest of the users.

Most Common Methods

Various methods adopted for the study of information use behaviour largely include survey methods used in social sciences, such as questionnaire, interview, participant observation and also experiments in field settings. Diary keeping by the researchers is also used extensively by the researchers in user behaviour. Connections among documents, rather than people, have been studied by citation analysis. A few studies have also tried participatory research, Computer content analysis, etc.

Most frequently used method is that of questionnaire. Paisley (1965) speaks of questionnaire as a compromise technique expedient to use when the sample is widely spread, but subject to such shortcomings as low response, respondents' understanding and interpretation of the questions and inability to clarify incomplete responses. Even with these drawbacks the self-administered questionnaire techniques is sounder with a high level of response for typical behaviour measurement.

Indirect Methods

Indirect methods in the context of information use

- Analysis of library records
- Citation analysis

Special and Unconventional Methods

- Computer feedback
- Unconventional methods

Mahabala advocates data-oriented approach. He suggests Delphi-based survey. Delphi technique enables one to arrive at group consensus with reasonable degree of reliability. According to him such Delphi studies are useful in determining the contents of a data bank.

Methods and techniques are to be determined on the basis of the objectives of an user need study. One may resort to a single method or more than one but the methodology must be in a position to enable the investigator to draw comprehensive information with an unbiased approach. The present study involves a questionnaire method.

User's Approach to Information

Information need is a composite concept, which is generally dynamic in users. The information requirement is generally affected by various factors like purpose of his work, stage of his work, diversity of interest. According to Melvin Voigt the user's different approaches to meet information requirements are current approach, everyday approach, exhaustive approach and catching up or brushing up approach. The current approach is that users want to keep themselves abreast of the nascent developments in their field of interest. Everyday approach is sought; to satisfy; the specific piece of information required by the user, during day-to-day investigation in the form of facts. The exhaustive approach is sought at when a researcher wants comprehensive detail about a specific topic on the field of study. Catching up approach is adopted in situations where a particular user requires information pertaining to relate subject fields.

Information seeking behaviour results form the recognition of some need experienced by the user. That behaviour may take several forms, e.g. user may make the demands upon formal systems (libraries) or upon systems which may perform information functions in addition to a primary non-information function. Alternatively the user may seek information from other people. In this context user studies do not aim to pattern information seeking behaviour, but to draw interrelationships among concepts used in the field.

Despite the doubts expressed regarding the user's ability to convey their needs investigations concerning user needs have been pursued for their practical value. Paisley has pointed out that the earliest studies of information needs and uses took place within libraries, information centers and labouratories because librarians and administrators needed data for service decisions.

QUESTIONNAIRE FOR USER STUDIES

Internet Users Study Research in University
Please make a tick mark against the relevant answer

1. Name:		
2. Gender:	1. Male	☐
	2. Female	☐
3. Age:	1. 20-25	☐
	2. 25-30	☐
	3. 30-35	☐
	4. 35-40	☐
	5. 40 and above	☐
4. Marital Status:	1. Married	☐
	2. Unmarried	☐
5. Religion:	1. Hindu	☐
	2. Muslim	☐
	3. Christian	☐
	4. Others	☐
6. Residing Sector:	1. Urban	☐
	2. Rural	☐
	3. Sub-Urban	☐
7. Name of the State:	1. Tamil Nadu	☐
	2. Other State	☐
8. Status:	1. Faculty Member	☐
:	2. Scholar: M.Phil	☐
	Ph.D.	☐
:	3. Student: P.G:	
	First Year	☐
	Second Year	☐
	Third Year	☐
9. Name of the School:		
10. Name of the Department		
11. Name of the Course	1. M.A.	☐
	2. M.Sc.	☐

3. M.Com ☐
4. M.C.A ☐
5. M.B.A ☐
6. M.Ed ☐
7. M.L.I.Sc ☐
8. M.P.Ed ☐
9. Others ☐

12. Educational Qualification:
    1. PG ☐
    2. M.Phil ☐
    3. Ph.D. ☐
13. Do you use Internet?
    1. Yes ☐
    2. No ☐
14. If yes, where do you access the Internet?
    1. Home ☐
    2. University ☐
    3. Home and University ☐
    4. Computer center ☐
    5. Internet café ☐
    6. Others ☐
15. What is your category of Internet Literacy?
    1. Novice ☐
    2. Intermediate ☐
    3. Expert ☐
16. How did you learn Internet Skills?
    1. Guidance from friends ☐
    2. Trial and error method/Self Instruction ☐
    3. Formal training ☐
    4. By attending courses ☐
    5. Others ☐
17. How long have you been using Internet?
    1. Less than 1 year ☐
    2. Between 1 and 2 years ☐
    3. Between 3 and 5 years ☐
    4. More than 5 years ☐
18. What is your frequency of use of Internet?
    1. Everyday ☐
    2. Two to Three times a week ☐
    3. Once in a week ☐
    4. 2-3 times a month ☐

5. Once in a month ☐
6. Occasionally ☐
7. Never use ☐

19. Time spent in Internet per day during the use
    1. ½ hour ☐
    2. One hour ☐
    3. Two hours ☐
    4. Three hours ☐
    5. More than Three hours ☐
20. What is the purpose of using Internet? (Indicate order of preferences by 1, 2, 3), etc.
    1. Ongoing research work ☐
    2. Subject specific information ☐
    3. Employment Information ☐
    4. Preparation of teaching/ Lecture notes ☐
    5. Writing a research paper for publication ☐
    6. Entertainment Information ☐
    7. E-mail ☐
    8. For Career Development ☐
    9. E-News papers ☐
    10. Others ☐
21. Which browser do you use for Information access?
    1. Internet Explorer ☐
    2. Opera ☐
    3. Google Chrome ☐
    4. Mozila firefox ☐
    5. Netscape Navigator ☐
    6. Others ☐
22. What is the Search Engine do you use in Internet?
    1. Google ☐
    2. Yahoo ☐
    3. MSN ☐
    4. Altavista ☐
    5. Google and Yahoo ☐
    6. MSN and Altavista ☐
    7. Others ☐
23. What type of methods do you use to download information?
    1. Hard disc ☐

2. CD-ROM ☐
3. Pen drive ☐
4. Print out ☐
5. Others ☐

24. Which format do you prefer to download information?
    1. PDF ☐
    2. Word format ☐
    3. HTML ☐
    4. Others ☐
25. Do you use E-mail for Communication?
    1. Yes ☐
    2. No ☐
26. If yes, what is the Name of the E-mail provider?
    1. Yahoo ☐
    2. Hotmail ☐
    3. G-mail ☐
    4. Rediffmail ☐
    5. VSNL ☐
    6. Others ☐
27. How often do you check your E-mail?
    1. Daily ☐
    2. Two times in a week ☐
    3. Once in a week ☐
    4. Fortnightly ☐
    5. Once in a month ☐
    6. Rarely ☐
28. What are the problems you face while using Internet?
    1. Slow access speed ☐
    2. Difficulty in finding relevant Information ☐
    3. Overload of information on the Internet ☐
    4. It takes too long to view/ download pages ☐
    5. Privacy problem ☐
    6. Lack of IT knowledge ☐
    7. Any other ☐
29. How do you access the required Information from the Internet?
    1. From the Web address directly ☐

2. Use search engines ☐
3. Use subscribed database ☐
4. Through Portal ☐
5. Any other ☐

30. Please indicate the use of the following services being provided through Internet give your preferences (Indicate your order of preference by 1, 2, 3), etc.
    1. E-mail ☐
    2. World Wide Web ☐
    3. Search Engines ☐
    4. List Serves/Discussion group ☐
    5. Chatting ☐
    6. Telnet ☐
    7. File Transfer Protocols ☐
    8. Access to E-Journals ☐
    9. Access to INFONET Journals ☐
    10. Any others ☐
31. How do you find out about new WWW pages/sites? (Please check all that apply.)
    1. Books ☐
    2. Friends ☐
    3. Follow hyperlinks from other Web pages ☐
    4. Internet search engines ☐
    5. Internet directories (e.g., Yahoo, McKinley, etc.) ☐
    6. Usenet newsgroups ☐
    7. Magazines/newspapers ☐
    8. Television advertisements ☐
    9. Other Sources ☐
32. Do you use internet mainly for getting Information on a topic?
    1. Rarely ☐
    2. Often ☐
    3. Always ☐
    4. No Opinion ☐
33. If you search a topic on the Internet and cannot find it, will you search it afterwards with conventional methods?
    1. Always ☐

2. Rarely ☐
3. Never ☐
4. No Opinion ☐

34. The Web is a versatile tool. Please indicate how often you have used the Web for each of the following categories.

...to access online news?

1. Daily ☐
2. Weekly ☐
3. Bi-Monthly ☐
4. Monthly ☐
5. Never ☐

...to access information about commercial products/services?

1. Daily ☐
2. Weekly ☐
3. Bi-Monthly ☐
4. Monthly ☐
5. Never ☐

...to access reference materials?

1. Daily ☐
2. Weekly ☐
3. Bi-Monthly ☐
4. Monthly ☐
5. Never ☐

...to access research reports and projects?

1. Daily ☐
2. Weekly ☐
3. Bi-Monthly ☐
4. Monthly ☐
5. Never ☐

...to access online chat groups?

1. Daily ☐
2. Weekly ☐
3. Bi-Monthly ☐
4. Monthly ☐
5. Never ☐

...to access online job listings?

1. Daily ☐
2. Weekly ☐
3. Bi-Monthly ☐
4. Monthly ☐
5. Never ☐

35. Do you access to UGC-INFONET Journals?
    1. Yes ☐
    2. No ☐
36. If No, give reason
    1. No Awareness about INFONET-Journals ☐
    2. No relevant Information ☐
    3. Lack of training to access ☐
    4. Others ☐
37. What is your rating of UGC-INFONET services?
    1. Very Good ☐
    2. Good ☐
    3. Satisfactory ☐
    4. Not Satisfactory ☐
    5. No Comments ☐
38. What is your frequency of accessing E-journals?
    1. Daily ☐
    2. Weekly ☐
    3. Fortnightly ☐
    4. Bi-Monthly ☐
    5. Monthly ☐
39. Influence on Academic Efficiency. The Impact of use of Internet is:
    1. Use of conventional documents decreased ☐
    2. Dependency on the Internet increased ☐
    3. Expedites the research process ☐
    4. Improve the professional competence ☐
40. Comparison of Conventional Documents and Internet in your opinion, using Internet as compared to use of conventional document is:
    1. Time saving ☐ or Time consuming ☐
    2. More informative ☐ or Less informative ☐
    3. More useful ☐ or Less useful ☐
    4. More expensive ☐ or Less Expensive ☐
    5. More preferred ☐ or Less preferred ☐

41. What is your level of Satisfaction while using Internet?
    1. Highly satisfied ☐
    2. Satisfied ☐
    3. Dissatisfied ☐
    4. No comments ☐
42. What is your present extent of use of traditional resources and Web resources?
    1. 50% WEB and 50% library resources ☐
    2. 20% WEB and 80% library resources ☐
    3. 80% WEB and 20% library resources ☐
    4. Other ratio————————
43. What is your favourite Web site for your Academic Information?
44. Do you use the University Central Library Internet Services?
    1. Yes ☐
    2. No ☐
45. What is your opinion about the Internet Services of the University Central Library?
    1. Very good ☐
    2. Good ☐
    3. No comments ☐
    4. Satisfactory ☐
    5. Poor ☐

CURRENT AWARENESS SERVICE (CAS)

Information is ever expanding rather exploding day by. It is very difficult for the information users to keep pace with the ever expanding "Information Explosion." So the need for developing an effective and efficient system for the maximal utilization of the available information has been felt.

Information need varies from library system to system. Hence, each system adopts a variety of services to meet the user's needs and one such service is "Current Awareness Service." CAS offers information identification only. CAS is a phenomenon common in special libraries. In western countries CAS is provided by the Academic libraries and Public libraries also.

Current Awareness has been defined as "Knowledge of recent developments." It relates to the special interest of users and it varies from professional and from individual to individual. It may derive from the following.

1. Self-Interest.
2. In working for the benefit of others.
3. Need for the information to devise the policies for an organization.
4. For the competitors in same field.

CAS involves the following four categories:

1. New Theoretical ideas and hypothesis.
2. New problems to be solved.
3. New methods and techniques for solving old and new problems.
4. New Circumstances affecting what people do and how they may do.

Current Awareness Service: Definition

According to Alasdair Kemp, Current Awareness Service may be defined as "Systems for reviewing newly available documents/relating terms relevant to the needs of an individual or group and recording them so that notifications may be sent those individual groups to whose needs they are related.

Therefore, Current Awareness service involves,

1. The review or scanning of documents,
2. The selection of item, and
3. The notification to those people of the items interest to them.

In some Current Awareness Services the concern is not only with the individual items, but also with the detection of any notification of general trends.

S.R. Ranganathan defines Current Awareness Service as: Documentation periodical listing the documents appearing during the period covered and without being selected to suit the requirements of a particular reader of a specific topic under investigation. This is the nature of a general appetizer. It tries to keep the user/reader informed properly of all nascent through created in their field of work and related fields.

To sum up Current Awareness Services,

1. It is an announcement mechanism usually in documentary form.
2. It is designed to meet or help cultivating the current approach to information.
3. This service is not intended to answer any specify query is aimed only for obtaining a broader view of current developments.
4. Recent developments in a subject field are shown in a current awareness list through a judicious selection from current literature in the field.
5. Since the service covers the broader subject area, the user gets a view not only in his subject field, but also of related subjects; developments in which areas may influence his own field of work.
6. CAS is mainly means for those people who cannot entirely depend upon information channel.
7. The speed and timeliness are the most essential ingredients of CAS.

Current Awareness Service—Needs

The following may be considered as reasons for providing CAS in libraries:

1. Large quantum of new information output.
2. Information requirements of users on recent/latest development in specific fields.
3. Documents in varied forms are the main sources of information.
4. Wasteful efforts of users in literature search are to reduced.
5. CAS saves the time of users.
6. Clients need not scan whole lot of publication in their field and moreover lack of ability or willingness to scan the publications on the part of the users require CAS.
7. CAS creates an awareness of the existence of library and its services.
8. The reader-library relations are promoted by CAS.

Current Awareness Service—Methods

Depending upon the user needs, an information centre offers a variety of CAS. It ranges from as simple as the display of new arrivals to the publication of abstracting and indexing periodical articles. Following are some of the methods of CAS:

1. Display of new arrivals.
2. Preparation of Accession list.
3. Routing of periodicals.
4. Current contents.
5. Library Bulletins.
6. Information Bulletins.
7. Data Sheets.
8. Indexing Services.
9. Abstracting Services.
10. Selective Dissemination of Information (SDI).
11. Selective Dissemination of Documents (SDD).
12. View data.
13. Casual telephone calls and visits.

1. Display of New Arrivals

A simplest service that can be offered by any library is display of new arrivals. Book jackets and sometime the books themselves are displayed in an elegant manner in a prominent place so as to attract the attention of the users. But this method is useful only to those people who visit the library regularly.

2. Preparation of Accession List

A list of new arrivals to the library is prepared with the appropriate feature headings and distributed among the users. This helps the users to be aware of the new arrivals in their library and also it helps the users who do not visit the library often.

3. Routing of Periodicals

The users of periodicals are automatically sent to individual clients for perusal and they pass from one client on a list to the next and finally to the library. Routing of periodicals may be circular or radical. The main disadvantage of this method is whenever a user wants a particular title the periodical may not be available either in the library or with the librarians. The change of losing the periodical is more in the process.

4. *Current Contents*

The contents pages of the periodicals may be photocopied and distributed among the users for quick intimation of the contents of periodicals. This method helps the user to select a particular title and the user may obtain the original copy of the periodical or the photo copy of the periodical article.

5. *Library Bulletin*

Consolidated bulletin can be brought by the library, so that the efforts of bringing different individual publications can be saved. The current accession list, current contents may be merged into library bulletins.

6. *Information Bulletin*

This information bulletin can be published at definite intervals to cater the needs of technicians and workers, since in some libraries library bulletin is restricted to researchers and management. This bulletin can be useful in knowing the current research activities of the organization, apart from the other usual information.

7. *Data Sheets*

Depending upon the interest of the users, the data sheet containing statistical data can be prepared and distributed among the interested users. This may comprise of Production, Sales, Demand and Inventory, etc.

8. *Indexing Service*

Exhaustive indexes can be prepared for the documents and published periodically with appropriate reference number but it is to be noted this service is more time consuming and costly also.

9. *Abstracting Services*

Abstracts are prepared for articles appearing in periodical and published with appropriate reading. This service helps the user to select particular document for further reading.

10. SDI

SDI involves the provision of a service where by the individual clients sent notifications of relevant items in the literature match a statement of this requirement called a profile. It is specialized service and this will be discussed in detail in a separate chapter.

11. SDD

The intention of SDD is to combine the selective element in SDI with the availability of documents especially in the case of clients at remote locations who lack direct access to the services and materials in the library. Copies of materials are sent to groups of clients at remote location. Usually such copies are in microforms.

12. View Data

View data is the current generic name of three services developed in Britain as means of conveying current information. Those three services are:

1. Ceefax (BBC),
2. Oracle, and
3. Prestel service.

Ceefax and Oracle are similar and they involves selections of information by the user using push buttons

Prestel service is run by the Post office telephones. In that the signals is carried from the post office to the user's T.V. set via the telephone line. The information demanded by the individual is transmitted to him only as long as he wants.

13. Casual Telephone Calls and Visits

Any information wanted urgently a user is conveyed by the librarian either by his visit or through telephone. This method helps to maintain a good rapport between the librarian and his clientele.

Computers can be very useful in promoting CAS. Some forms of CAS such as SDI, Key word and Citation Index can be performed more effectively. It is evident that CAS is one of the best alternatives to combat the environment polluted by information explosion. Remember CAS may sometimes take the simple form of news clipping services also. Any method to keep the user abreast of the latest information may suitably adopted under CAS.

SELECTIVE DISSEMINATION OF INFORMATION (SDI)

People are in constant process of acquiring new information and are keen abreast of new developments. People select various communication media for this purpose like reading newspapers listing to radio or watching TV, etc. So it is needless to say that, for researchers it is absolutely essential that he keeps himself up-to-date in the field of his work and must know the new developments in other broader and peripheral areas. So the types approach to information in other broader and peripheral areas. So the type approach to information is known as current approach to information. And service that fulfils his current is known as "Current Awareness Service."

Services vary from system to system. The following services are essential for research libraries which come under special library system.

1. CAS (Current Awareness Service),
2. Document service,
3. Inter-library loan, and
4. Bibliographical services, etc.

The important characteristic of current awareness service is the speed with which current information is made available to users. The current awareness service includes the following:

1. Current Awareness
2. Automatic loan
3. Selective dissemination of document
4. View data
5. Selective dissemination of information
6. Content by journal service
7. Research in progress bulletins
8. Newspaper clipping service, etc.

So, Selective dissemination of information services is an intensified form of Current Awareness Service. With the advent of computers, the attempts were made to automate Current Awareness Service. Hands Peter Luhn in 1961 proposed a method for the same and he called this method of providing Automatic Current Awareness service as "Selective Dissemination of Information" (SDI).

Definition of SDI

Hands Peter Luhn defines SDI as "that service within an organization that concerns itself with machine assisted channeling of new items of information from whatever source to those points within the organizations were the probability of usefulness in connection with the current work or interest is high."

SDI is personalized service and hence Alasdair Kemp says that I in SDI stands for Individual in selective Dissemination of information. Hence, "SDI is a service where by one individual client is sent notification of items in the literature which matches a statement of his requirements called a profile."

Principles/Components of SDI

The following may be considered the Principles/ Components of SDI.

(a) A description of "Interest" called "Profile" is prepared and is known as User profile.
User profile is a file describing the users and their subject interest and is a computer readable files. The building up of user profile is a very important activity.

(b) For every new document, a document records is prepared both in machine readable form. It consists of a file containing document description and terms representing the subject contents of the documents being described.

(c) Reader's/User's profile and document records are matched with the help of computers. Actually computers match the user's interest with documents record and there will be a hit when reader's profile and document record are matched and is sent to the clientele.

(d) User—SDI system interface:
It comprises of the following:
- SDI notification,
- Getting the feedback from the user for the notification sent to them, and
- Intermediaries of the system operators.

Operation of SDI

Operation of SDI can be both manual as well as with the use of Computers. It comprises of the following:

- The input and storage of profiles, and
- Output means of notifying clients.

Input

The early concept of SDI was that it would be a batch process in which all the profiles are matched at regular intervals against a collection of the new document records input to the system. Profiles can be fed into computers in the following three ways:

1. Vendor supplied,
2. Saved, or
3. Rekeyed.

In vendor supplied SDI the profile is stored in services computer and run by the service at regular intervals against batches of new data.

In saved SDI the same method is adopted as in vendor supplied for the compilation and inputting the data, but difference is the responsibility for running lies with the customer.

In the rekeyed SDI the method of operation is the same as those for on line retrospective search but the profiles contain a date, so that the search obtains hits only for recent items.

Output: Means of Notifying Clients

The output is in the form of printed details of the hits for which the profile together with the details of the client (names and address of the client). These printed details act "as notifications."

The alternative method can be notifications can be made for each and this may help the client to keep a file reference or to add them to his notes.

Profiles and Search Statements

According to A. Kemp, "a profile is an expression of the current interests and needs of a client, stated in a way which enables it to be used to identify the records of documents which will meet those interests and needs."

Search Statements

It is essentially the same definition and it is mostly for retrospective information rather than current interests. It comprises of the following elements:

(a) Descriptors,
(b) Identifiers, and
(c) Key terms.

(a) Descriptors

Descriptors represent in the sense of a word or phase which represents, more or less precisely, a concept or idea that are related to subjects. The subjects interest of a client is represented by the descriptors.

(b) Identifier

It represents a feature of a document other than its subjects. This includes names of author, of issuing institutions, the name of the series, dates of publications, etc.

(c) Key Terms

Terms represent all the things which may be used to enable the discovery and retrieval of records representing documents which will meet the needs of clients.

Indexing Languages

Controlled and Natural Language Vocabularies

A set of descriptors which may by used in profiles and document records to represent subject is called an indexing vocabulary. This consists of an indexing vocabulary, and its syntax (i.e., the rules for its use).

Vocabularies are of two kinds:

1. Controlled vocabulary, and
2. Natural language.

1. Controlled Vocabulary

Controlled vocabulary so that only one descriptor controlled vocabulary is that descriptor should be available and used for a concept and used both in profiles.

2. Natural Language Vocabulary

Natural language vocabulary consists of any words used in documents, or by clients are used as descriptors. Use of natural language complicated the compilations of profiles the cost of compiling document records.

3. Text Searching

Searching parts such as title and abstracts are referred to as "text searching." In some database it is possible to limit the search for descriptors in a profile to that part of document records which contain the descriptors assigned by indexers/abstractors who parts of document records such as title and abstracts, or every part of the record.

4. Logical Relations and Weighing

We know that the profiles consist of descriptors, and that they may also include the relationship between the descriptors. The relationship may be shown in one or other or both or two-way by showing the logical relationships between the descriptions and by showing the relative importance of the descriptors, i.e. by weighing. There are three possible logic relationships between terms and is known as Boolean logic.

AND (logical product)
OR (logical sum)
NOT (logical difference)

Weighed terms may be used instead of or in conjunction

with the use of logical relationships. The relative importance or weightness of the descriptors used in a document record should be recorded.

Steps involved in SDI

SDI can be operated both manually and with the machine (i.e. Computer) and major operation includes—

(a) Selection,
(b) Notification,
(c) Feedback, and
(d) Modification.

(a) Selection

In this stage of SDI computer program tries to find a match between user interests expressed as a combination of subject interest and those of new document in the database. When a close match is observed, as per instructions between any user profile and document records the details of both the records are noted.

(b) Notification

The user receives notification from the system when a close match is observed. The notification may be include the following:

1. The bibliographical details
2. Abstracts
3. Bare citations
4. Document itself or
5. Copy of the document

(c) Feedback

The user in turn furnished feedback on the actual relevance of the document. According to Luhn "a recipient might instruct the system that a particular document notified to him would be interest to another member." He called it Referral Service.

(d) Modification

The user's feedback received is carefully analyzed and

necessary adjustments are made for the profile or the level of match altered. The user's profiles thus continuously revised on such feedback, which results in an increasing ratio of relevant information. This leads to the possibility of the better understanding of user needs and this could lead to a better acquisition of documents, indexing and abstracting services.

Evaluation of the SDI Services

The following are the factors which influence clients on assessing the value on an SDI Service:

1. Recall
2. Precision
3. Cost effectiveness and efficiency
4. Quantum of relevant information

In general, the clients of an SDI seem to prefer high call rather than high precision and low costs are also preferred to high precision.

User Profile

1. Name
2. Qualification
3. Institution
4. Phone number
5. Address
6. Area of specialization
7. Language ability Read/Write/Translate/Speak
8. Topic(s) of interest
9. Key words
10. Journals to be scanned.

DOCUMENTATION SERVICE

In the past, Libraries were document-oriented, manually operated systems. The world wars changed the outlook and functioning of many concepts including libraries. The post-war world has been witnessing the impact of information explosion which has caused complexities not only in the physical form of documents but also the organization of information in documents. The net result is that the user becomes increasingly helpless. The passive role of libraries in providing the users with Macro-documents has become outdated. The changed information environment has found suitable means to provide information to specialists with a wide range of services. Documentation is the service that gives a coverage to information in Micro-documents.

Documentation—Definition

In 1925, Paul Otlet, one of the founders of FID, used this term for the first time. He published a book in 1934 entitled "Traits de Documentation." He defined as "a process by which are brought together, classified and distributed all documents of all kinds of all the areas of human activity."

Later in 1948 S.C. Bradford published his book 'Documentation'. According to him, "documentation is an art of collection, classifying and making readily accessible the records of all kinds of intellectual activity to the specialists." This definition of Bradford closely resembles that of Otlet.

ASLIB defined documentation precisely as "recording, organization and dissemination of specialized knowledge."

Documentation according to S.R. Ranganathan "Involves all the library practices evolved from the stage when new knowledge is generated and published to the ultimate stage of dissemination." With all the process included in the definitions, documentation aims to put before the specialists the existing literature in his narrow specific field in a library way.

Documentation—Characteristics

Documentation is not mere bibliographic organization alone. It is something more than that.

1. It handles nascent micro thought rather than old thoughts.
2. It considers micro documents rather than macro documents.
3. It aims to career to the information needs of specialists rather than general readers.

In general, documentation scans through sources and makes an exhaustive literature search. It brings to the attention of specialists the current and latest information in their respective fields. Documentation provides information not only on demand but also in anticipation.

Documentation—Needs

1. Information explosion caused by unprecedented proliferation of scientific literature.
2. Social pressure (Demand) from the side of specialists and document pressure (Literature output) by contributors, writers and publishers.
3. Lack of time on the part of specialists to obtain information directly from the sources. While the quantum of literature output is an ever increasing phenomenon, individual specialist's time is a fixed (limited) factor.
4. Impact of innovative technology on information systems and services. Microforms of literature and library automation have evolved documentation.

All the above reasons attribute collectively to the introduction of documentation services in special libraries.

Documentation—Work and Service

Documentation undertakes the processing and repackaging in between procurement and dissemination. S.R. Ranganathan identifies two states involved in documentation, namely:

1. Documentation Work
2. Documentation Service

Documentation Work

Documentation works involves:

- Acquisition of periodicals and other forms of micro document, i.e. serials, monographs, transitions, patents, standards, specifications, reports of scientific or other types of current researchers;

- Selection and making of the items to be included in the documentation list;
- Indexing documents or cataloguing the selected items;
- Abstracting document or the selected articles; Classification and arrangement of the item/s selected;
- Provision of author index, title and subject index; and
- Producing documentation list-typed cyclostyled, mimeographed or printed.

Documentation Service

Documentation service concerns the search, location and the dissemination of information or information containing documents, it is also called passive documentation or documentation service on demand. It consists of the following steps:

- Document finding, and for this purpose conducting a trilouge between the research worker, the reference librarian; and the documentations lists;
- Supply of documents needed by the research workers;
- Checking up at intervals whether the research worker gas go fall that he needed and whether he would to have some thing more;
- Processing documents on inter-library loan of not available in the library;
- Reproducing documents photographically when the user wants to have a copy; and
- Providing translation service to overcome the language barrier.

REPROGRAPHY

The term reprography evolved from two English terms "Reproduction" and "Photography." Reproduction means producing single or multiple copies, and photography means an act of producing picture or image by means of light on sensitive paper. Thus literally the term reprography is producing a copy with the help of photographic technique. But in broad sense reprography includes all types of duplication methods.

Definition

According to M.A. Galfand, "Reprography" a term increasingly applied to copying process as whole—has served to expedite the transmission of knowledge on a worldwide scale and to improve library resources and services accordingly."

In the words of Dr S.R. Ranganathan, the term "Reprography" denotes all the process and methods used for both copying and for duplicating documents whether printed, typed or manuscript.

Ronold E. Stevens defines that "Reprography is a term more commonly used...for the process of facsimile reproduction of documents of all kinds, photocopies, microcopies, blue-prints, electrocopies, thermocopies, etc.

Harrod's Librarians Glossary defines it as "the reproduction in faceimile of documents of all kinds by any process using fight heat or electronic radiation—photocopies, microcopies, blue-prints, electrocopies, thermocopies, etc. also reproduction by methods of duplicating and office printing."

Reprography as a term has recently gained international recognition as an accepted expression substitution for 'Copying', 'Photocopying' and 'Reproduction'. It was first introduced at the first international Congress of Reprography held in Cologne, Germany in October 1963.

Need for Reprography

1. The need of rare and important documents in the field of research in multiple copies.
2. The problem of space for storage of documents.
3. Microcopies facilities much greater expansion of the system of inter-library loan.
4. For preserving the costly and rare materials.
5. For enlargement of as graph, map, diagram or specifications, etc.
6. For having a copy of page(s) of a book which are missing.
7. For economical reproduction and for saving buildings and maintenance cost.
8. For a book easily damageable due to its old age.
9. As a source of income to institution by selling the copies nominal rate.

Advantages

1. It enables the production of an exact replica of the original document.
2. It enables to reproduce all the contents of the original irrespective of the language and the diagrams, charts, tables, etc. contained therein.
3. Copies can be made quickly.
4. It is economical since it does not necessitate redrawing, retyping or rewriting the original before making copies.
5. The handing storage and transportation of the copy, if necessary posed no problem since the copy can be reduced by suitable techniques.
6. Economical updating of files of back volumes of journals.
7. Speedy retrieval and recording of information.
8. Minimizing mutilation and loss of documents.
9. Easy replacement of lost copies.
10. By suitable reprographic technique, permanent copies of the original copy may be obtained even in those cases where the original document itself may be on poor paper or otherwise physically not durable.

Kinds of Reproduction

The two main kinds of reproduction of documents are:

1. Microcopy;
2. Eye-legible copy.

1. *Micro-Copy:* In micro copy, the image of the text is of such a reduced size that some optical apparatus in the form of a magnifier or projection device, is required to read it.
2. *Eye-Legible Copy*: In an eye-legible copy the image of the text is either the same size or larger than the original document but it is be read without magnification.

The individual process and products of reprography are of

two types: (1) full-size duplication, and (2) Micrographics. The full size duplication and micro duplication have somewhat different purposes and uses.

Most full size duplication processes do not require trained personnel to carry them out. The duplication of printed documents is technically simpler. There are large number of document duplication processes available such as elect fax, auto positive, xerograph, etc. Eye-legible copying might be a more significant than full size, for it includes macro size duplications that are enlargements or miniatures of the original, in other words, are duplication which is not the real of microforms.

Development of Methods

For over a century, document copying was done largely by a few different methods of photography, i.e. based on the fact that certain substances are sensitive to the action of light.

A major advance was the use of heat energy in document copying process. Dr. Cal S. Miller's 'Thermorax' was the first successful example of the thermal processes. It was followed by either process, the Eltafax processes and the Imagic process and the fixation of image by heat in Xerography and Electrofax.

Further, the best is if used for the development of the latent image formed photographically in such processes as the Dual Spectrum, Dry Silver, Thermaldiazo and Kalvar. These dry processes facilitate fast reprography service.

The development of electro photography methods using the principles of photo conductivity and electrostatics are the landmarks Xerography and Electrofax are examples.

Till about 1950, eye-legible copies were made largely by silver Halide process or its variations such as photo stating and auto positive printing. Most of these methods required costly and cumbersome equipment. Their handing and operation required appreciable skill. As a result, the cost of a copy made by these processes was comparatively high.

Eye-Legible Copy: Method of Production

Eye-legible copy of a document can be made by following methods:

1. Contact Copying

(a) Print-through or Direct Method, and
(b) Reflex Method.

2. Optical Copying

(a) Projection printing

Automated Office Copier: An increasing variety of automated 'Office Copier' using optical systems are being produced. They usually give a copy of the same or slightly reduced size as the original. Control over exposure range is limited. The built-in processing unit delivers the finished copy in about a minute's time.

The 'upside down' copying arrangements works well with loose sheet, but techniques are to be adopted for copying from a bound volume.

Xerox 914 Electrofax process copier and coin operated copier using stabilization techniques are examples of automated copier.

Organizing Reprographic Services: In setting up reprographic unit, the factors to be taken into consideration are:

(1) Purpose of the copies—acquisition, preservation, dissemination or class room use.
(2) Quantity required of each kind copy.
(3) Anticipated loss of work.
(4) Kind of equipment needed.
(5) Reprographic facilities already available in the country/region/area.
(6) Availability, at a reasonable cost of the raw materials and equipment.
(7) Facility for serving and replacement of the parts of the equipment.
(8) Availability of personnel required for operating the equipment.

Micrographics

Harrod's Librarians glossary defines micrographics as "the science and technique of reproducing documents in so small scale that enlargement is necessary to make that legible.

Micrographics is "a generic term indicating any form of micro record whether on flat or roll form, paper or other material."

The term micrographics apparently is replacing the term microphotography which pertains to the production and use of miniaturized records.

Microphotography, micro-production or micro-recording is the process of copying the objects at an extremely small scale in which the copy of the film or paper cannot be read with naked eye but required enlargement by projection or in a reader.

Though the term micrographics may be recent, the history of the field goes back to 1832 when J.B. Dancer is said to have made first microphotography using Daguerre's newly invented photographic process. The recent history of micrographics began with the invention of the Rotary camera in 1952 by Georde McCarthy.

Libraries use micro-reproduction to reserve old and deteriorated record, to disseminate knowledge and to meet the space problem.

Micro Forms

Microfilm: A best known and most used from of the micro reproduction processes. Microfilms of various size are viz. 8 mm, 16 mm, 70 mm, and 105 mm. Mostly 16 mm width is for the normal size document and 70mm width for large sized drawings and charts, etc. Roll microfilm stores document images at reduction ratio typically around 15:1 to 20:1 on reels of film.

Very Sensitive cameras are required for copying documents. Loose sheets are copied with flow cameras and bound volumes with planetary cameras. Microfilm cameras are very costly and poses a highly complicated machinery having many controls, levels, and switches and meters for producing accurate and fast copies. Only a skilled man can operate the machine properly. A microfilm reader is required for making use of microfilm.

Advantages

1. Fantastic storage capacity it affords.
2. Old newspapers rate and out of print fragile books can be copied and preserved.

3. Optimum dissemination and consumption of literature.
4. The cost of production and dispatch of microfilms is cheaper than the cost involved in sending the original document.
5. Copies can be produced quickly.

Microfiche: It is a rectangular sheet of negative or positive film containing a number of micro images arranged in rows according to a set pattern depending on the area of the film and reduction ratio of the images size to that of original document. Fiche is the French word for card. A microfiche is generally of 4"×6" sheet of film containing multiple micro or reduced images. The prevailing formats carry 60 to 98 images per sheet.

Ultra Microfiche: The most significant development in microfiche in recent years has been the reductions of greater than 150:1 as documents. The 1:0:1 ratio make it possible to store 3000 page images on a single 4"×6" fiche.

Each image representing a printed page or an illustration.

Advantages

1. It has good storage capacity.
2. It can easily be reproduced by the Silver halide, Diazo or Kelvar processes.
3. Card to card reproduction is easy.
4. It is economical to transfer, because weight is less than 1/8 of an ounce.

Microcard: Microcard is an opaque paper of 5"×3" size usually contains 80 pages. It is used for making microscopic photographic reproduction of printed material.

Advantages

1. Microcard is comparatively cheaper than other microforms.
2. Microcard saves about 92 to 96% space as compared with 70 to 90% saved by microfilm.
3. As microprint is supplied with standardized title

description it further saves 80 to 100% cataloguing cost.

4. Microcard is easier to handle than the microfilm. For instance easy in one pocket and especially easy to send by post.

Limitations of Microforms

Though the micro publications are very economical media for reproduction, recording and retrieval of information, they suffer from the following limitations:

1. It violates the copy right acts.
2. It needs magnifying glasses.
3. It needs to invest a large amount in purchasing microreader.

However, the advantages of micro publication outweigh the limitation.

Copyright and Reprography and Micrographics

For centuries earlier to the invention of printing from microvabmetallic types, copying document was considered a legitimate Pursuit. Many great classical works of the pre-printer have been preserved through the works of the scribes. The first specific law on copyright was enacted in England in 1710. Since then copyright laws have been enacted in many countries.

A Library just cannot go ahead and reproduce copyright material just as it likes. It has to operate within the law. Consequently it is a standard and obligatory procedure for every photo copying transaction which involves copyright text. The person who is to be the recipient of the copy made by the library must sign a copyright declaration form which states that the copy is strictly for the purposes of research or private study also only a single copy can be made and the amount of text copied must not exceed a reasonable portion.

For instance by convention a scholar getting a reprographic copy of a page a few pages of a document made for use in his study does not deprive the author or the publisher from sale of the document. This is fair use. The general consensus as contained in the statement of the Royal Society of London and of the US Joint Committee on Fair use in photocopying is that:

(1) When a library makes a single copy of a document for the use of a reader. It is a natural extension of services traditionally given by the library; and
(2) The present demand of readers for copies of a document can be satisfied without greatly harming the interests of the copyright owners and of the publisher.

The use of computer for storage and retrieval of documents and television and facsimile transmission of document images from general point are also a raising new problem in copyright law.

In recent years, the use of reprography has steadily increased. Reprography facilities to reproduce quickly and conveniently well high perfect copies of parts of books, periodical articles and documents and records. It has revolutionized library loans especially interlibrary loans. Having a photocopy made of an article from a journal is often very less trouble than borrowing it. As a part of document procurement and exchange programme there is an increasing flow of reprographic copies not only from one library to another within a country, but also one country to another.

As far as scholars and researchers are concerned, it has removed the chorea of manual transcription. It has increased the availability of texts for teaching purposes. It has its affects too on library routines: all sorts of records (lists of overdues, lists of desiderata, catalogue records) can manufactured easily in any number of copies.

BIBLIOGRAPHY

The term "bibliography" was first used by Louis Jacob de Saint Charles in his Bibliographia Parisiana (1645-50), and become popular in the eighteenth century. It is derived from the Greek words, "biblion" and "graphein", "biblion" means "books", and "graphien" is "to write." Thus etymologically bibliography means the writing of books. This is the original meaning given the Oxford English Dictionary, which prevailed during the seventeenth century. Thus, bibliography was originally defined as the writing (in the mechanical scene) and transcription of books.

The great German bibliography, F. Ebert defined bibliography as, "in the broadest sense that deals with literary productions."

Developments

Early bibliographies were mostly publishers' trade lists of books, and in libraries a few catalogue of books were available. The next important step was the compilation of regional catalogue called Messkataloge (fair catalogue) in the second half of the sixteenth century. It was during this period also that Konard Gesner attempted to list all scholarly publications in the world, and the Bibliotheca universalis appeared in 1545. Towards the beginning of the eigthteenth century critical bibliographies also came to be complied, and subject book lists covering one or more subjects became rather common by the middle of the century.

Aims

This basic aim of a bibliography is to assist the user in locating the existence of or identifying a book or any other material which may be of interest to him. In the case of a research, a bibliography enables him to find out what has already been written on his subjected allows him to keep himself well-informed and up-to-date. This avoids duplication in research saving him both time and money. The secondary aim of a bibliography is to serve as a tool for books selection, the identification and verification of bibliographic details, location of materials (in terms of place of publication, location in the library or point of purchase. More often a reader is concerned with what is available of a given subject in various forms).

BRANCHES OF BIBLIOGRAPHY

There are three branches of bibliography, namely, (i) Systematic or enumerative bibliography, (ii) Analytical or critical bibliography, and (iii) Historical bibliography.

Systematic or Enumerative Bubliography

Whenever a layman or an average librarian speaks of bibliography, he usually means systematic or enumerative bibliography. It is certainly the easiest of all aspects of bibliography. The straightforward listing of individual items with minimum details is known as systematic bibliography.

The object of a systematic bibliography is to collate and list information about individual books and related material in a logical or useful order. Such a bibliography is usually enumerative, which means that some sort of selection has prevailed in determining what to include.

Types

The field of systematic bibliography can be divided in a number of ways depending upon the characteristic used. Due to the fact that many characteristics are available for such a division, we are able to obtain a wide veriety of types of bibliographies. Within each type, we can have a large variety of bibliographies depending upon degree of comprehensiveness, selectivity, amount of information, arrangement, etc.

The following characteristics may be used to distinguish bibliographies: kinds of materials covered; the purpose or point of view of the compiler; geographical area of coverage; language; time; primary and secondary; and enumeration.

Kinds of Material Covered

The following are some of the kinds of material:

(a) Books: incunabula, modern books, pamphlets
(b) Periodicals and articles in periodicals
(c) Pictures, illustration, etc.
(d) Microfilms, etc.
(e) Gramophone records.

Purpose or Point of View of the Compiler

The purpose or point of view of the compiler of a bibliography depends upon the agency responsible for creating that bibliography. Every such agency has a purpose of its own, thus leading to different types of bibliographies, each type corresponding to a particular agency. Dr. S.R. Ranganathan has recognized ten such agencies, which form links in the economic-bibliographical chain.

Geographical Area of Coverage

Area of origin of publisher can be used as the basis to get types of bibliographies. Thus we obtain an international, national or regional bibliography, etc.

Language

We may obtain linguistic bibliography by listing documents in a specific language. This will give us grouping by language.

Time

It is usually necessary to limit a bibliography in time. This means that it should be either a closed or open bibliography. A closed bibliography is one which covers material published up to a particular point in time and is not kept up to date.

Primary and Secondary

Esdaile, in his Student's manual of bibliography, has divided bibliographies into two categories, namely, primary and secondary bibliographies. Primary bibliographies are "those which are the original record of the whole or part of their contents." Secondary bibliographies are "those in which material registered elsewhere is rearranged for the convenience of research."

Enumeration

Commonly recognized types of systematic bibliography are enumerated below:

Universal bibliography (including printed catalogues of great national libraries (e.g., Bibliotheca universalis).

National bibliography (e.g., Indian national bibliography, British national bibliography).

Trade bibliography) including book trade records and catalogues, e.g., Cumulative book index, Indian in print).

Selective or elective bibliography (e.g. World's best books).

Incunabula or book rarities bibliography (e.g., Index to the early printed books... by Robert Proctor).

Bibliography of anonymous and pseudonymous works (e.g., Dictionary of anonymous and pseudonymous literature by S. Halkett and J. Laning).

List of periodicals (including lists of current periodicals, lists of retrospective, location and finding lists, e.g., Ulrich's international periodicals directory).

Subject bibliography (including indices and abstracts, e.g., Library literature, Bibliography of Chaucer).

Author bibliography (e.g., Chaucer; a bibliographical manual).

Bibliography of bibliographies (e.g., Bibliographic index, Besterman's Works bibliography of bibliographies).

Analytical or Critical Bibliography

An analytical or critical bibliography involves "investigation of the physical nature of the book which can be, and frequently is, sufficiently exhaustive to enable all the circumstances of the book's manufacture and history to be revealed."

Analytical bibliography has an important relationship to descriptive cataloguing and the history of the book.

Descriptive Bibliography

This is the end product of analytical or critical bibliography. "Its function is primarily that of recording the bibliographic detail of a book which has been established during the process of analytical bibliography." Due to the recording function, it has some relationship with enumerative bibliography but the difference lies in different purpose as well as in the degree of bibliography detail required to record a document. Descriptive bibliography is also the application of analytical bibliography to the physical form of the book.

Textual Bibliography

This is the end-product of analytical of critical bibliography. It is the application of analytical to the contents of books. It is a bibliography applied to textual studies. The chief purpose of such a bibliography is to determine the effect of writing or the printing process on the correctness or completeness of a text. It helps ascertain the variety of authorship, edition, etc. Thus, textual bibliography deals with textual variations between a manuscript and the printed book or between various reprints or editions. An analytical bibliography is concerned more with the physical aspects of the book, whereas textual bibliography is more interested in the author's words and tries to determine the exact words that the author intended should constitute his work.

Historical Bibliography

The study of books "as object of art" may be termed a historical bibliography. It is concerned with art of writing, printing, illumination and binding. Historical bibliography makes an attempt to achieve a broad understanding of the milieu of the book in the context of the world of book, and social and cultural conditions in existence at the time. Historical Bibliography looks a book itself and its history to assess its influence on the social and cultural developments of a country. Bibliography, to whatever type it may belong, has certain common functions to perform.

Functions of Bibliography

In general, a bibliography has the following reference functions and values. It helps to—

(1) Verify individual titles
i.e. What are the documents available under a particular subject. Obtains information on book and other reading materials available on a particular subject.
(2) Works by a given author. Obtains information on the complete work by an individual author.
(3) Find out the basis and best books on a particular subject.
(4) Appraise books with the help of annotations or references to critical and evaluative reviews.

According to Gates, a Bibliography is a valuable reference tool and he enumerated the following as its general functions.

(a) They locate materials on the subject in question.

(b) They provide means for verifying such items as author's name, complete title of the work, place of publications, date of publication, edition, total number of pages, price, etc.

(c) If they are annotated they indicate the scope of the subject and the manner in which it is treated. If the annotation is critical and evaluating, it comments on the usefulness of the publication.

(d) They point out materials including parts of books, which cannot do analyses in a card catalogue.

(e) They group works according to from location and period.

Identification of Specific Bibliographies

Other than the three broader types of bibliographies mentioned above, there exist different categories having specific purposes. The criteria for identifying different types of bibliographies are as follows:

(1) Kinds of documents listed.
E.g., Periodicals—Ulrich's International Periodicals Directory.

(2) The purpose of the point of view of the compiler.
E.g., Indexing—Current Contents.

(3) Place of origin of documents.
E.g., National Bibliographies—INB, BNB.
(Books published in a country)

(4) Language: e.g. Cumulative Book Index, A World List of Books in English Language.

(5) Time: The period of coverage either current or retrospective as found in the book.
E.g., "Current Contents."

Restrospective-eg. Union List of Serial Holdings in South-East Asia covered up to 1957-64.

Apart from these a different categorization identifies the following types:

(1) Incunabula or book rarities Bibliography.

(2) General or Universal Bibliography.

(3) National Bibliography.
(4) Selective or Elective Bibliographies.
(5) Trade Bibliographies.
(6) Subject Bibliographies.
(7) Author Bibliographies (or) Bio-Bibliographies.
(8) Bibliography of Bibliographies.

Any research investigation begins with a bibliography and ends with a bibliography as well. It has become an indispensable tool for scholars in pursuit of information whatever be their subject. Bibliography being one of the vital, secondary sources of information which enables bibliographic control becomes a reality. Finally, it should be remembered that Bibliography of Bibliographies is a tertiary source of information.

INDIAN NATIONAL BIBLIOGRAPHY

The Indian National Bibliography (INB) appeared as an experimental fascicle in 1957 and the first quarterly pertained to October-December 1957 subsequently it has been cumulated in annual volumes. The Annual have been supplemented by a five-year (1958-62) cumulated index volume an alphabetical list of 4,500 subjects used in the Bibliography. The proposal to bring out cumulated language fascicles has not been very successful due to lack of Co-operation by authorities at the State level.

The Indian national bibliography, a classified record of current publications published in India, is based on publications deposited in the National Library, Calcutta under the Delivery of Books Act of 1954, as amended by Act No. 99 of 1956. At present INB is brought out monthly and then cumulated in annual volumes. The following categories of publications are excluded from its purview:

(a) maps,
(b) musical scores,
(c) Periodical publications, (except the first issued new periodical and the first issue of a periodical under a new title),
(d) Keys and guides to textbooks, and
(e) Ephemeral material.

INB is a subject list of books published in India in Assamese, Bengali, English, Gujarati, Hindi, Kannada, Malayalam, Marathi, Oriya, Punjabi, Sanskrit, Tamil, Telugu and Urdu.

The bibliography was published initially in two parts—Part I, general publications, and Part II, the issue of January 1973, the two parts have been amalgamated. Now there are two sections, namely, classified and alphabetical. In the classified section, the entries have been arranged by subject according to the Dewey decimal classification scheme supplemented by Colon class numbers assigned at the right hand bottom corner of each entry.

Full bibliographical details are given under each entry in the classified section, which consists of the class number, author's name, full title, place of publication, publisher's name, year of publications, pages, nature of illustrations if any, size, nature of binding, price, series note and annotations, whatever necessary.

Because of the variety of scripts prevalent in this country, it was decided to use the Roman script for the bibliography. Names of authors and titles of books in Indian languages are translated into Roman script with diacritical marks and then arranged in one alphabetical order under each class. The language of the book is denoted by symbols given at the left hand bottom corner of each entry.

The publication programme of INB is too much delayed. November 1976 issue was received in May 1979. Besides, the same lists a number of publications published in 1973, 1974, and 1975, which shows that a special effort should be get the publications in time. Latest annual volume is for 1973. Although it is a national bibliography, it is far from comprehensive. It is estimated its coverage is not more than 60 percent.

INB records all publications in regional languages in Roman script. But most Indian readers do not recognize the Roman script and cannot therefore, benefit from INB. Besides, the subscription price is beyond the reach of small libraries. Therefore, separate annual bibliographies for each of the Indian languages in their respective scripts are issued. These are prepared and edited at the Indian National Bibliography Unit at Calcutta. The State government's print manuscripts provided by them. This leads to uniformity in standards. However, bibliographies in Indian languages scripts are not being issued regularly.

BRITISH NATIONAL BIBLIOGRAPHY

British National Bibliography (BNB), 1850-, London, British Library, Bibliographic Services Division, 1950-, Weekly, publisher varies.

BNB is a list of new books published in Great Britain prepared by the Bibliographic Services Division of the British Library on the basis of books received by the Copyright Receipt Office of the British Library.

It is weekly listing of all published in the British sales excluding the following categories publications:

(1) Periodicals;
(2) Music Maps;
(3) Certain Government Publications ;
(4) Publications without a British imprint; and
(5) Cheap novels, etc.

Each weekly list contains classified and alphabetical parts. The alphabetical part consists of an index under authors, titles and series two separate indexes of authors and subjects, covering all items in the weekly lists of the month. The entries in the classification are prepared according to the British text of the Anglo-American Cataloguing Rules.

Each main entry given in the classified part contains the usual bibliographic details as per the rules of the AARC and in addition includes the ISBN number, price and BNB Serial number. It also contains entries derived from advance information supplied by publishers, identified as CIP entry. Index entries contain complete bibliographic details except tracing. However, subject index entries contain the name of the subject and the class number as well. A large number of feature headings in the classified part and detailed subject heading and cross-references are also provided.

Cumulations of weekly lists are published for the periods—January-April, May, August and January-December.

Thus there are interim cumulations and annual cumulations. Besides, cumulated subject catalogues and cumulated indexes are available for long periods, generally five years. Cumulated subject catalogues cumulated indexes provides subject, author and title approaches, whereby these are regarded as very handy tours for retrospective searches.

The BNB printed card service provides copies of each entry included in the weekly lists as unit author entries on standard sized catalogue cards.

COMPILATION OF BIBLIOGRAPHY

A reference librarian has to prepare various types of bibliographies on demand or in anticipation. It is an important part of the job. Now-a-days, full time bibliographers are also being appointed for job in library for this work.

Bibliography generally falls into two, namely, that is Retrospective and Current. A Current bibliography as its name implies, lists the records of all kinds currently published. While a retrospective bibliography lists only past production as a comprehensive record.

Who should undertake Compilation?

For a long time field of subject bibliography was identified by subject materials, librarians have entered this field only recently. Compilation of a bibliography requires:

1. Knowledge of the subjects.
2. Knowledge about location.
3. Evaluation and organization of documents that is knowledge about classification and cataloguing.

A subject bibliography will have good subject background but he may lack knowledge about organization of documents. A librarian is likely to lack in subject field, but expertise in the organization of documents. A librarian with proper training in the art and science of bibliography and having practical experience would require undertaking the compilation of bibliography.

1. Planning

It is the first stage in the compilation. It is almost important and should be given proper consideration. At the beginning the complier that the amount of material too extensive on these circumstances, he might decide to make it selective. In order to avoid repenting later, a better planning is a must.

The following are the steps involves in planning:

1. Definition of the subject.
2. Scope of the subject in terms of the coverage to be achieved by the bibliography.
3. Items of information to be included for each document.
4. Kinds of entries to be prepared.
5. Arrangement of entries to be followed.
6. Other adjuncts to bibliography to be prepared.
7. Form of bibliography in which it is be finally presented to users.

1. Definition of the subject

Consult a document, text book or subject Encyclopaedia on the subject to determine its definition.

2. Scope of the subject

The scope of the subject must be determined in terms of comprehensiveness period, form of materials (book, articles, patterns, etc.) Language and level of readers, taking into consideration the specific subject and its related areas. The decision regarding the scope of the subject of the bibliography will depend upon factors like:

1. User's need.
2. Availability of user's resources and requirements of area.

(a) Comprehensiveness or Selectivity

The vastness of the subject, quantity of materials available in it and the resources for compilation of a bibliography should be taken into consideration, while deciding the element of selectivity.

(b) Period

Bibliographies are generally of two, namely:

1. Current.
2. Retrospective.

A current bibliography records the current output as soon as possible after publication and retrospective bibliography is concerned with literature of the past. In case, the subject is too vast or the amount of material available on a subject is enormous, it becomes essential to fix the cut-off period.

(c) Form of Materials

There are different forms of materials available like books, periodical publications, articles from periodical publications, pamphlets, Gramophone records, tapes, films, micro cards, micro films, etc. In practice one is required to limit one self in respect of forms of materials. Very often bibliographies are confined to books and periodicals.

(d) Language

In science, significant quantum is being published in Russian, German, French and Japan besides English. Therefore, a comprehensive science bibliography for research scholars must include material in these languages also. Translation is necessary to the research scholars.

(e) Area

The area can be interpreted as either the area of coverage of the subject or place of publication.

It is essential to determine for whom the bibliography is intended. It may be research scholar's specialist, school students (or) any other category of users.

3. Items of Information

The information about author collaborators, full title, edition, illustration, bibliography, place of publication, year of publication, publisher's name and number of volumes is the minimum that must be provided in the main entries.

A strong case can be made for including annotation or an abstract in certain types of lists:

We may recognize two types of annotation, namely:

1. Descriptive.
2. Critical and appraisal or evaluatíve.

Descriptive annotation

It consists of factual description regarding the intellectual contents of the documents.

An evaluative or critical and appraisal annotation

It describes whether the aim of the author has been fulfilled or not. The first type is used for library catalogues and the second is usually provided for book lists and similar works.

4. Kinds of entries

It is essential to satisfy the approaches through author. Collaborators, title and subject sufficient number of references should also be provided to take care of alternative approaches. Indexes are a must for a bibliography unless it is short (Containing less than 40 or 50 entries)—or arranged alphabetically. Usually author, title and subject indexes are needed. An author index includes entries for authors, Collaborators such as editors, translators, illustrators, etc. Subject indexes are provided almost in all bibliographies. Index refers to the main entries with the help of a serial number or class number.

5. The arrangement

The arrangement should be determine on the basis of subjects, purpose and the length of bibliographies. The arrangement of a bibliography for a researcher is chosen, because it saves the time energy and also convenient to the user. There has been variety of arrangement.

(a) Alphabetical,
(b) Classified,
(c) Combination of alphabetical and classified,
(d) Chronological, and
(e) Annalistics.

(a) Alphabetical

(1) Alphabetical by author, and
(2) Alphabetical under subject heading.

A bibliographer finds it easy to arrange entries by author's name. This method is used where users are likely to approach through the author.

We may follow one kind of arrangement (such as subject arrangement or graphical arrangement or chronological one for main and sub-heading as a primary arrangement, and within each main and sub-heading, further arrangement may be alphabetical by author.

(b) Classified arrangement

A subject bibliography compiled to serve the requirements of a subject specialist should be arranged in a systematic order based on a scheme of classification.

(c) Chronological arrangement

It according to the periods on which the books are written is the most logical and useful arrangement for topics like history of a country, region or place.

The subject has many aspects and each can be divided by period.

E.g: "Developments in chemistry during 19th century."

(d) Annalistic Arrangement

This is an arrangement by year of publication. This enables a user to easily locate works on a topic.

6. Physical forms of entries

The entries should be prepared either as slips or cards of the size "3.5×5." One card or slip should be used one for one entry. This should be prepared on the front and an annotation abstract should be given at the back.

7. Other Adjuncts

The following other adjuncts can be provided to a bibliography:

(a) Preface, describing the purpose, scope limitations, History of the bibliography, etc.,
(b) Lists of contents,
(c) Method of arrangement,
(d) List of periodicals and other documents consulted,
(e) How to use the bibliography, and
(f) Directory of publishers.

8. Forms of final presentation

Once the bibliography is ready guide cards should be added to it. The final form of presentation may be on slip, cards or magnetic tapes. It may be typed or printed.

9. Search for documents

Before starting the actual work of search for material, one should prepare a list of subject headings under which materials is likely to be found. For a comprehensive bibliography, one should try to exhaust divisions as well as sub-divisions of the topic and related areas documents.

First of all, find out if a bibliography has already been compiled on the given topic. For this, consult library catalogue general guides to list bibliography of bibliographies.

DIGITAL LIBRARY

Libraries are the storehouse of knowledge as they maintain the book and other knowledge resource available—mostly in printed form. However, with the advent of digital technology and Internet connectivity, the library scenario is changing fast. Digital technology, Internet connectivity and physical content can be dovetailed resulting in Digital Library. Data available in physical form can be preserved digitally in Digital Library. Digital Libraries have the ability to enhance access to information and knowledge. They also Bridge barriers of time and space

A digital library is a library in which collections are stored in digital formats (as opposed to print, microform, or other media) and accessible by computers. The digital content may be stored locally, or accessed remotely via computer networks. A digital library is a type of information retrieval system. The first use of the term digital library in print may have been in a 1988 report to the Corporation for National Research Initiatives. The term digital libraries was first popularized by the NSF/DARPA/NASA Digital Libraries Initiative in 1994. These draw heavily on As We May Think by Vannevar Bush in 1945, which set out a vision not in terms of technology, but user experience. The term virtual library was initially used interchangeably with digital library, but is now primarily used for libraries that are virtual in other senses (such as libraries which aggregate distributed content).

A distinction is often made between content that was created in a digital format, known as born-digital, and information that has been converted from a physical medium, e.g., paper, by digitizing. The term hybrid library is sometimes used for libraries that have both physical collections and digital collections. For example, American Memory is a digital library within the Library of Congress. Some important digital libraries also serve as long-term archives, for example, the ePrint arXiv, and the Internet Archive.

Digital Libraries are a set of electronic resources and associated technical capabilities for creating, searching, and using information. In this sense they are an extension and enhancement of information storage and retrieval systems that manipulate digital data in any medium (text, image, sound) and exist in distributed networks. Nowadays Libraries are in the infant stage of the digital revolution. However, whether it is a digital library or a traditional library we can observe that one way or another, all libraries have some common functions of housing, organizing, and providing access to information. That is, the primary function of any library is collection and organization of information for future use.

DEFINITION

As the name indicates, a digital library is one where all the reading materials are in the digital format. The basic concept behind a digital library is to exploit the facilities of information technology with a mission of sharing resources available globally for providing right and nascent information to the user community at right time. Computer and Telecommunication Technologies along with tools and Techniques used for digitization are essential for the digital library that is to be designed in a distributed environment. This offers the facilities of accessibility to each and every piece of information of any format from any remote area.

The DELOS Digital Library Reference Model defines a digital library as:

An organization, which might be virtual, that comprehensively collects, manages and preserves for the long-term rich digital content, and offers to its user communities specialized functionality on that content, of measurable quality and according to codified policies.

The Association of Research Libraries, (Waters, 1998) one of the leaders in collaborative digitization programs in US, assigns following tenets to a digital library:

- The digital library is not a single entity;
- The digital library requires technology to link the resources of many;
- These linkages between many digital libraries and information services are transparent to end-users;
- Universal access to the digital libraries and information services is the goal; and
- Digital Library collections are not limited to documents surrogates, they also include digital artifacts that cannot be represented or distributed in printed formats.

Arms (2000) defines digital libraries as managed collection of information, with associated services, where the information is stored in digital formats and accessible over a network.

Leiner, B.M. (1998), The digital library is the collection of services and the collection of information objects that support users in dealing with information objects available directly or indirectly via electronic/digital means.

Clifford Lynch (1995), a well-known expert on digital libraries and new technologies, defined digital library as a system providing a community of users with coherent access to a large, organized repository of digital information and knowledge. The digital library is not just one entity, but multiple sources seamlessly integrated.

Digital libraries are organizations that provide the resources, including the specialized staff, to select, structure, offer intellectual access to, interpret, distribute, preserve the integrity of, and ensure the persistence over time of collections of digital works so that they are readily and economically available for use by a defined community or set of communities.

Hence, digital libraries provide an organized and structured access to information contents in a distributed environment and assist users in searching, evaluating and utilizing resources irrespective of their format.

Digital libraries combine collection and expertise in a

seamless interface, and therefore, require specialized staff to select, organize, evaluate, interpret, offer intellectual access, preserve the integrity and ensure the persistence over time of digital works so that they are readily and economically available for use by a defined community or set of communities.

OBJECTIVES OF THE DIGITAL LIBRARY

The main objectives of the digital library are:

- To capture, store, manipulate, and distribute information.
- To introduce and produce new services.
- To have large number of databases in CDs.
- To avoid routine and redundant activities.
- To provide facility for networking and resource sharing.
- To access national and international journals which are being published only in machine-readable form.
- To improve the cost effectiveness of library operations.
- To support library functions such as circulations, serial control, acquisition control, stock maintenance and other routine office works and developing in house databases.

ADVANTAGES OF DIGITAL LIBRARY

The advantages of digital libraries as a means of easily and rapidly accessing books, archives and images of various types are now widely recognized by commercial interests and public bodies alike. Traditional libraries are limited by storage space; digital libraries have the potential to store much more information, simply because digital information requires very little physical space to contain it. As such, the cost of maintaining a digital library is much lower than that of a traditional library. A traditional library must spend large sums of money paying for staff, book maintenance, rent, and additional books. Digital libraries may reduce or, in some instances, do away with these fees. Both types of library require cataloguing input to allow users to locate and retrieve material. Digital libraries may be more willing to adopt innovations in technology providing users with improvements in electronic and audio book technology as well as presenting new forms of communication such as wikis and blogs; conventional libraries may consider that providing online access to their OPAC catalogue is sufficient. An important advantage to digital conversion is increased accessibility to users. They also increase availability to individuals who may not be traditional patrons of a library, due to geographic location or organizational affiliation.

No physical boundary: The user of a digital library need not to go to the library physically; people from all over the world can gain access to the same information, as long as an Internet connection is available.

Round the clock availability: A major advantage of digital libraries is that people can gain access 24/7 to the information.

Multiple access: The same resources can be used simultaneously by a number of institutions and patrons. This may not be the case for copyrighted material: a library may have a license for "lending out" only one copy at a time; this is achieved with a system of digital rights management where a resource can become inaccessible after expiration of the lending period or after the lender chooses to make it inaccessible (equivalent to returning the resource).

Information retrieval: The user is able to use any search term (word, phrase, title, name, subject) to search the entire collection. Digital libraries can provide very user-friendly interfaces, giving clickable access to its resources.

Preservation and conservation: Digitization is not a long-term preservation solution for physical collections, but does succeed in providing access copies for materials that would otherwise fall to degradation from repeated use. Digitized collections and born-digital objects pose many preservation and conservation concerns that analog materials do not. Please see the following "Problems" section of this page for examples.

Space: Whereas traditional libraries are limited by storage space, digital libraries have the potential to store much more information, simply because digital information requires very little physical space to contain them and media storage technologies are more affordable than ever before.

Added value: Certain characteristics of objects, primarily the quality of images, may be improved. Digitization can enhance legibility and remove visible flaws such as stains and discoloration.

Easily Accessible

Searching

Most digital libraries provide a search interface which allows resources to be found. These resources are typically deep web (or invisible web) resources since they frequently cannot be located by search engine crawlers. Some digital libraries create special pages or sitemaps to allow search engines to find all their resources. Digital libraries frequently use the Open Archives Initiative Protocol for Metadata Harvesting (OAI-PMH) to expose their metadata to other digital libraries, and search engines like Google Scholar, Yahoo and Scirus can also use OAI-PMH to find these deep web resources.

There are two general strategies for searching a federation of digital libraries:

- distributed searching,, and
- searching previously harvested metadata.

Distributed searching typically involves a client sending multiple search requests in parallel to a number of servers in the federation. The results are gathered, duplicates are eliminated or clustered, and the remaining items are sorted and presented back to the client. Protocols like Z39.50 are frequently used in distributed searching. A benefit to this approach is that the resource-intensive tasks of indexing and storage are left to the respective servers in the federation. A drawback to this approach is that the search mechanism is limited by the different indexing and ranking capabilities of each database, making it difficult to assemble a combined result consisting of the most relevant found items.

Searching over previously harvested metadata involves searching a locally stored index of information that has previously been collected from the libraries in the federation. When a search is performed, the search mechanism does not need to make connections with the digital libraries it is searching —it already has a local representation of the information. This approach requires the creation of an indexing and harvesting mechanism which operates regularly, connecting to all the digital libraries and querying the whole collection in order to discover new and updated resources. OAI-PMH is frequently used by digital libraries for allowing metadata to be harvested. A benefit to this approach is that the search mechanism has full control over indexing and ranking algorithms, possibly allowing more consistent results. A drawback is that harvesting and indexing systems are more resource-intensive and therefore expensive.

CHARACTERISTICS OF DIGITAL LIBRARY

- A digital library is not a single entity, it may also provide access to digital material and resources from outside the actual confines of any one digital library;
- Digital libraries support quick and efficient access to a large number of distributed but interlinked information sources that are seamlessly integrated;
- Digital libraries have collections that (i) are large and persist over time; (ii) are well-organized and managed; (iii) contain many formats; (iv) contain objects and not just their representations; (v) contain objects that may be otherwise unobtainable; and (vi) contain some objects that are digital ab origine; and
- Digital libraries include all the processes and services offered by traditional libraries though these processes will have to be revised to accommodate difference between digital and paper media—
  - Global infrastructure
  - Network accessibility
  - User-friendly interface
  - Advanced search and retrieval
  - Supporting multimedia content
  - Accessibility from anywhere, home, school, libraries, etc.
  - 24/365 Accessibility
  - Greater opportunity for publishing
  - Equal opportunities of access
  - Reduce physical space

- Break the time, space and language barriers
- Searching and retrieval facilities
- Usage of electronic information will steadily increase, and usage of printed material will decrease
- Access to the digital library is not bounded in space or time. It can be accessed from anywhere in any time
- Jobs, training and recruitment will be re-profiled

DIGITISATION PROCESS

The term 'digitisation' is a shorthand phrase that describes the process of making an electronic version of a 'real world' object or event, enabling the object to be stored, displayed and manipulated on a computer, and disseminated over networks and/or the World Wide Web. The physical or analogue object is 'captured' by some device such as a scanner, digital camera or a recorder, which converts the analogue features of the object to binary values, enabling them to be 'read' electronically

The numerical system used by computers is called binary and is made up of a series of ones and zeros. These ones and zeros are commonly referred to as 'bits' of information. A fundamental point to note from any digitisation process is that the binary or digital channels are relatively narrow, and only a partial representation of an analogue object can ever be rendered in digital form. In other words, the digital object can ever only be a version of the real thing. The digitiser therefore has to make informed decisions about what level of detail is required in the digital version of an object, for that digital version to serve its intended purpose.

Digitisation—Points to be Considered

To make decisions on any technical issue, the digitiser must have a clear understanding of how they expect the digital object to be utilised. This could include, for example: increasing access; facilitating new research; aiding conservation; adding value, by perhaps including the objects in a learning and teaching environment; or comparing and searching objects alongside electronic resources of a similar nature. The possibilities are many, and none are mutually exclusive. Questions such as: who is expected to use the resource and why, and what are users expected to do with the resource should be addressed at the outset. When answers to these questions are known, the digitiser can then make effective and proper technical decisions about how.

Compression

The level of detail stored in a digital file has a corresponding increase in its file-size, which in turn impacts on storage and dissemination of the object. If a high resolution object is created, it is considered best practice to store at least two versions of the object:

1. the master high resolution uncompressed file that is archived at point of capture, and
2. a surrogate compressed version derived from the master for dissemination purposes.

The uncompressed master or archival version should, wherever possible, be stored in an open source file format.

Types of Compression

There are two types of compression available are—

(a) 'lossless', and
(b) 'lossy'.

Lossless compression enables a reduction in file size without losing any information within the file, hence lossless. It does this using algorithms (or software routines) that reduce the number of bits used to represent data in a file, thereby reducing its size while retaining all the original information. Lossless compression typically achieves space savings of up to thirty percent.

Lossy compression, on the other hand, reduces file size with a corresponding loss of data. It works by eliminating information from the file that the program deems superfluous. The lost information is either unnoticeable to the user, or can be recovered during decompression by extrapolation of the existing data. Lossy is probably the appropriate type of compression for data that is originally analogue rather than digital, such as video and sound clips, and continuous-tone greyscale or colour images. Joint Photographic Experts Group (JPEG) and Motion Pictures Experts Group (MPEG) are two common types of lossy compression, and the file reduction can be quite dramatic, resulting in possibly ninety percent smaller files.

Pathways

When starting to digitise it is thought best to capture as close an analogue object as possible. Depending on the nature of the source this could mean capturing directly using, for example, a flatbed scanner to digitise a text document, a digital camera to capture an object, or a digital camcorder or audio recorder to capture moving images or sound. However, it may be that the source is one step removed from the original in, say, capturing a slide or photograph of an object, or digitising an interview stored on analogue audio tape. It is further removed from the original photocopy of a document, or a second analogue recording of a recording. The resulting file is the less likely to be a true representation of the original object or event, and the more likely that erroneous data could have crept into the file.

Making the decision about the method of capture is very much a project decision based on—

- the type of source material being digitised,
- the equipment,
- staff skills available, and
- the budget allocated, for both equipment and staff time.

Different Types of Digital Scanning

Sometimes decisions about how to capture are self-evident and easy to make. For example, if digitising a collection of 35 mm slides, then a slide scanner is probably the best solution.

If scanning a series of flat documents, an A4 flat bed scanner would be a good choice.

If capturing a museum collection that includes flat paintings, 3-dimensional objects and written documents, there is more than one way to go about digitising the collection.

If digitising a manuscript, there is often the need to have text transcribed beside an image.

If filming an event there is likely to be moving image, sound, and text transcription and perhaps also still images as part of the final resource.

Digital Objects

There are various issues concerned with the capture of digital objects depending on the nature of the object itself. There are three broad types of digital object:

- text-based,
- image-based, and
- time-based.

Text-based

Text processing and the scholarly use of digital texts is relatively long established, going back to the early days of computing in the late 1960s. The early text format used in computing was the American Standard Code for Information Interchange, more commonly known as ASCII text, sometimes referred to as plain text. ASCII is usually an adequate format for sharing documents between computers and applications when the text contains only simple, modern English prose. Simple US-ASCII uses 7 bits of information for character encoding, reserving the 8th bit for control and formatting information. Thus, ASCII can encode only the upper and lower case characters of the Roman alphabet, along with the more common punctuation characters.

A second and later text format is Unicode. Unicode solves the problems of limitation evident in the use of ASCII plain text. The aim of Unicode is for all of the characters in all of the world's languages, including some languages of the past, to be mapped unambiguously onto a distinct numerical code. Unicode is certain to become the standard for character encoding in the future, and is already supported by the latest versions of the major operating systems. To date, Unicode offers mappings for all major languages and coverage of less commonly supported languages is on-going

There are two main methods used to digitise existing texts-transcription and Optical Character Recognition (OCR).

Text Transcription

Transcription is the simplest method of digitisation, as it requires only a person, keyboard and monitor. This denotes manual keying in of text into a computer.

Transcription can be very accurate, particularly when working on documents with complex layouts and passages of text that are difficult to read. Perhaps, for example, hand-written diaries with notes in margins and text flowing at odd angles, or newsprint made up with blocks of unrelated text on the page. However, text transcription can also be time consuming, particularly if the work is outsourced. Also, spelling and other errors made by the transcriber can be difficult to find and fix as they are random. It is best practice for any text transcription to have two people working on a document, one person transcribing and another proof reading.

Optical Character Recognition (OCR)

The second method used to digitise text is scanning using OCR software. This is a more automated method of digitisation, and OCR works by scanning a document and using a computer programme to 'read' the resultant digital image. OCR software employs various methods to achieve its results, such as:

- *Pattern Recognition*: which uses pre-recorded images in a database, which is good for documents with a uniform typeface.
- *Feature Extraction*: which recognises characters by their shape; again this is good for high quality prints.
- *Structural Analysis*: which examines the structure of each character (how many lines, vertical and horizontal it contains), and is better with poor quality texts.
- *Neural Networks*: which works by comparing each character with characters the software has been trained to recognise. The neural nets therefore change and 'grow' over time. Each character is given a confidence level, and, again, this is better with texts of poor quality.

OCR has the benefit of being much faster than

transcription, and therefore more economical, especially for clear type-written documents with simple layout. Furthermore, errors made by the software tend to be systematic, and therefore easier to find and fix. OCR is less good when document layouts are complicated and text is difficult to read. Again, as with text transcription, it is best practice to error and spell check documents thoroughly, ideally using two people.

Images

Raster (or Bit-mapped) Images

Raster images are made up of pixels (picture elements), and each pixel stores information about the colour of an image.

A black and white (bi-tonal) image has one 'bit' of information, either black or white. A greyscale image will be made up of 8 bits, going from white to black through shades of grey. The abbreviation RGB stands for Red, Green, and Blue. For an RGB colour image there are commonly 8 bits. making a 24 bit image.

At the time of writing, the latest capture equipment has the possibility of going up to 48 bits, with 16 bits of information per red, green and blue channel.

Raster images are the most common image type on the web, for example in the file formats JPEG and GIF, and Raster data models are often used in geographic information systems (GIS) to represent continuous surfaces—such as satellite images or historic maps. Geographical information systems are explained further in 'Data Models' section below.

Resolution

The resolution of an image concerns the number of pixels held within the digital file, and is measured in pixels per inch (ppi). The more pixels stored per inch, the greater the density of the colour information, and therefore the greater the detail evident in the image. This is known as 'scan' resolution, and it is important to scan at an appropriate resolution. The appropriateness of the resolution chosen depends on the intended purpose of the digital image. However, resolution or ppi is only an indicator of image size, and therefore 'quality'.

For example, scanning an A4 document (9 × 12 inches) at

300 ppi will produce a digital image that is 2700 pixels x 3600 pixels (the dimensions of the original multiplied by the ppi). Scanning a postage stamp that is 1 inch x 1 inch in size, will produce a digital image that is 300 pixels x 300 pixels.

Both these images are scanned at the same 300 ppi resolution, but produce vastly different sized digital images. The correct way to refer to the size of a digital image should, therefore, always be its pixel dimensions.

In the context of a GIS (Geographical Information System) each pixel represents a known area on the surface of the earth. In this context, each pixel summarises a square of known dimension: for a high resolution aerial photography a pixel may have a 'ground resolution' of 25 cm—while for a low resolution satellite image it may summarise an area of several square kilometres.

Vector Images

Another type of image is a vector graphic. Rather than being made up of pixels, these images are co-ordinate-based; so two points a and b define a line, and three or more points, define an area.

A common file format used to create vector graphics is Encapsulated Postscript (.eps). Scalable Vector Graphics (.SVG) is a newer format that utilises XML technologies, and may well, at time of writing, become industry standard. A significant benefit of vector images is that because they are co-ordinate-based—as opposed to pixel-based raster images—they can be zoomed to any size without pixilation. It is best practice to store the topology, in other words, the order, contiguity and relative position of the points. Vector graphics are used often in virtual reality and 3-D modeling, as well as in Macromedia Flash applications.

A good simple example of a vector graphic at work is a font used in a word processor. These fonts, or rather the images used to represent the fonts, are vector-based, and when you increase the size say from point 10 to point 28, the image increases in size without any degradation. Vector data is also widely used in architecture and cartography, such as in computer-aided design (CAD) or in geographic information systems. In these contexts the ability to use a single co-ordinates system allows diverse types of information to be reconciled.

Time-based

Digitising time-based media (sound and video) throws up some different concerns for the digitiser.

The first major issue to be addressed is the large size of the digital files produced, relative to most other forms of digitisation. To give an idea of scale, one second of digitised sound produces the same size of file as around one quarter of the complete works of Shakespeare digitised as text. One and a half seconds of digitised video, is the same size as the entire digitised works of Shakespeare.

The second issue, related to the size of the files, is how to enable sound and video to be disseminated and displayed over the web. Like large raster images, some form of file compression is required to do this, and types of appropriate compression are listed below.

Finally, unlike most other types of digital object that are readily viewable on screen, to view most compressed sound and video on screen a plug-in or viewer is often required to use the file.

Sound

The process of moving from analogue to digital sound is called sampling. To reproduce an analogue sound to digital, one must sample the signal many times per second. The frequency of this sampling rate is measured in Hertz (Hz), and the range of each sample is measured in bits. For lossless digitisation a minimum sampling rate of 36 kHz is normal, and the standard highest frequency for most computers is 44.1 kHz. In terms of bit rate, 16 bits per sample is considered good enough, giving an overall bit rate of 192 kb/s. Common types of uncompressed sound file formats are Microsofts' WAVeform PCM encoding (.wav), the default sound format on the MS Windows platform, and Audio Interchange File Format (.aiff), the default format for the Apple MacOS. These formats provide accurate, high quality and lossless sound files. However, the file sizes are large and therefore suitable for archival master versions of files, but not for dissemination over the web.

Compressed 'lossy' audio formats use specialist codecs (Compressor/DECompressor) to compress audio data. Popular variants include MPEG2 Layer 3 (MP3), Ogg and Real Audio.

MP3 is the most common compressed format. A sample rate of 44.1 kHz and bit-rate of 192 kbps or higher is advised to preserve quality. Using MP3 it is possible to achieve relatively big reductions in file size of up to about one twelfth of lossless .wav files.

Moving Image

A digital video file is a sequence of still images (frames) played in rapid succession, usually accompanied with audio data played in tandem. When played at a set rate (12 frames per second, or higher), the image sequence creates the illusion that the onscreen object is moving.

Some common video formats are MPEG-1, MPEG-2, Audio Video Interleaved (.AVI) and Quicktime (.QT). Higher compression rates and therefore smaller files may be achieved by using a third party codec such as DivX.

For example, a 450 mb MPEG-1 file, may be compressed by more than half to around a 180 mb DivX file. MPEG-1 is a stable and documented format, which can be played back by most current computers and digital video players without the need for additional software. However, MPEG-2 and, more recently, MPEG-4, are better suited to high quality video, and do not place restrictions on resolution and dimensions, as happens with MPEG-1. MPEG-2 and MPEG-4 are likely to be the recommended archival formats for digital video in the next few years. There are many proprietary Codes available for playing desktop video, such as, Quicktime, Real Media and Windows Media Video, which are useful for specific tasks, but none of these formats should be considered for a master archival version of a file.

Data Models

The digital objects referred to above, are, of course, single entities. The outcome of any digitisation process, will likely have many hundreds, sometimes thousands of these objects created. These may consist of objects of one type, say, one hundred digital images, or, sometimes combinations of text, image and time-based objects. It is necessary, therefore, to manage and organise these resources efficiently to enable their effective use and retrieval. In essence this is an information management issue, and is sometimes referred to as 'data modeling'. In other words, data modelling is the mechanism by which individual digital objects are stored, organised and managed together. For the purposes of this paper, there are essentially four conceptual methods of organising data: Lists, Hierarchies, Sets, and Geometric or Co-ordinate-based systems. Each one is explained in further detail below.

Choosing a Data Model

Choosing a data model for your project's digital output, is based on three fundamental questions. How is the data organised naturally? What is the intended purpose of the resource, going back to the idea of 'fit for purpose'? And, following on from this, what are the intended users' expectations and experience when using resources of a similar nature?

Lists

A simple example of a data model would be if you had a list of contact details giving, say, contact name and email address. The best way to model this list data is in a tabular format, either in a spreadsheet, or if slightly more complex data manipulation and searching is required, in one table of a database. The wrong way to organise this data would be to store it in a text file, say an MS Word document. This would prohibit the effective use of the digital resource, as sorting and finding contacts would be made more difficult.

Hierarchy

Another method of modelling data is in a hierarchy. This is the classic tree structure, common for storing files inside folders on a computer. This structure can be seen graphically by viewing files on a Windows machine, using the Windows Explorer option. There are various resources that suit such organisation. Most texts are organised naturally in a hierarchical fashion, e.g. a book, inside which are chapters, which consist of pages, which consist of sentences and so on. Or a poem, which has stanzas, which has lines, which have words, etc. As a result, all text mark-up, whether Extensible Mark-up Language (XML), Hypertext Mark-up Language (HTML) or Standard Generalised Mark-up Language (SGML), follows this pattern. This is sometimes referred to as 'parent-child' model. It is common also, for archival resources to be organised in a hierarchy, as they are logically ordered in this way in the analogue world, for example, in boxes, that contain files, that contain documents. Therefore, most electronic archives will be stored in some form of hierarchical database.

Sets

Sets are an effective method of storage particularly for objects that have clear relationships with one another. A good example of the set data model is a relational database, where one object can have many related objects. This is known as a 'one to many' relationship. The advantage being here, that more objects can be added to the many sides of the relationship without unnecessary repetition of information pertaining to the main object. For example, a relational database that contains images may have one main image with six related images showing different views. In this case, the main image information would be entered once only. Thus, relational databases avoid the unnecessary duplication of the same information in a database, sometimes known as avoiding redundancy.

Geography/Geometry

Some data sets can be reconciled and explored most effectively by exploiting shared geography. So, for example, modern and historic maps could be plotted together, with observations taken in the field or digitised from another source. A common model for storing such data is a Geographical Information System (GIS) . GIS combine many of the features of relational databases with image processing tools and thus present a powerful set of tools for unifying diverse data sets and for analysing relationships between them. In simple terms it uses geography as a primary key for data. So, for example, it is possible to ask questions such as 'show me all the information within 500 metres of where I am' or to produce visualisations of data that would not normally lend itself to being shown in this way—tasks that would be impossible or very time consuming by other means. This is made possible when the different sets share a common vocabulary of co-ordinates.

Choosing Software

It is more important to get the data model right, than it is to choose a particular piece of software to represent that data model. In principle, for example, if you choose to organise your data in a relational database, it does not matter whether you choose MS Access, Filemaker Pro, Paradox, MySQL, Postgresql or any other relational database software. In essence these products all store data in the same way. There are caveats to this depending on use. For example, if the database is to be searchable over the web, or if a large amount of data is being stored and retrieval speeds are important, then the more robust MySQL would be preferred over MS Access. However, this strays from the basic premise that the underlying data is being designed and stored in the same model, whatever software is chosen. Similarly, a Lotus Spreadsheet will store information in the same way as an MS Excel Spreadsheet and Corel Word Perfect, stores text in the same way as MS Word.

Having said this, there are important considerations to bear in mind when choosing software. Such as:

- making sure the software performs the tasks required,
- picking software that is well used and has good support,
- choosing software that has good import and export functions, and
- choosing software that supports recognised international standards

DIGITAL LIBRARY SOFTWARE—DSPACE

In March 2000, Hewlett-Packard Company (HP) awarded $1.8 million to the MIT Libraries for an 18-month collaboration to build DSpace, a dynamic repository for the intellectual output in digital formats of multi-disciplinary research organizations. HP Labs and MIT Libraries released the system worldwide on November 4, 2002, under the terms of the BSD open source license , one month after its introduction as a new service of the MIT Libraries. As an open source system, DSpace is now freely available to other institutions to run as-is, or to modify and extend as they require to meet local needs. From the outset, HP and MIT designed the system to be run by institutions other than MIT, and to support federation among its adopters, in both the technical and the social sense. The DSpace Federation will be explored in a later section.

It is an attempt to address a problem that MIT faculty have been expressing to the Libraries for the past few years. As faculty and other researchers develop research materials and scholarly publications in increasingly complex digital formats, there is a need to collect, preserve, index and distribute them: a time-consuming and expensive chore for individual faculty and their departments, labs, and centers to manage themselves. The DSpace system provides a way to manage these research materials and publications in a professionally maintained repository to give them greater visibility and accessibility over time.

DSpace was built breadth-first: it supports every function that a research organization needs to run a production digital repository service, but as simply as possible. The project focus was on building a production quality system. It complements and was influenced by previous research in computer science and digital library architectures. Our goals were to build a system that: would be immediately useful at MIT, and hopefully at other institutions; could be expanded and improved over time; and could serve as a platform for future research. With the help of developers at other institutions that adopt DSpace under its open source license, we will work to add features and improve the different functions of the system as we learn what users actually want, and how to best support such complex requirements as digital preservation and digital rights management.

DSpace is designed to make participation by depositors easy. The system's information model is built around the idea of organizational "Communities"—natural sub-units of an institution that have distinctive information management needs. In the case of MIT (a large research university) "Communities" are defined to be the schools, departments, labs, and centers of the Institute. Each Community can adapt the system to meet its particular needs and manage the submission process itself.

Metadata

DSpace uses a qualified Dublin Core metadata standard

DSpace Information Model

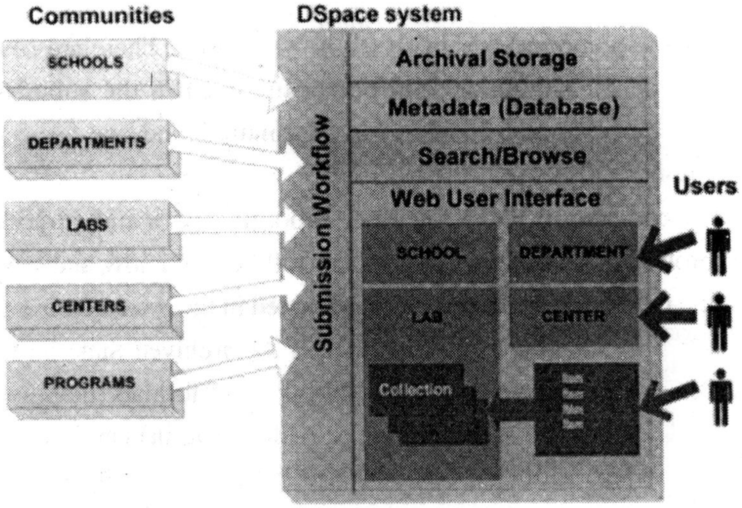

for describing items intellectually (specifically, the Libraries Working Group Application Profile). Only three fields are required: title, language, and submission date, all other fields are optional. There are additional fields for document abstracts, keywords, technical metadata and rights metadata, among others. This metadata is displayed in the item record in DSpace, and is indexed for browsing and searching the system (within a collection, across collections, or across Communities). For the Dissemination Information Packages (DIPs) of the OAIS framework, the system currently exports metadata and digital material in a custom XML schema while we work with the METS community to develop the necessary extension schemas for the technical and rights metadata about arbitrary digital formats.

User Interface

DSpace's current user interface is web-based. There are several interfaces: one for submitters and others involved in the submission process, one for end-users looking for information, and one for system administrators.

The end-user or public interface supports search and retrieval of items by browsing or searching the metadata (all fields for now, and specific fields in the near future). Once an item is located in the system, retrieval is accomplished by clicking a link that causes the archived material to be downloaded to the user's web browser. "Web-native" formats (those which will display directly in a web browser or with a plug-in) can be viewed immediately; others must be saved to the user's local computer and viewed with a separate program that can interpret the file (e.g., a Microsoft Excel spreadsheet, an SAS dataset, or a CAD/CAM file).

Workflow

DSpace is the first open source digital repository system to tackle the complex problem of how to accommodate the differing submission workflows needed for a multidisciplinary system. In other words, different DSpace Communities, representing different schools, departments, research labs and centers, have very different ideas of how material should be submitted to DSpace, by whom, and with what restrictions. Who is allowed to deposit items? What type of items will they deposit? Who else needs to review, enhance, or approve the submission? To what collections can they deposit material? Who can see the items once deposited? All of these issues are addressed by the Community representatives, working together with the Libraries' DSpace user support staff, and are then modeled in a workflow for each collection to enforce their decisions. The system models "e-people" who have "roles" in the workflow of a particular Community in the context of a given collection. Individuals from the Community are registered with DSpace, then assigned to appropriate roles. For example, a department may choose to have two collections: one for working papers and another for datasets. They may then decide that any member of the faculty can deposit items to either collection directly, and that any member of the general public can have access to these collections. In this example the workflow is very simple, and the only "role" is that of submitter.

In a more complex example, the same department may have a working paper collection that requires tight editorial control by the head of the department. In this case, they may choose to again designate all faculty as "submitters", but also designate a small group of people as "reviewers", an administrative staff person as a "metadata editor", and the head of the department as the final "coordinator." An item deposited by a faculty member would then go through a process of review, cleanup and approval before finally being deposited to the relevant DSpace collection. Each person with a role to play in this process is notified of the new submission, and goes to a personal workspace in the system to perform their assigned task. Items that do not make it through the process are not archived in the system.

Technology Platform

DSpace was developed to be open source, and in such a way that institutions and organizations with minimal resources could run it. The system is designed to run on the UNIX platform, and comprises other open source middleware and tools, and programs written by the DSpace team. All original code is in the Java programming language. Other pieces of the technology stack include a relational database management system (PostgreSQL), a Web server and Java servlet engine (Apache and Tomcat, both from the Apache Foundation), Jena (an RDF toolkit from HP Labs), OAICat from OCLC, and several other useful libraries. All leveraged components and libraries are also open source software. Libraries are bundled where possible (exceptions are described in the installation instructions). The system is available on SourceForge, linked from both the DSpace informational web site and the HP Labs site.

While DSpace is open source and freely available, neither MIT Libraries nor HP offer formal support for DSpace adopters. It is our assumption that institutions that use DSpace will have resources to use the system, including adequate hardware that runs the UNIX operating system, and a UNIX systems administrator to install and configure the system. Most institutions using DSpace will also want the services of a Java programmer who can localize and customize for them, or enhance it, although this is not absolutely necessary to run the system. As DSpace continues to be improved by staff at HP, the MIT Libraries, and other institutions that adopt it during the coming year, MIT will take responsibility for evaluating and reincorporating these improvements into the main open source system available to the public. Plans for building a more sustainable open source maintenance strategy through the DSpace Federation will be discussed later.

System Architecture

The DSpace architecture is a straightforward three-layer architecture, including storage, business, and application layers, each with a documented API to allow for future customization and enhancement. The storage layer is implemented using the file system, as managed by PostgreSQL database tables. The business layer is where the DSpace-specific functionality resides, including the workflow, content management, administration, and search and browse modules. Each module has an API to allow DSpace adopters to replace or enhance that function as desired. Finally, the application layer covers the interfaces to the system: the web UI and batch loader, in particular, but also the OAI support and Handle server for resolving persistent identifiers to DSpace items. This is the layer that will get much of the attention in future releases, as we add web services for new features (e.g., to support interoperation with other systems) and define Federation services across the range of institutions adopting DSpace.

Open Archives Initiative (OAI)

To further its goal of supporting interoperability with other DSpace adopters, and with other digital repositories, preprint, and e-print servers, the system has implemented the Open Archives Initiative Protocol for Metadata Harvesting (OAI-PMH). DSpace used the OCLC-OAICat to accomplish this, and is currently exposing Dublin Core metadata for every item in the system. For material that is restricted to local access, the item metadata is exposed to OAI harvesters but the system will enforce the restriction when a user requests the associated bitstream(s). DSpace at MIT has recently been added to the OAI registry, and as the system is deployed at other institutions, we intend to investigate what added-value services might be built on top of this promising piece of infrastructure to work across the Federation. For example, we may examine the possibility of defining and building preprint and e-print collections for a particular academic discipline with individual items distributed among many institutionally-based multidisciplinary repositories, all OAI compliant.

Persistent Identifiers (Handles)

One goal of persistent digital repositories is that it be possible to find and retrieve deposited items far into the future. In particular, it is considered crucial that citations to archived material, whether found in printed articles or online, remain valid for long periods. To this end, DSpace chose to implement CNRI handles as the persistent identifier associated with each item. The Handle System covers assignment, management, and resolution of these persistent identifiers (or "handles"). Although CNRI has not registered with the IETF for an official namespace, handles are compliant with the IETF's Uniform Resource Name (URN) specification.

Handle resolution can be done using a special client, or handles can be packaged in the form of URLs and a proxy server used to resolve these into the handle form, which is, in turn, resolved to the local system location for the item. This second approach is the one we have taken in DSpace. The main alternative to using handles is to use persistent URLs with HTTP redirection to allow items to move around over time. The long-term viability of these alternatives is not yet sufficiently understood.

We plan to discuss this decision and its implications with other institutions adopting DSpace over the coming year, to see if the DSpace Federation can support other systems of persistent identification while supporting distributed services.

DIGITAL LIBRARY SOFTWARE—GREENSTONE

Greenstone is a suite of software for building and distributing digital library collections. It provides a new way of organizing information and publishing it on the Internet or on CD-ROM. Greenstone is produced by the New Zealand Digital Library Project at the University of Waikato, and developed and distributed in cooperation with UNESCO and the Human Info NGO. It is open-source, multilingual software, issued under the terms of the GNU General Public License. Read the Greenstone Fact Sheet for more information.

The aim of the Greenstone software is to empower users, particularly in universities, libraries, and other public service institutions, to build their own digital libraries. Digital libraries are radically reforming how information is disseminated and acquired in UNESCO's partner communities and institutions in the fields of education, science and culture around the world, and particularly in developing countries. We hope that this software will encourage the effective deployment of digital libraries to share information and place it in the public domain. Further information can be found in the book.

The Greenstone digital library software is an open-source system for the construction and presentation of information collections. It builds collections with effective full-text searching and metadata-based browsing facilities that are attractive and easy to use. Moreover, they are easily maintained and can be augmented and rebuilt entirely automatically. The system is extensible: software "plugins" accommodate different document and metadata types. Greenstone incorporates an interface that makes it easy for people to create their own library collections. Collections may be built and served locally from the user's own web server, or (given appropriate permissions) remotely on a shared digital library host. End users can easily build new collections styled after existing ones from material on the Web or from their local files (or both), and collections can be updated and new ones brought on-line at any time.

The Greenstone Digital Library Software from the New Zealand Digital Library project provides a new way of organizing information and making it available over the Internet. Collections of information comprise large number of documents (typically several thousand to several million), and a uniform interface is provided to them. Libraries include many collections, individually organized—though bearing a strong family resemblance. The structure of a collection is determined by a configuration file. Existing collections range from newspaper articles to technical documents, from educational journals to oral history, from visual art to videos, from MIDI pop music collections to ethnic folksongs.

Making information available using Greenstone is far more than just "putting it on the Web." The information becomes searchable, browsable, and maintainable. Each collection, prior to presentation, undergoes a "building" process that, once established, is fully automatic. This creates all the structures used for access at run-time. Searching utilizes various indexes of text and/or metadata, while browsing utilizes metadata such as title and author. When new material appears, it is incorporated into the collection by rebuilding.

To address the broad demands of digital libraries, the system is public and extensible. Issued under the Gnu public license, users are invited to contribute modifications and enhancements. Widely used internationally, Greenstone supports collections in many different languages. Greenstone CD-ROMs have been published by the United Nations and other humanitarian agencies for distribution in developing countries.

Information collections built by Greenstone combine full-text search with browsing indexes based on different metadata types. There are several ways for users to find information, although they differ between collections depending on the metadata available and the collection design. Searching is full-text, and — depending on the collection — users select indexes built from different parts of the full text or the metadata. Some collections have separate indexes of full documents, sections, paragraphs, titles, and section headings, each of which can be searched for particular words or phrases. When browsing, users examine data structures created from metadata: lists of authors, titles, dates; hierarchical classifications; and so on. Structures for both searching and browsing are specified by instructions in the configuration file, and can be rebuilt entirely automatically. No information is inserted by hand.

Each document may be hierarchically organized into logical sections, each of which comprises paragraphs. Metadata such as author, title, date, keywords, may be associated with documents, or with individual sections. This is the raw material for indexes. It must either be provided explicitly (for example, in an accompanying spreadsheet) or be derived automatically from the source documents. Metadata is stored with the document for internal use.

The software is organized so that "plugins" import documents and transform them into a standard XML form with metadata included. There are plugins for plain text documents; HTML, Word, PostScript and PDF files; email; and common bibliographic formats. New plugins can easily be written — several have been specially produced for proprietary formats. If the collection contains source documents in different forms, it is just a matter of specifying the necessary plugins. Plugins also perform metadata conversion, whether from internal sources such as HTML's <title> and <meta> tags or Word's "summary" properties, or from externally-specified XML or spreadsheet files. Many collections express metadata in *ad hoc* ways: these require bespoke plugins. Some plugins also extract metadata from documents using text mining techniques. There are plugins that identify languages and extract acronyms, historical dates, email addresses, keyphrases, etc.

Modules called "classifiers" build browsing structures from metadata—alphabetic lists, dates, hierarchical classifications, etc. The Digital Library collection shown in the example above has four metadata indexes. One can access publications through a subject hierarchy using the subjects button; by title, which displays a list of books in alphabetic order; by organization (i.e., Dublin Core "publisher"); or by a list of hints defined by the collection's editors (how to). Dublin Core forms a base that is extended to accommodate idiosyncratic requirements of collection designers.

The Unicode character set is used throughout, so documents—and interfaces—can be in any language. Collections have been produced in English, French, Spanish, German, Maori, Chinese, Russian, and Arabic, and Greenstone has interfaces in all these languages. This also includes a text-only version for visually impaired users. Collections can contain text, pictures, audio and video clips, and music. Most non-textual material is linked to textual documents or accompanied by textual captions to support searching and browsing. Compression technology is used throughout to ensure best use of storage.

The system includes an "administrative" function whereby specified users can examine the composition of all collections, protect documents so that they can only be accessed by registered users on presentation of a password, and so on. User activity logs record all queries made to every Greenstone collection. Although primarily designed for web access, collections can be printed on self-installing Windows CD-ROMs with a built-in web server and the same web interface. These operate standalone on all Windows versions—a requirement that complicates the software design but is crucial for users in underdeveloped countries seeking access to humanitarian aid collections.

Greenstone—Platform

The system operates under Unix, Windows, and Mac OS/X, and works with standard Web servers. A flexible process structure allows different collections to be served by different computers and yet presented to the user as part of the same digital library — and even, seamlessly, as part of the same collection. Existing collections can be updated and new ones brought on-line at any time, without bringing the system down — the interface process checks periodically and automatically adds new collections to the list presented to the user.

SAMPLE OF VARIOUS DIGITAL LIBRARIES

Academic Info, http://academicinfo.net/

"Gateway to Quality Educational Resources", International in scope, Includes great many academically-oriented links, many not covered by other search engines.

Bartleby Library—Great Books Online, http://www.bartleby.com

"The preeminent Internet publisher of literature, reference and verse providing students, researchers and the intellectually curious with unlimited access to books and information on the Web, free of charge. Our ever-expanding list of great books—currently thousands of works by hundreds of authors—meets the needs of students, researchers, and pleasure readers alike and forms the preeminent electronic publishing enterprise of the twenty-first century." A great site for original literature.

Library of Congress, http://www.loc.gov/

Provides entrance to the catalog and a number of collections, projects and a large directory of links.

American Memory: Historical Collection for the National Digital Library, http://lcweb2.loc.gov/ammem/ammemhome.html

American Memory is the online resource compiled by the Library of Congress National Digital Library Program. With the participation of other libraries and archives, the program provides a gateway to rich primary source materials relating to the history and culture of the United States. Now over 90 collections are online.

Library and Informations Science Resources http://lcweb.loc.gov/global/library/A rich directory of links to state and national libraries, and great many other library resources.

The Collaborative Digital Reference Service (CDRS), http://lcweb.loc.gov/rr/digiref/

Project involving several institutions. "... delivering answers to your desktop now, when you need them." "CDRS will provide professional reference service to researchers any time anywhere, through an international, digital network of libraries and related institutions."

Rutgers libraries, http://www.libraries.rutgers.edu/

A long-term strategic plan for development of a digital library (also on the site). Various electronic sources and numerous links. Includes information guides and sources for various fields; e.g. for sources in library and information science go to: Subject Research Guides; Social Sciences and Law; Library and Information Science.

Tuffts University—The Perseus Digital Library, http://www.perseus.tufts.edu/

"Perseus is an evolving digital library, engineering interactions through time, space, and language." A most remarkable collection of sources dealing with culture from antiquity to English renaissance to some pioneering American sources.

United States National Library of Medicine (NLM), http://www.nlm.nih.gov/hinfo.html

NLM is the world's largest medical library and online system. Includes MEDLINE, MEDLINEplus, and links to numerous other health-related resources, including to research programs for computational biology and medical informatics.

University of California, Berkeley, http://sunsite.berkeley.edu/

Maintained by the University of California and Sun MicroSystems. Renowned for its wealth of digitized collections, its breadth of information and aides for the digital library designer.

University of California: Digital Library, http://www.cdlib.org

Digital library for the nine universities in the University of California system.

University of Michigan: Internet Public Library, http://www.ipl.org/

Started at Michigan Library School. Has a service Ask a Question at the IPL Reference Center—answered by students, librarians, etc.

University of North Carolina, Chapel Hill—Ibiblio the Public's Library and Digital Archive, http://www.ibiblio.org/

Constructed and maintained by collaboration of Center for Public Domain and University of North Carolina—Chapel Hill. "Welcome to ibiblio.org—the Public's Library—home to one of the largest "collections of collections" on the Internet, ibiblio is a conservancy of freely available information, including software, music, literature, art, history, science, politics, and cultural studies."

Bibliothèque Nationale de France—National Library of France, http://www.bnf.fr/

Includes a version in English. In addition to catalogues, includes a number of virtual exhibitions (such as on short photographic poems), Gallica digital library, and cultural events.

Cambridge University Library, U.K., http://www.lib.cam.ac.uk/Digital

A number of interesting and rare collections such as: images of a verse on the life of King Edward the Confessor (written probably in the later 1230s or early 1240s), and the "Taylor-Schecter Genizah Research Units." (Taylor and Schecter are two scholars who added significant discovery contributions to the collection of rare Judaica and Hebrew documents). The networked electronic services supported by the library include references to books, articles, dissertations, reports, and electronic journals.

Die Deutsche Bibliothek—National Library of Germany, http://www.ddb.de/

Includes a version in English. Catalogs and databases in a number of national collections and in museums. Not very impresive in comparison to Library of Congress digital presence.

Oxford University, U.K.—Bodley Library, http://www.bodley.ox.ac.uk/welcome.html

Bodley (one of the most prestigious academic library in the world) has developed a site of digital resources, images, and full-text journals dating back from the 16th century. Among others, content includes CJK allegro Catalogues, the Internet library of early journals covering journals of 18th and 19th century, Bodley Library Broadside Ballads Projects with 30,000 ballads of which the original printed materials range from the 16th to the 20th century, an Image Catalogue, and many other resources.

Strathclyde University, U.K.—Centre for Digital Library Research—BUBL Information Service, http://bubl.ac.uk/

"A national information service for the higher education community." A rich site including among others, access to over 200 journals, a catalogue of 12,000 selected Internet resources organized by subject, links to collection development tools, and more.

The New Zealand Digital Library, http://www.nzdl.org/

Includes several demonstration collections—computer science technical reports and bibliographies, literary works, humanitarian and development information, magazines, newspaper links from throughout the world, etc. It also provides digital library software that they developed free of charge.

Toronto Public Library—Canada, http://vrl.tpl.toronto.on.ca/

A good example of public library efforts.

Virtual Library—Switzerland, US, UK and other countries, http://vlib.org

"The VL is the oldest catalog of the web, started by Tim Berners-Lee, the creator of html and the web itself. Unlike commercial catalogs, it is run by a loose confederation of volunteers, who compile pages of key links for particular areas in which they are expert; even though it isn't the biggest index of the web, the VL pages are widely recognised as being amongst the highest-quality guides to particular sections of the web." Yes, this is an accurate statement.

Digital Libraries in India

- Indian National Library in Engineering Science and Technology Consortium (INDEST), IIT-Delhi—www.indest.iitd.ac.in
- Indira Gandhi National Center for Arts (IGNCA), New Delhi—www.ignca.gov.in
- Vidyanidhi Digital Library, University of Mysore.—www.vidyanidhi.org.in
- ERNET, India New Delhi, Digital Library—http://www.digitallibrary.ernet.in
- Information and Library Network Centre, Ahmedabad-Gujarat—www.inflibnet.ac.in
- National Institute of Science Communication and Information Resources (NISCAIR), Dr. Krishanan Marg, New Delhi-110012—http://www.niscair.res.in
- V.V. Giri National Labour Institute, Noida—www.vvgnli.org

ELECTRONIC SCHOLARLY JOURNALS

Information underpins the learning, research and debate that drive research forward. Access to information is essential for describing and understanding the deficiencies of the present, building visions of a better future, developing practical ways to achieve these visions. Validation and distribution of academic knowledge is primarily based on peer review publication.

There have been astounding developments and widespread adoption by many segments of society over the past few years in our ability to move and manage information. We have been told that we live in "The Information Age" for some time now, but it has truly been the explosive growth of the global computer network known as the Internet that has brought this somewhat tired phrase home to many. What began as an exclusive network for academics and military installations has blossomed into a unique public communication and publishing medium used by millions of people around the world everyday.

The electronic revolution is narrowing the gap of information. The power of web technology lies in the ability to redefine research reporting and transform the nature of scholarly communication in ways not feasible in traditional print media. Increasingly, the Internet provides enhanced opportunities for visual, audio and video interactivity. The potential to incorporate features that advance or surpass those traditionally used in print journals is yet to be realized by authors and publishers of e-journals. In their early development there had been a tradition of creating/offering free access to e-journals, perhaps taking advantage of the lower production costs of e-distribution. It also frees the users from limitations, for example, size, limitations that are heavily imposed by high print cost.

Although it might seem that "everybody knows what an electronic journal is," editors and librarians have not reached consensus in their definitions or classification of electronic Journals. An early definition described electronic journals as "any serials produced, published, and distributed via electronic networks. Later descriptions distinguished between electronic journals available only electronically and electronic editions of journals available both in print and electronically; and among types of electronic journals, such as online, CD-ROM and networked journals.

A journal is referred to be free journal, when access to the journal is not dependent on a subscription or membership in an organization. 'Scholarly' is defined to be peer reviewed and with a scholarly treatment. Functionally, a journal, whose articles contain references is said to have scholarly treatment. 'Electronic Journal' includes both online only journal and also journals, which have a print counterpart. The restrictions made for a journal to be considered electronic is that the online version contains equal context as the print publication, published earlier or simultaneously.

In an academic environment scholarly communication is a critical component of generation of knowledge. It is important to know what other researchers in our discipline are doing so as to improve our professional and academic efforts and to avoid duplicating theirs. Hence, scholars generally want access to a broad range of academic journals demand to publish in a scholarly journal is high, since these are highly read and visible amongst the community of academicians and researchers.

Although electronic journals (or e-journals) have been under development since 1976 e-journals in their nonexperimental phase did not begin until the 1990s, with a few exceptions. The first peer-reviewed electronic, full-text e-journal including graphics was Online Journal of Current Clinical Trials (OJCCT). It is estimated that there are more than 150 scholarly, peer-reviewed e-journals in Science, Technology and Medicine and equal number in the Humanities and Social Sciences. These can be said to be the first generation of electronic journals, with more revolution yet to come into this field.

Initiatives

The appearance of PubMed Central, BioMed Central and e-print servers at the Lancet and BMJ have made it possible to bring to the notice of the world the research findings. Few such repositories are:

BioMed Central (www.biomedcentral.com), access to primary research articles published in BioMed Central is free to all. BioMed Central is a repository for digitized articles from UK's Current Science Group (CSG) has print journals, and also aims to publish peer-reviewed, online only biomed journals. The online journals will permit the authors to retain the copyrights of their works, in contrast to print journals, which retain copyright for themselves and thus benefit from sales of articles reprint.

PubMed Central (http://www.pubmedcentral.nih.gov/) aims to be a secure central representative for research articles. Peer-reviewed journals provide their original research articles, usually a month after publication.

Mathematics e-Print Archive (http://front.math.ucdavis.edu/) is a potential source of preprint and e-print archives. The archive at Los Alamos National Labs is a comprehensive archive of e-prints in mathematics. The author, title, and abstract information are searchable, and the citations are given for papers that have subsequently been published, but there are no links, as yet, to the published versions of the papers. An e-mail list of the users of the research community is maintained and they are notified of any new papers in the area of their interest.

Math-Net Link (http://www.math-net.de/links/). This is a collection of mathematical resources and related links into the Internet. This has links to the Electronic Publications in Mathematics, which is a near to complete collection of electronic mathematical journals (all electronic and electronic versions of paper journals) which are accessible free of costs at present in the Internet. It gives links to almost 40 journals in mathematics.

PhysNet—Physics related free-access Journals (http://physnet.unioldenburg. de/PhysNet/physnet.html)

Organized under the auspices of the European Physical Society (EPS) and several national societies. This site lists Physics-related fulltext Journals, which are freely available on the net, offers links to offers a set of lists of links to nearly all Physics Institutions worldwide, provides lists of links to document sources of the distributed Physics Institutions.

International Consortium for the Advancement of Academic Publication (http://www.icaap.org/)

The International Consortium for the Advancement of Academic Publication is a research and development laboratory and standards organization devoted to the advancement of electronic scholarly communication. Our mission includes the support and enhancement of scholarly journal production as well as the enhancement of online delivery of course and educational content. ICAAP specializes in developing technology for the delivery of scholarly content. There are currently 74 open access resources affiliated with ICAAP and 152 resources in the ICAAP journals database.

All these and many such more repositories provide full text search capabilities. This is due to the advancement of Web-technologies. Web-journals have an upper hand over print journals at this point. Print journal also provide search aids, however, none match the capabilities of e-journal search engines that facilitate searching with Boolean logic. Full text searching of e-journals is bound to develop further and will be a universal feature.

Free Journal Resources on the Web

The web is a host to loads of free journals. A few of these links are given here:

Scholarly Electronic Journals

(http://www.library.msu.ac.th/arec/e-journal/nid.html)

This is a list of scholarly electronic journals available FREE on the Internet selected as per subjects. The Academic Resource Center Mahasarakham University, Thailand has compiled this list. Journals can be selected, subject-wise or by alphabetically.

University of Houston Library: Scholarly E-journals
(http://info.lib.uh.edu/wj/webjour.htm)

The University of Houston Library maintains a directory with links to online scholarly journals available free on the net. An alphabetical list is available of all journals included in this directory.

Free Medical Journals Site
(http://www.freemedicaljournals.com/)

The Free Medical Journals Site is dedicated to the promotion of free access to medical journals over the Internet. Created basically to promote the popularity of free journals on the web. The site also includes links to Medical Journals, whose archives are available free, trail period journals. It mentions that within the next three years, the most important medical journals will be available online, free and in full-text, else they will loose their popularity.

SocioSite: Electronic Journals and Magazines
(http://www.pscw.uva.nl/sociosite/Journals.html)

An annotated collection of electronic journals and magazines in social science from around the world. Electronic journals are listed country-wise, thematically. Contains lots of reference links also.

Serials in Cyberspace: Collections, Resources, and Services
(http://www.uvm.edu/~bmaclenn/)

A good reference source for E-journals and related topics. World Wide Web Resources in Economics (http://www.helsinki.fi/WebEc/journals.html/)

WebEc is an effort to categorize free information in economics on the World Wide Web. Contains a list of journals available in Economics.

All Academic
(http://www.allacademic.com/)

All Academic is an academic index. It is designed to

provide scholars and researchers with useful on-line source information about scholarly works. All Academic catalogs free publications only! Links to commercial and fee-based scholarly publications are not included in this database. Users can browse and magazines alphabetically by title within specified academic disciplines.

Scholarly Electronic Journals
(http://netjunk.com/users/sej/maiy.htm)

Gives an alphabetical list of scholarly electronic journals arranged alphabetically and also subject-wise. This list also includes journals, which don't fall under the free journals category.

Psychology Journals
(http://www.clas.ufl.edu/users/gthursby/psi/journals.htm)

A virtual library of all Psychology journals, both print and electronic.

Health Science E-Journals
(http://www.ispub.com/ejournals.htm)

Internet Scientific Publications LLC is an International medical publishing house on the web. Publishes about forty (40), e-journals, which are available free on the web.

CD-ROM RESOURCES

Early 1980s dawned with efforts for a High-density electronic storage media for music scoring. What started for storing music could not fill its space to its full capacity. The manufacturers looked up for larger quantum of information to test the full capacity of the CD-ROM disc and the library provided the solution readily. Voluminous information of the encyclopaedia came to be stored and tested and at last they found that it was more meaningful for library databases than music store.

CD-ROM stands for Compact Disc Read-Only Memory, a mass storage medium utilizing an optical laser to read microscopic pits on the aluminized layer of a polycarbonate disc. The same format is used for audio Compact Discs. Because of its high storage capacity, reliability, and low cost, CD-ROM has become an increasingly popular storage media.

The storage capacity of a CD-ROM disc is approximately 650 megabytes, equivalent to over 500 high density 3.5" floppy disks or roughly 250,000 typed pages.

First generation drives (known as single speed), provided a transfer rate of approximately 150 kilobytes per second. Hardware manufacturers then introduced double speed (300 kB/sec), quad speed (600 kB/sec), and higher. Current drives operate at up to 40 times speed, although the maximum rate is only achievable over certain portions of the disc surface.

Most CD-ROM drives use either the Small Computer Systems Interface (SCSI), ATAPI enhanced IDE interface, or a vendor proprietary interface. They also typically support playing audio CDs via an external headphone jack or line level output. Most drives also allow reading the frames of data from audio CDs in digital form.

CD-ROMs are usually formatted with an ISO-9660 (formerly called High Sierra) file system. This format restricts filenames to the MS-DOS style (8+3 characters). The Rock Ridge Extensions use undefined fields in the ISO-9660 standard to support longer filenames and additional Unix style information (e.g. file ownership, symbolic links, etc.). Microsoft has defined a proprietary ISO file system extension called Joliet which supports long filenames using the 16-bit UNICODE character encoding.

Types of CD-ROM

PhotoCD is a standard developed by Kodak for storing photographic images as digital data on a CD-ROM. With appropriate software, you can view the images on a computer, manipulate them, or send them to a printer. Information can be added to a PhotoCD at a later date; this is known as multi-session capability.

CD recordable (CD-R) drives allow writing onto a special "gold" CD which can then be read by any CD-ROM drive. Data can only be written once, although using multi-session new data can be appended to a disc.

CD-RW (rewritable) drives can be erased and rewritten with new data. They use special discs which can be read by most recent CD-ROM drives (but not older ones or most audio CD players).

DVD-ROM (Digital Video Disc) expands the storage of a CD to as much as 17 gigabytes. They are commonly used as a medium for distributing full length motion pictures encoded using the MPEG-2 format. The MPEG video decoding is performed using specialized decoder software and/or hardware. DVD-ROM is a writable version of DVD.

Characteristics of CD-ROM

A CD-ROM disc is 12 cm in Diameter with a spindle hole measuring 1.5 cm in diameter and has a thickness of 0.12 cm. The width of a track is 0.00006 cm and the lateral distance between two tracks (center to center) measures 0.00016 cm. It is said that the total length of tracks is 4.828 kms.

A CD-ROM disc has a single spiral track like a gramophone record. The track starts near the center and is divided into sectors of equal length. Data is stored on the track in the form of pits and lands which are impressed by the manufacture on a transparent polycarbonate substance. The pits are 0.000012 cm. deep depressions created on the substance. The area between two pits is called land.

One side of the CD-ROM disc is plain which is the bottom while the topside usually contains prints which are identified as the top side. The disc is inserted/placed in the CD drive with the printed side on the top. The plain surface is at the bottom. In the read head assembly, the laser beam is passed through a set of lenses to fall on the lower surface of the disc, which passes through the transparent substance layer. The land reflects the light back however the pits scatter it (hence do not reflect). If the light is reflected, it falls on a one-way mirror which diverts the reflected light towards photo diode. The reflected light finally falls on the photo diode and thus the presence of reflected light is sensed by it to detect the presence of each bit on land.

Advantages of CD-ROM

- CD-ROM facilitate unreadable storage of information and as such a permanent storage media.
- CD-ROM discs have longer life than print media and hence considered to be durable.
- The high-density nature of the disc allows to store roughly about 25,000 pages of textual information.

- They are removable from the drive and hence portable
- In terms of cost, technology has made the CD-ROM discs cheaper.
- They facilitate multiuse environment as CD changers have been introduced.
- Stored Data is fully protected from corruption due to mishandling of disc and electrical fluctuation, etc.
- It is a space saving storage device.
- It does not require heavy hardware or software.
- In an unreliable telecommunication environment, CD-ROM is found to be a better alternative.

Resources

CD-ROM databases are of three types:

Bibliographic: e.g. Compendexplus (KR Information on disc UMI-PRO QUEST) ASTI.

Full text: e.g. IEEE/JIEE periodicals on disc (UMI-IPO) polymer encyclopaedia.

Referral: e.g. ULRICH'S PLUS (Ulrich's international periodicals directory on disc).

Process of CD-ROM Publication

CD-ROM has begun to be accepted as the new medium of publishing, which is particularly suitable for large volumes of information. Since it is stored in digitized form, the information may be the collection of data, Text, Graphics, Images and Voice too. Moreover, it is stored on the Disk in a permanent form. The reflective disk with spiral tracks on which information is stored as pits and flat areas is covered on both sides by transparent layers. This makes CD-ROM durable and much easier and safer to handle than magnetic media.

In the information storage phase, data in first recorded on a master disk in a form of shallow pits along a spiral track. The master is then used to replicate a quantity of CD's usually between 50 and 100. The process involves five steps, namely,

- Data generation
- Data preparation
- Pre-mastering
- Replication
- Standardization

CD-ROM Applications

The major applications of CD-ROM include bibliographic data bases, encyclopaedias, and as replacement for large mainframe on-line data bases. Large reference books such as the city telephone directories, airline guide, railway tables, years of old newspaper fully indexed and fully searchable can be of old newspaper fully indexed and fully searchable can be packed in to CD-ROMs. For example, an Indian newspaper fully with about 20-25 pages every day, the equivalent of 80-100 A4 pages amounts to a maximum of about 37,000 pages in a year. In digitized mode this will need a maximum of 2 CD-ROMs. Imagine the space savings and the absence of paper and dust in the library! The CD-ROM phone book is almost cheaper than paper directory already in the U.S.A. and some other countries.

Bibliography

Akst, D. (2003). The Digital Library: Its Future has Arrived. Carnegie Reporter, 2(3), 4-8.

Arms, W.Y. (2000). *Digital Libraries,* MIT Press, Cambridge, MA.

Ashburner, E.R. Libraries: Their Planning and Design. New Delhi: Roliance, 1986.

Bemge, Ronald C. Libraries and Cultural Change. London: Clive Bingley, 1970.

Bishop, Ann Peterson, *et al.* Digital Library Use. New Delhi: Ane Books, 2005.

Breeding, Marshall. Preserving Digital Information. Information Today 19:5 (2002).

Buinchat, C. and Menon, Michel. General introductory analysis. London: Clive Bingley, 1981.

Candela, L *et al.*: *The DELOS Digital Library Reference Model—Foundations for Digital Libraries.* Version 0.98, February 2008.

Denstman Harold and Mortan J. Schultz. Photographic Reproduction: Methods, Techniques and Application for Engineering and the Graphic Arts. New York: Mc Graw Hill, 1963.

Ekbots, Gopal Rao. Public Libraries System, Hydrabad: Ekbote Brothers, 1987.

Gerard, David. Librarian in Society. London: Clive Bingley, 1977.

Girija Kumar and Krishan Kumar. Bibliography. Rev ed. 3. New Delhi: Vikas, 1990.

Gonalves, M.A., Fox, E.A., Watson, L.T., and Kipp, N.A. (2004). Streams, Structures, Spaces, Scenarios, Societies (5S): A Formal Model for Digital Libraries. ACM Transactions on Information Systems (TOIS), 22(2), 270-312.

Greenstein, Daniel I., Thorin, Suzanne Elizabeth. The Digital Library: A Biography. Digital Library Federation. ISBN 1933645180. Accessed June 25, 2007.

Highman, Norman. The Library in the University: Observations on a Service. London: Andre Dentsch, 1980.

Jefferson, G. Library Co-operation. London: Andre Dontsh, 1977.

Joltfee, H. Public Library Extension Activities. Ed. 2. London: LA, 1968.

Kahn, R.E. and Cerf, V.G. (1988). The Digital Library Project Volume I: The World of Knowbots, (DRAFT): An Open Architecture for a Digital Library System and a Plan for its Development. Reston, VA: Corporation for National Research Initiatives.

Kawatra, P.S. Library User Studies. Bombay: Jaico Publishing House, 1992.

Lrpsman, Clare. The Disadvantaged and Library Effectiveness. Chicago: ALA, 1972.

Mc Garry, Kelvin J. Changing Context of Information: An Introductory Analysis. London: Clive Bingley, 1981.

Murison, W.J. The Public Library: Its Origin, Purpose and Significance as a Social Institution. London: George G. Harrap, 1955.

Pande, S.K. Sharma. Public Libraries in India, 1985.

Radhakrishna kashyap, K.A. Selective Dissemination of Information Services. New Delhi: Anmol Publications Pvt. Ltd., 1998.

Ranganathan, S.R. and Neelamegam, A. Public Library System: India, Sri Lanka, UK, USA. Bangalore: Saratha Ranganathan Endowment, 1972.

Ranganathan, S.R. and Neelameghan, A. Ed. Public Library System, 1972.

Ranganathan, S.R. Physical Bibliography for Librarians, Ed. 2, Asst. by Neelameghan, A. Bombay: Asia, 1974.

Ranganathan, S.R. Model Public Libraries Act, in Public Library System, ed. by S.R. Ranganathan and A. Neelameghan, 1972.

Ranganathan, S.R. Five Laws of Library Science, 1957.

Sengupta, B. and Mokerjee, K. Library Organisation and Administration, 1977.

Venkatappaiaih, V. Model State Library Policy and Legislation. (For States and Union Territories), Delhi: ILA, 1995.

Wilson, T.D.O. and Stephenson, J. Dissemination of Information, Ed. 2, London: Clive Bingley, 1969.

Index